ENGAGING THE
STATE AND BUSINESS

ENGAGING THE STATE AND BUSINESS

The Labour Movement and Co-determination in Contemporary South Africa

Edited by
Glenn Adler

WITWATERSRAND UNIVERSITY PRESS

Witwatersrand University Press
1 Jan Smuts Avenue
2000 Johannesburg
South Africa

Published by Witwatersrand University Press in association with the National
Labour and Economic Development Institute (NALEDI)

© NALEDI 2000
First Published 2000

ISBN 1-86814-360-0

Cover design and typesetting by Sue Sandrock
Printed and bound by ABC Press

'Industrial policy-making in the automobile and the textile and clothing sectors:
Labour's strategic ambivalence' by Philip Hirschsohn, Shane Godfrey and Johann
Maree was first published in *Transformation* (41) 2000.

CONTENTS

———— ✦ ————

ABBREVIATIONS / ACRONYMS

———— ✦ ————

ACTU	Australian Council of Trade Unions
AMEO	Automobile Manufacturer's Employers' Association
AMIETB	Automobile Manufacturing Industry Education and Training Board
ANC	African National Congress
ATEASA	Amalgamated Technical and Electronic Association of South Africa
BIFAWU	Banking, Insurance, Finance and Assurance Workers' Union
BSA	Business South Africa
BTT	Board of Tariffs and Trade
CCMA	Commission for Conciliation, Mediation and Arbitration
CITB	Clothing Industry Training Board
CLOFED	Clothing Federation of South Africa
CODESA	Convention for a Democratic South Africa
COIDA	Compensation for Occupational Injury and Diseases Act
COSATU	Congress of South African Trade Unions
CUSA	Consultative Unions of South Africa
DCC	Duty Credit Certificate
DITSELA	Development Institute for Training, Support and Education for Labour
DPSA	Department of Public Service and Administration
DTI	Department of Trade and Industry
ELRA	Education Labour Relations Act (1993)
ELRC	Education Labour Relations Council
ESOP	Employee Share Ownership Scheme
EXCO	Executive Committee
FEDSAL	Federation of South African Labour
FEDUSA	Federation of Unions of South Africa
GATT	General Agreement on Tariffs and Trade
GDP	Gross Domestic Product
GEAR	Growth, Employment and Redistribution
GNU	Government of National Unity
HRD	Human Resource Development

HWU	Health Workers' Union
ICU	Industrial and Commercial Workers' Union
IDC	Industrial Development Corporation
ILO	International Labour Organisation
JUMEC	Joint Union Management Executive Committee
LRA	Labour Relations Act of 1995
MIDC	Motor Industry Development Council
MIDP	Motor Industry Development Programme
MITG	Motor Industry Task Group
MITI	Ministry of International Trade and Industry
MMD	Movement for Multiparty Democracy
MSOA	Mine Surface Officials Association
NAACAM	National Association of Automotive Component and Allied Manufacturers
NAAMSA	National Association of Automobile Manufacturers of South Africa
NACTU	National Council of Trade Unions
NAFCOC	National African Federated Chambers of Commerce
NALEDI	National Labour and Economic Development Institute
NBF	National Bargaining Forum
NEDLAC	National Economic Development and Labour Council
NEF	National Economic Forum
NEHAWU	National Education, Health and Allied Workers' Union
NGO	Non-governmental Organisation
NMC	National Manpower Commission
NNF	National Negotiating Forum
NQF	National Qualifications Framework
NUM	National Union of Mineworkers
NUMSA	National Union of Metalworkers of South Africa
PAS	Personnel Administration Standard
PPWAWU	Paper, Printing, Wood and Allied Workers' Union
PSBC	Public Service Bargaining Council
PSCBC	Public Service Co-ordinating Bargaining Council
PSF	Public Service Forum
PSLRA	Public Service Labour Relations Act of 1994
PSTF	Public Service Transformation Forum
PTA	Parent Teacher Association
PTSA	Parent Teacher Student Association

RDP   Reconstruction and Development Programme
RPL   Recognition of Prior Learning
SACP   South African Communist Party
SACTU   South African Congress of Trade Unions
SACTWU   Southern African Clothing and Textile Workers' Union
SADNU   South African Democratic Nurses' Union
SADTU   South African Democratic Teachers' Union
SALB   *South African Labour Bulletin*
SALFS   South African Labour Flexibility Survey
SAP   Structural Adjustment Programme
SAPS   South African Police Services
SASA   South African Schools Act of 1996
STOA   Surface and Technical Officials Association
SWOP   Sociology of Work Unit (University of Witwatersrand, Johannesburg)
TCA   Textile and Clothing Authority
TCLC   Tripartite Consultative Labour Council
TDC   Trade Development Council
TEXFED   Textile Federation of South Africa
TITB   Textile Industry Training Board
TPQ   Total Productivity and Quality
TU   Transformation Unit
TUACC   Trade Union Advisory Co-ordinating Committee
UNESCO   United Nations Economic, Social and Cultural Organisation
UOA   Underground Officials Association
VAT   Value-added Tax
WCM   World-class Manufacturing
WTO   World Trade Organisation
ZCTU   Zambian Congress of Trade Unions

PREFACE

———— ✦ ————

Democratisation in South Africa has been accompanied by the growth of a range of institutions and processes through which workers and their organisations may gain varying degrees of control over economic and social decisions that directly affect their lives. These developments are themselves varied, and have been known by a variety of names: co-determination, worker participation, concertation, tripartism or multipartism. They, in turn, have sparked robust debates on appropriate strategic and tactical directions for the labour movement, yet they remain generally un-theorised and seriously under-researched.

In late 1996, the National Labour and Economic Development Institute (NALEDI) embarked on a long-term research project to investigate what we define as labour's 'engagement' with the state and business. NALEDI is a not-for-profit research NGO, established in 1993 by the Congress of South African Trade Unions (COSATU) to conduct research and policy analysis on issues of relevance to the labour movement.

Engagement stresses working in concert with the state and business towards certain mutually accepted goals, but also emphasises disagreement and conflict, and the fact that the parties may have very different bases for seeking a concertation of interests. It implies a common meeting place, not a common starting point, nor even a common end-point.

In launching a long-term research project on engagement in South Africa, NALEDI's objective was to combine theoretical reflection and empirically-grounded research to investigate systematically the dramatic changes that are occurring regarding worker representation at the workplace, industry and societal levels. To this end, NALEDI commissioned eight original research papers from labour-based researchers and academics for whom this is a specialised field of study. The contributions thus combine depth of research and critical appraisal with privileged insight into current policy developments. The project examined a number of key questions. What are the forces behind the development of the new institutions of engagement? Who are their champions? What impact do they have on power relations between labour, the state and business? Are they likely to survive the democratisation period? How can they be strengthened?

These and other issues are examined in a series of chapters specifically commissioned by the editor to develop a multi-faceted perspective on engagement in its most significant forms. Two chapters, by Jarvis and Sitas and by Satgar examine broader theoretical issues relating to co-determination and social transformation. These are followed by four chapters that examine engagement from the macro to micro level: Gostner and Joffe on societal-level engagement through NEDLAC; Hirschsohn, Godfrey and Maree on engagement at the industry level; Webster and Macun on engagement in enterprises; and Patel on the public service. Finally, Buhlungu and Godfrey, Hirschsohn, and Maree separately examine labour and management as strategic actors: their vision(s) and capacities for engagement.

The results were first made available to COSATU's central executive committee in 1997 and to affiliates in a two-day workshop in late March 1998. They were subsequently published in a specialist legal journal – *Law, Democracy and Development,* 2(2), 1998. We are grateful to the Witwatersrand University Press for agreeing to publish the revised contributions in this collection so that the work may be communicated to a broader audience in South Africa and abroad. Chapter 5 by Hirschsohn, Godrey and Maree was first published in *Transformation* (41) 1999. The chapter by Buhlungu was first published in *The African Sociological Review* 3(1) 1999.

While the research began soon after the formal development of institutions of engagement, it is being published at a time when engagement remains unconsolidated. Indeed, the late nineties have witnessed a number of calls from business interests and even from various state officials to downgrade certain institutions. Moreover labour – the putative beneficiary of the expansion of democratic decision-making – has been sceptical of engagement, and has cold-shouldered one key institution, the workplace forum created under Chapter 5 of the Labour Relations Act of 1995.

If scepticism about engagement is warranted, predictions of its imminent decline are probably premature. Engagement certainly developed as a consequence of South Africa's transition to democracy. However, NALEDI would not have launched the project if we believed it to be a mere passing phenomenon. Though we shy away from predicting future directions, we feel that these processes and insitutions will remain important long after the transition that provided their impetus. In part, this is because some key pressures behind engagement – the restructuring of the economy, the extension of processes of accountability and participation – are not once-off events with a definable beginning and end point. Rather, these will remain highly contested issues for the foreseeable future, even if specific institutional expressions of engagement decline. Moreover, the entrenched position of representative trade unions ensures that workers' views on these matters will continue to be expressed. Policy-oriented research always runs the risk of becoming dated before it finds its way into print, not only because the research addresses ephemeral questions, but because the object of research is itself rapidly changing. However, for the reasons mentioned above, we hope that the research presented here will remain valuable well beyond the period in which it was conducted and the moment in which it is published.

Though all the researchers are keenly interested in engagement, they represent a spectrum of views on the matter and include both proponents and strong critics of many aspects of the issue. Though we held three researchers' workshops to develop common questions and methodological approaches, no attempt was made to present a common set of conclusions, which remain the responsibility of the authors alone. Moreover, while NALEDI is closely linked to COSATU – many current and former trade unionists and allied scholars sit on its board – the organisation is independent of the federation, and its research findings do not reflect nor are they bound by COSATU's policies.

If the research reflected in the contributions to this collection is a first assessment of the institutions of engagement, it is also by definition incomplete and tentative. We will have achieved our purpose not only if our work can contribute to labour's efforts to clarify its positions, not only if we generate debate, but if our efforts stimulate further research work on these important developments.

We wish to thank the Friedrich Ebert Stiftung, especially Ulrich Golaszinski, Bethuell Maserumule and Sven Schwersensky, for valuable support at all stages of the project, and for fiancial support for our trade union workshop and for this publication. We wish to thank the NALEDI staff – Edson Phiri, Emily Radebe and Dolly Vundla – for their administrative support. We also wish to thank the Human Behaviour and

Work Programme of the Human Sciences Research Council for the support provided under the auspices of their 'Priority Theme: People and Work'. The shop stewards, organisers and office bearers from the COSATU affiliates who participated in our 1998 conference in Johannesburg gave the authors valuable inputs which were of enormous help in their efforts to clarify their work. Finally, we wish to thank the editors at Witwatersrand University Press for bringing this collection to readers.

Ravi Naidoo
NALEDI Director
Johannesburg, March 2000

ACKNOWLEDGEMENTS

———— ◆ ————

This book has its origins in an intense debate in the mid-1990s over forms of engagement between labour, business and the state, sparked off by apparent possibilities to extend worker control in the context of South Africa's democratisation.

In 1996 NALEDI initiated a long-term research project on labour's engagement with the state and business, commissioning a number of participants in these debates to generate sustained original theoretical and empirical investigations of the new developments. The products of their research efforts are presented in this collection. The chapters were written between 1997 and 1998 and were revised for inclusion here.

One acquires a number of debts, and a fair share of joy in a collective effort such as this, enough to provide balm for the stray bruises that come along the way. I wish to thank Jeremy Baskin, NALEDI's founding Director, for inviting me to join the institute's staff to develop the project on engagement. It was his encouragement that persuaded me to exchange – temporarily – the Ivory Tower for COSATU House, or (more prosaically) to move from the top of Braamfontein ridge to the bottom. I owe a debt to my NALEDI comrades Steven Rix, Roseline Nyman and Rob Rees – whose superb labour research is not presented in this collection, but whose ideas and critical suggestions shaped many of its contours nonetheless.

I am grateful to the Sociology of Work Unit at the University of the Witwatersrand for seconding me to NALEDI, and to the Staff Development Committee of the Sociology Department and the Dean of the Arts Faculty, Gerrit Olivier, for approving the arrangement.

Hyreath Anderson, Commissioning Editor at Witwatersrand University Press did a sterling job collaborating on the production of the volume. Darcy du Toit and Jeanne Rossouw first saw the merit of publishing a selection of the reports in the journal they edit, *Law, Democracy and Development*. Finally, I wish to thank the twelve contributors, whose insights, hard work, and persistence made the project – and this book – possible.

Glenn Adler
Johannesburg, March 2000

1

ENGAGING THE STATE AND BUSINESS

Labour and the deepening of democracy in South Africa

———— ♦ ————

Glenn Adler [1]

INTRODUCTION

One of the most innovative aspects of South Africa's democratisation has been the emergence of institutions and processes through which workers and unions may engage the state and business to gain varying degrees of control over important economic decisions. These features are entirely unprecedented when compared to old modes of economic decision-making in South Africa. In the past, workers were systematically excluded from such decisions except where – by dint of periodic exercise of power – they had won a tentative purchase in limited areas, such as wage setting. Moreover, these institutions and processes are unique among developing countries in Africa and elsewhere that are undergoing democratisation. Indeed, they appear to have few precedents among advanced industrial countries, even those with well-established systems of co-determination. Taken together, these features of South Africa's transition have the potential to deepen significantly the political democracy won in 1994 by dramatically expanding the participation by a range of citizens and their organisations.[2]

These new institutions and processes were the subject of vigorous debate among scholars, trade unionists and industrial relations practitioners when the ANC government began enacting the new labour dispensation after the 1994 elections. These interventions were generally speculative – an inevitable consequence of the newness of the legislation – and tended to examine the new order's impact on trade union solidarity and power and on economic development. Moreover, they tended to focus on parts of the change, such as the National Economic Development and Labour Council (NEDLAC), or the workplace forum provisions of the new Labour Relations Act (LRA, no. 66 of 1995). Most analysts tended to miss its more systematic features: its wide scope from the factory floor to the societal level, and the extent to which workers and their organisations obtained strong decision-making and consultation rights founded in both statute and agreement.

These institutions promise to be more enduring than the voluntary forums that grew during the transition to democracy in the early nineties which usurped functions of the discredited regime, but quickly faded once a legitimate government was established. Not only do they have a basis in statute and formal agreement, but both labour and business have their own reasons to seek greater worker involvement in decision-making, though their reasons for doing so are dramatically different. Finally, engagement is rooted in the extensive and long-entrenched institutional association between labour and business growing out of the employment relationship.

Oddly enough, it is the very newness of these institutions which – for different reasons – causes great hesitation among labour, business and the state to engage through them. Each, to some extent, must give up long-standing ways of operating and accept new processes that are frighteningly open-ended. Despite the possibilities held out by engagement, the actors' hesitation may, sooner rather than later, render these institutions a dead letter.

This chapter reviews the variety of forms of engagement, examines the reasons for their emergence, and discusses the possibilities for and impediments to their survival beyond South Africa's transition.

NEW FORMS OF INTEREST REPRESENTATION AMONG LABOUR, THE STATE AND BUSINESS

Corporatism, concertation, engagement: Capturing South African conditions

Industrial relations reforms in the 1990s have had to look both backwards and forwards. One major thrust has been to make labour legislation consistent with the provisions of the Bill of Rights in the new constitution. In practice, this has entailed a massive effort to eliminate discriminatory provisions of the old labour relations dispensation, while extending existing rights to all workers. The revision and repeal of old legislation also provided an opportunity to look forward and create an order appropriate to a modern democracy at the end of the twentieth century.

Three prominent innovations now complement the traditional emphasis on collective bargaining in labour law: provision for forms of joint decision-making and consultation at the workplace level; the creation of industry (or meso-level) accords; and the establishment of NEDLAC. At each level, workers and their organisations have won possibilities for increasing control over the content of policies that directly affect them. Following Bayat, control is taken to mean organisational and institutional arrangements through which ordinary workers have the power to make decisions affecting the processes and administration of production. It 'implies a change in power relations from authoritarianism to a more democratic and egalitarian work environment'. While control is generally focused on the workplace, this need not be the case: 'The areas which workers may bring under their control,' he argues, 'and the degree to which they exert control in these areas, vary in different experiences and arrangements' (Bayat, 1991: 3-4).

The multi-layered character of engagement between labour, the state and business in South Africa defies easy definition in the conceptual categories of industrial relations. In some respects, the engagement takes on a corporatist character in that it features 'regularised peak or subpeak negotiation between relatively cohesive units of business and labour, with the formal or informal backing of the state' (Turner, 1991: 16).[3]

However, trends towards *corporatism* are highly uneven. Not only are labour, the state and business relatively disorganised when compared to the participants in strong corporatist systems elsewhere, but such peak-level negotiation is firmly established in but a few industries.[4] Moreover, peak-level negotiations have not subsumed plant-level processes. Centralised agreements tend to set minimum rather than actual wages and benefits, with the latter to be worked out in plant-level agreements where factory-level unionists retain the right to negotiate and take action independently of their national unions.

Nor can the system be easily described by the term *co-determinist*, if the latter is meant to suggest the development of a strong statute-based system of collective interest representation and participation at the workplace. While there are certainly trends in this direction, such as Chapter 5 of the LRA, these are distrusted by labour and, for the moment, remain relatively peripheral to traditional adversarial bargaining between shop stewards and employers. As of 1998, only six workplace forums had been established by trade unions under the LRA, and three of these were subsequently cancelled by the same unions (Psoulis et al., 1999).

Finally, as Jeremy Baskin has argued, labour's involvement in decision-making extends well beyond the borders of the industrial relations system to include involvement in multipartite processes as diverse as university transformation structures, the selection of constitutional court judges, and (until recently) budget formulation. To capture such diversity, Baskin has employed the term *concertation* to describe a looser, less structured, policy bargaining arrangement (Baskin, in Friedman and de Villiers, 1996). According to Baskin (2000), concertation means 'an institutional role for interest organisations (mainly economic) in the formulation and implementation/regulation of state policy':

> In practice, this involves not one event or institution, but a *web of collaborative interchanges* [emphasis added] between state, labour and capital. It may include, but is not limited to, forms of tripartism or even multipartite institutions.

For its part, COSATU (1998) resolved at its recent 6th National Congress to 'develop strategies that engage both the state and business for the improvement of the material conditions of the majority, while developing a long-term vision of a socialist society'. The idea of *engagement* has certain advantages over concertation. In particular, while it allows for an emphasis on working in concert towards certain mutually accepted goals, it also emphasises disagreement and conflict, and that the parties may have very different bases for seeking a concertation of interests. Engagement implies a common meeting place, not a common starting point, nor even a common end-point. For these reasons, the term engagement will be employed here. But whatever the term, it is crucial to stress Baskin's emphasis on a 'web of collaborative interchanges between state, labour and business' which traverse every level of society.

Engagement at enterprise level:
African and European comparisons

Chapter 5 of the LRA for the first time enabled representative unions in workplaces with more than 100 employees to create co-determinist-type institutions called workplace forums, which possess broad consultative and joint decision-making powers. While consultation means that an employer must, in a timely fashion, canvass plans with a workplace forum, decision-making power rests with the employer, though the latter must provide reasons to the forum for overriding their objections. Joint decision-making means exactly that: both the employer and the council make the decision, with clear and agreed procedures for breaking deadlocks. While one may be seen as a 'soft' and one a 'hard' form of interest representation, in practice the two tend to blur. Employers are more likely to heed a forum's objections on a matter of consultation if they know that tomorrow they will need the same council's agreement on a matter of joint decision-making. (For a discussion of issues subject to consultation and joint decision-making, see the chapter by Satgar in this collection.)

As originally envisaged, workplace forums would be composed of all employees in a workplace and their powers would be focused on non-distributive (non-wage) matters, while registered trade unions would continue to be responsible for collective bargaining over wages and working conditions.

Workplace forums are examples of what Rogers and Streeck (1994) call 'second channel institutions': 'workplace-based institutions for worker representation and labour-management communication'. But the notion of a 'second channel' as specified in the draft of Chapter 5 of the LRA became a subject of considerable dispute. Not only did the proposed legislation carry with it strong notions of co-operation, at odds with the adversarial nature of the South African workplace, but this vision was to be embodied in the twin separations mentioned above between wage and non-wage issues and between the forum and a representative trade union. Taken together, these proposals were read by many unionists and labour-linked researchers as a formula for weakening unions. These perceptions were reinforced by historical experience in South Africa and elsewhere in Africa, and by a tendency of the South African left to interpret co-determination in terms of the German model with which many are uncomfortable.

Non-union workplace representative structures have a rather unfortunate precedent in South African labour law which, in large part, explains the hostility unions possess for Chapter 5. The 1953 Native Labour (Settlement of Disputes) Act – a notoriously anti-labour piece of apartheid legislation – included a provision for 'works committees' for African workers whose representatives were directly elected by workers themselves. However, these bodies had no statutory rights to joint decision-making or consultation, and were a clear attempt at union avoidance.[5] Disputes between works committees and employers would be automatically referred to hierarchical state bodies chaired by whites appointed by the Minister of Labour. An even weaker body – the infamous liaison committee – was created in legislative revisions in response to the resurgence of black trade unionism following the 1973 Durban strikes. The Wiehahn Commission advocated the retention of a weak form of works councils that were to replace both works and liaison committees. Though embodied in section 34A of the old Labour Relations Act, this recommendation remained a dead letter.

Despite being enacted by a succession of racist governments, the works and liaison committees were ironically similar to those introduced in a number of post-independence African countries. During the turn to socialism in Tanzania, these took the form of compulsory workers' councils which included worker representatives, but were essentially dominated by management and party officials. Combined with the wide use of 'essential service' declarations – prohibiting strikes across entire industries – and the top-down party control of union structures, these features were intended to harness workers' efforts to the project of national development by undermining unions' independent collective power. Roughly similar developments occurred in Zambia in the early 1970s, as well as in Zimbabwe after independence. (Lwogo and Mapolu, n.d.; Rakner, 1992; Maphosa, 1992; Bayat, 1991: 152ff). However, in Tanzania a solely worker-run body, the workers' committees, had a narrow brief – ensuring 'discipline' – but were in fact often independent of management (see Shivji, 1976 and 1986).

These experiments in union avoidance generated considerable opposition from workers. In Tanzania, the relatively independent workers' committees enabled workers to mount a powerful critique of corruption and poor conditions in state-owned enterprises, cleverly subverting their formal brief by attacking their managers' 'indiscipline'. In Zambia, the attempt to bypass unions created more confusion than control. In the early 1970s, the Kaunda government introduced employee- rather than union-based works councils on the West German model in every workplace of 100 or more workers. Works councils enjoyed wide co-determining power which tended, however, to cut across the unions' traditional collective bargaining prerogatives and representational rights. A works council, a party political committee and a shop stewards council might all be operating within the same factory, blurring lines of authority and responsibility. For this reason, they were viewed with scepticism by unions and employers alike, and both tended to ignore them (Rakner, 1992).

If these experiments were not always effective in controlling workers' collective organisation, neither did they enable workers to make sustained inroads into managerial prerogatives. This sad history certainly contributed to black South African workers' continuing perception that non-union workplace structures are little more than an attempt to weaken legitimate trade union representation. After years of building independent shop-floor organisation, unionists were deeply suspicious of legislation which proposed a new and potentially rival body in their midst. Such anxiety was heightened by the fact that workplace forums would include all employees, including supervisors and lower and middle managers who are mostly white.

Though it would be tempting to view South African workplace forums in this manner – and many commentators have done precisely that (Etkind, 1995; Lehulere, 1996) – there are substantial differences between workplace forums and their predecessors elsewhere in Africa or in South Africa's past.

Workplace forums are not compulsory institutions; indeed, they may be triggered only by a registered trade union in a particular workplace. Nor must they replace trade unions as workers' collective voice – though in draft form Chapter 5 certainly held this potential. However, the original provisions of the draft Bill were changed at NEDLAC. Unions won amendments that allow for a variety of types of workplace forums, including a union-based model which is essentially an extension of the union shop steward committee. This change simultaneously addressed the other contentious features in Chapter 5, the institutional separation of distributive from non-wage matters and the pressure towards co-operation. Many commentators noted the potential for competition between shop steward committees and workplace forums, and predicted that employee-based workplace forums would undermine union power and bargaining. Under the union model, however, a union could continue to represent its members in collective bargaining while simultaneously claiming the consultative and joint decision-making rights on a range of non-distributive issues, as well as extensive rights to information.[6] A union would retain its strike powers, and would be able to decide whether or not to take issues to the 'second channel'.

If the draft provisions catalysed unionists' suspicions based on local and African experience, they also activated their hostility to the German model of co-determination where works councils are separate from trade unions, involve all employees, and are not permitted to strike. Many analysts simply slide between discussions of forms of workplace representation, co-determination, and the specifically German system of co-determination, *mitbestimmung*. (See, for example, Barchiesi, 1998.) Not only is this a misreading of European experience where co-determination takes many institutional forms, but it fails to capture the revisions accepted in NEDLAC.

In fact, the model enacted in the LRA varies markedly from any extant overseas system. As Satgar shows in his chapter in this collection, its form is derived less from European models and more from responses to perceived South African political and economic exigencies and from bargaining in NEDLAC.

The LRA's permissiveness allows for a variety of forms of workplace representation and, in this context, it is helpful to review the diversity of European experience rather than assume that any experiment in co-determination must follow a specific institutional model. In many European countries, the rights and obligations of second channel institutions ('councils') are statutorily entrenched, and may include powers of joint decision-making, consultation and information-sharing. The issues addressed by such institutions vary widely but, according to Rogers and Streeck (1994), these are largely determined by the character of extra-firm collective bargaining. Where this is strong and centralised, councils are prevented from dealing directly with matters addressed in collective bargaining, such as wage-setting. Indeed, councils are obliged to uphold and monitor any collective agreements applying to their enterprise. By contrast, in countries with weak systems of extra-firm wage-setting, councils function like local trade unions and, in some cases, are able to bargain over wages and call strikes.

In some countries, most notably Germany, councils are established on a non-union basis. But this is not the case everywhere. In Italy local unions perform council functions, while in Sweden, which has both strong centralised bargaining and strong 'second channel institutions', the latter are run by shop stewards. But whether or not they are union bodies, councils are institutions that represent *collective* rather than individual interests of workers. Insofar as they are *participatory* bodies, they are distinct from managerial schemes to 'involve' workers in production through, for example, quality circles or communication schemes. Significantly, councils are independent of management: they are not organised along functional production lines and stand outside channels of managerial authority (Rogers and Streeck, 1994: 102).[7]

Whether or not councils are union bodies, their functions are meant to complement collective bargaining by taking on tasks for which bargaining is not well suited. But 'well suited' is a relative term: there is no fundamental distinction between issues appropriate for collective bargaining or for councils. Council competencies may include matters that are best decided at the level of the enterprise, such as work organisation and technological change. Furthermore, where extra-firm bargaining takes place on an annual or triennial basis, councils provide a means for addressing issues that require either constant monitoring or rapid responses. But there are no absolutes: matters that in Germany are decided by a non-union works council, in Sweden are determined by shop stewards; issues that councils decide in Spain at the work-place level are the subject of collective bargaining in Germany.

The general point is that in different countries similar institutions can perform different functions while different institutions may perform similar functions. Indeed, the distinction between councils and unions blurs in practice, as in the modern workplace the valorisation of worker consent as a productive asset makes it increasingly impossible to separate technical and representative processes (Streeck, 1994). On the one hand, labour movements that sought to preserve their identity by eschewing council-type institutions (as in Sweden) find their factory-level structures becoming 'councilised'. On the other hand, the non-union works councils in Germany have essentially been colonised by strong centralised unions. Councils have helped unions to broaden their membership and power such that Streeck can describe them, in a well-known phrase, as the 'extended arm of the union at the workplace'.

International experience provides a variety of co-determination systems, many of which have features which address the explicit concerns voiced by critics of Chapter 5. Yet unions in South Africa remain reluctant to pursue workplace co-determination, a stand that has less to do with institutions and models and more to do with ambivalence about co-management itself.

Engagement beyond the workplace: Industry accords

If the LRA provides workers with new rights of engagement at the workplace level, other developments provide for engagement between labour, business and the state beyond the enterprise. These trends point to the development of corporatist-style bargaining in South Africa. (Maree, 1993; Baskin, 1993 and 1993a; Vally, 1992; Desai and Habib, 1996)

The new unions of the 1970s and 1980s grew from the shopfloor, where they focused their organisational power around strong shop steward-controlled locals capable of extracting concessions from employers in plant-level bargaining (Friedman, 1987; Adler and Webster, 1995). This strategic emphasis proved to be insufficient as employers and conservative unions could box unions into unfavourable conditions of employment through industry-level bargaining in industrial councils over which the unions exerted little influence. Many unions refused to participate in such structures which required formal registration with the Department of Manpower. However, as shop-floor strength and union density grew, many unions reassessed this strategy and chose to challenge management in industrial councils.[8] Since the late 1980s, centralised bargaining has in fact become a core demand of the labour movement and was a major point of contention between labour and business in revising the LRA.

But the unions' move towards centralised bargaining unleashed a series of organisational problems which have never been fully resolved. The need to combine disparate local demands into a common negotiating position created the possibility of destructive and embarrassing defections from the central bargain (Von Holdt, 1990). Furthermore, the skilled staff required to conduct the negotiations generated tensions for a movement that had long prioritised the power of elected semi-skilled worker leaders over full-time officials. These tensions between the centre and locals remain: Marie (1992, 1995) traces the widely acknowledged and chronic weakening of locals in large part to these original centralising tendencies.

Nonetheless, increased centralisation remains an imperative, compelling COSATU to identify an even more vexing problem: the creation of larger affiliates through the merger of existing unions along broad sectoral lines.[9]

In the early 1990s, COSATU's strongest affiliates were able to use their power to engage with broad questions of industry restructuring. This issue had been placed on the agenda as a result of South Africa's impending reintroduction into global markets as a consequence of political democratisation. The adjustment required would be enormous, given the long history of protectionism associated with import substitution industrialisation. Unions feared that such adjustment would occur on neo-liberal terms, entailing massive job losses unless they developed appropriate restructuring plans and the institutional means for establishing these as government policy. Thousands of jobs were at stake in many sectors, including textile and clothing, automobile, and mining. These were not only the largest sectors in manufacturing and the most densely organised, but the unions in these sectors were among COSATU's largest and most influential.

In the years prior to the 1994 elections, the unions sought to ensure that industrial policy would be developed on a tripartite basis by government, business and organised labour. While the 'mining summit' of the early 1990s largely stalled, efforts in the other two sectors ultimately produced agreements.[10] The unions were able to bring business to the negotiating table, in large part because the employers were as threatened as the unions by restructuring. Furthermore, the unions were able to impose industry bargaining on the weakened apartheid state which feared the disruptive political effects rapid restructuring would generate, and saw agreements with business and labour as a means to gaining some legitimacy for itself. According to Chapter 5 by Hirschsohn, Godfrey and Maree in this collection: 'The political transition thus created a unique opportunity for the three social partners to develop and implement consensus-based industrial policies to restructure their industries to ensure their long-term viability.' But they stress that the unions – rather than the state or business – drove the process by virtue of their ability to develop creative policies and to realise these through a combination of skilled negotiators backed up by their organisations' mobilisational power.

In both industries, the three parties agreed progressively to reduce tariffs and rapidly integrate South African industry into the global economy; in return, both labour and business sought numerous supply-side inputs, including retraining and trade incentives, to offset the likely shocks of adjustment. In addition, they sought the creation of industry authorities to implement these measures and to monitor progress. In principle, these agreements provided workers with substantial powers to restructure their industries according to their own agendas, rather than responding reactively to adjustment imposed from without.

However, engagement over industrial policy has been flawed in that the institutions through which engagement occurs are not statutorily-based, but depend on the goodwill of the participants. The parties – most especially government – were not bound by the agreements produced. Indeed, once in power, the ANC government 'cherry-picked' both the textile and clothing and automobile agreements, endorsing those aspects consistent with the policies of the Department of Trade and Industry, such as tariff reduction, while rejecting those that meant increased state expenditure or the creation of multipartite implementation and monitoring authorities which could usurp state functions. While COSATU could impose industry bargaining on the weakened National Party government, it could not achieve the same result with a legitimate government, even one headed by its alliance partner!

Curiously, unions displayed considerably less hostility to industry-level as compared to enterprise engagement. Where the latter suggested 'co-managing apartheid' and ran up against the unions' anti-capitalist ideological commitment, the former opened possibilities to reshape capitalist relations of production while maintaining some distance from actual enterprise management. Moreover, union negotiating and research capacity were greatest at the industry level as were the gains to be realised relative to the resources invested. Clearly, however, the two forms of engagement were deeply connected: in the absence of some type of enterprise-level engagement by workers, managers would likely subvert or ignore industry-level agreements. Unions' inability to develop a coherent approach to enterprise-level engagement would in turn compromise the best industrial accords.[11]

The public service remains a fascinating challenge to the development of engagement. It was deliberately excluded from the provisions of Chapter 5, and was instead to be regulated for the purposes of workplace forums by a schedule to be promulgated by the Minister for Public Service and Administration (LRA, Section 80(12); see also Satgar's and Patel's contributions to this collection).[12]

According to Patel's analysis in this collection engagement in the public service is both under- and over-developed relative to the rest of the economy. Even without a Ministerial proclamation, institutions of engagement are potentially widespread in the public service. These include interesting institutional innovations that have given unions wide-ranging co-determination powers at the enterprise level through participation in workplace transformation committees, governing committees and enterprise boards. These rights are available in Germany but were not included in Chapter 5. Meanwhile, centralised bargaining in the Public Service Co-ordinating Bargaining Council occurs over qualitative 'non-distributive issues' that extend well beyond wage-setting. Thus, public service co-determination includes workplace and sectoral transformation committees; board-level participation; and strong centralised bargaining over a wide array of distributive and non-distributive issues. Such practices may not survive fiscal austerity and the trend towards commercialising the public service. The public service has nonetheless produced institutions that could guide discussions of engagement elsewhere in the economy.

Engagement beyond the workplace: NEDLAC

Most significantly, and in contrast with the experience of engagement in industry restructuring, an Act of Parliament extended and entrenched workers' rights to engagement at the level of the society as a whole. The National Economic Development and Labour Council Act (Act 35 of 1994) provides labour and other collective actors with unprecedented rights to shape a range of government policies.[13]

According to Gostner and Joffe in their chapter in this collection, with the transition to democracy in the early 1990s the unions sought a dramatic extension of corporatist-style initiatives to questions of broad social policy. Though this was in some ways a logical development of labour's efforts to increase worker control over decision-making at the centre, Gostner and Joffe argue that the unions were primarily motivated by the goal of preventing the NP and business from undertaking unilateral restructuring of the economy prior to the election of an ANC government. (See also Schreiner, 1991; Friedman and Shaw, 2000; Webster, 1995)

For much the same reasons that labour was able to win the co-operation of business and the state on industry restructuring, the unions succeeded in drawing both parties into a tripartite National Economic Forum in the dying days of the old regime (Friedman and Shaw, 1999). Rather than fading away with the installation of a new government, the NEF and the National Manpower Commission – a policy advisory body created in the labour reforms of the 1970s – were replaced by NEDLAC.

Though labour's ability to achieve its goals in NEDLAC has been uneven, the Council provides the opportunity for wide-ranging interventions on the most important government policies. These possibilities are not only a radical departure in South Africa, but are largely unprecedented in the world, especially given the trend towards neo-liberal deregulation.

Examples of societal engagement from southern Africa serve to highlight NEDLAC's distinctiveness. One of the first labour reforms enacted in Zambia by the popularly elected government of Frederick Chiluba was the creation in 1993 of a Tripartite Consultative Labour Council (TCLC) with power to 'advise the government on all issues relating to labour matters, manpower development and utilisation ...' (Akwetey, 1996: 13). Though the TCLC granted the Zambian Congress of Trade Unions (ZCTU) a limited purchase on policy-making, the Council has not performed the role expected by labour. It has no permanent secretariat, nor does it have any statutory right to review legislation. Its role is merely advisory, and its decisions are not binding. Furthermore, it meets at the convenience of the Minister of Labour who, for the first years of the first Movement for Multiparty Democracy (MMD) government was Newstead Zimba – the former ZCTU Secretary General – identified by current ZCTU leaders as the most anti-labour member of Chiluba's cabinet! In 1996, the TCLC was convened only once. A top official of the Ministry of Finance referred to it as 'that consultative body where once a year government informs labour of decisions that have already been taken' (Gostner, 1997: 59-60; Ministry of Finance, 1996: confidential interview).

A similar institutional innovation in Namibia seems to have suffered the same fate. In 1992, the recently elected South West African People's Organisation enacted new labour legislation which established a tripartite Labour Advisory Council to advise the Minister of Labour on any labour-related matters (Bauer, 1994). However, the Council lacked a secretariat, was plagued by difficulties over labour's representation at the table, and was often ignored by the government.

NEDLAC does not – yet – suffer from the same shortcomings. For the time being at least, it enjoys a relatively large and capable secretariat, and is not organised at the convenience of a minister of state. All parties are publicly committed to its existence, though – as will be seen below – each has defected at critical moments on matters of self-interest.

Why should engagement have become so common in South Africa? The next section will explore a number of general explanations for its development.

EXPLAINING ENGAGEMENT: PASSING FASHION OR ENDURING FEATURE?

Engagement is not simply the latest managerial vogue, nor an obsession of the ministerial legislative drafting team that developed the LRA. Its emergence is part and parcel of the broader transition to democracy in South Africa which has prioritised practices of bargaining and pacting between opposed societal interests. Such co-operation – and the inherent compromises on which it hinges – was a necessary condition for transition under conditions of political stalemate. In this sense, engagement is an era-bound product, precipitated by the exigencies of collaboration between an illegitimate state which governed but did not rule, and a legitimate democratic opposition which ruled but did not govern. However, where most transitional multipartite bargaining withered away after the election of a legitimate government, engagement between labour, the state and business has survived the negotiated settlement that gave it such a strong impetus.[14]

There are four main reasons why forums for engagement have endured. First, South Africa's transition to democracy has coincided with the advance of globalisation and new forms of competition in the international political economy. Locally this has posed the simultaneous challenges of democratisation amidst profound economic restructuring. Given its historical strength and the imminent threat to its members' interests, the labour movement vaulted into negotiation with business and the state over the form and pace of restructuring. But, as described above, both the state and business – for different reasons – had an interest in some form of engagement over these same issues.

Similar processes are occurring at enterprise level. Market demand for quality puts a premium on employee performance, while new forms of work organisation allow for the potential decentralisation of decision-making and increase employees' influence over work. In many sectors management cannot simply tell employees what to do, but must trust them not to misuse their increased discretion. One approach is to increase employees' commitment to the enterprise, and many managements have undertaken some elements of organisational restructuring aimed at increasing 'employee involvement' and other forms of co-operation. Such initiatives are often tied to varieties of 'adjustment' aimed at improving productivity and competitiveness, and have often brought with them demands for retrenchment and wage restraint. In other words, engagement has persisted because many employers themselves desire that it continue as an adjunct to their development strategies, albeit with extremely important limitations on the nature and extent of participation.

Second, notwithstanding their refusal to participate in statutory structures during the apartheid era, most of the unions that emerged in the 1970s and 1980s were committed to a vision of socialist transformation, and advocated the radical extension of worker control at the enterprise, industrial and societal levels. Though the principled policy of 'militant abstentionism' during the anti-apartheid struggle emphasised minimum co-operation with the state and business (though it did not exclude routine collective bargaining and even registration under the LRA), with the onset of the transition to democracy, labour gave force to its commitment to worker control (Von Holdt, 1991 and 1991a). While there are some ambiguities about the approach, labour sought direct engagement with the state and business at the national and industrial sectoral levels.[15] If business sought to make contact with labour over certain limited forms of co-operation, then labour – in pursuit of worker control – sought engagement with business and the state.

Third, engagement has grown out of and has been sustained by the regular, institutionalised interactions between organised labour and business founded in the employment relationship. This relationship, exemplified by the welter of recognition agreements, bargaining councils and other institutions of the industrial relations system, existed prior to the transition itself. Thus, engagement is rooted in the extensive and long-entrenched relationship between labour and business which is formally independent of political parties and the state.[16] The historical embeddedness of engagement between labour and business in capitalist relations of production constrains the options available to the state for unilateral restructuring of the economy and society. Indeed, the LRA of 1995 has significantly bolstered the industrial relations system and its independence from the state.

Finally, most multipartite transitional negotiating processes emerged because of the crisis in legitimacy of the apartheid state and existed on a voluntary basis, with unstable and shifting membership. By contrast, the cornerstones of institutional engagement between labour, business and the state – NEDLAC and workplace forums – are enshrined in law. The existence of such forums and the rights conferred upon them do not depend primarily on the exercise of power by the participants; rather, the power of the participants enabled the creation of entrenched powers that will maintain the institution even if the parties' strength wanes. Gostner and Joffe argue in their contribution to this collection that the NEDLAC Act gives labour and business the right to influence the policy process and, therefore, the kinds of policy that government adopts before legislation goes to Parliament. As such, labour need only mobilise in those instances in which negotiations deadlock as it no longer has to expend considerable resources on getting a place at the table.

If engagement is not simply a passing fashion, it may be too soon to declare that it is an enduring feature. It is important to survey the difficulties each party has with engagement, to which the discussion now turns.

ENGAGEMENT:
CONFLICTING HOPES, CONFLICTING FEARS

If one speaks to trade unionists elsewhere in Africa or to their counter-parts in Asia or North America, they often express deep envy at the forms of engagement available to South African unions. Indeed, unionists else-where have spent considerable time studying the NEDLAC Act and the LRA of 1995 while strategising how to achieve similar gains in their own countries. Yet one of the most intriguing ironies of the experience of engagement in South Africa is that, while each party has reason to be thankful for its existence, engagement generates little enthusiasm among its supposed beneficiaries, most especially labour.

Indeed, at critical moments each party has opted out of engagement when it suited their interests to do so. As Gostner and Joffe demonstrate, NEDLAC has been particularly prone to such defections. Since 1996, for example, the unions have bypassed the council by insisting on treating the restructuring of state assets as a bilateral issue between them and government. Business judges that it can better secure its interests by quietly lobbying friendly government politicians and senior civil servants than by entering complicated negotiations in NEDLAC over macro-economic fundamentals. For its part, government treated GEAR as a non-negotiable issue, and manoeuvred to ensure that it was never formally discussed in NEDLAC's Public Finance and Monetary Policy chamber. According to Hirschsohn, Godfrey and Maree in Chapter 5 in this collection, government has similarly refused to be bound by industry restructuring accords, unilaterally rejecting crucial items in the textile and clothing and automobile industry agreements, thereby eroding their effectiveness.

Each party resembles a prosecutor or defence attorney 'shopping' for the most suitable judge to hear their case. Rather than being bound by decisions that limit their options, the parties seek another venue where an unpopular result can be overturned, as if on appeal. In this respect, engagement serves not to bind parties to unfavourable outcomes, but is more or less an extension by other means of a zero-sum adversarial bargaining process.

By definition, engagement cannot allow any actor to maximise his or her rewards at the expense of another. It is rather a way of producing compromises: sub-optimal or 'least-worst' outcomes (Baskin, 1998: 18). Ambivalence arises, however, because engagement is a deeply contested concept with different meanings for each actor. On labour's side, advances towards involvement in decision-making appear to satisfy long-standing goals to deepen worker control and constrain the unilateral decision-making power of both business and the state. As Satgar argues in his chapter in this collection, the LRA's provisions allowing for the establishment of a workplace forum through agreement between employers and a representative trade union hold out the possibility for a radical extension of worker control. In addition to expanding the areas of joint decision-making beyond those identified in Section 81(1) of the Act, Satgar identifies the possibility of including within the agreement an autonomous self-management competency which goes beyond co-determination in that workers begin to usurp managerial functions.

But these very possibilities threaten managerial prerogatives and heighten business's fears that engagement is labour's Trojan Horse that must at all costs be kept outside the gates. Hence, for the most part, as

Godfrey, Hirschsohn and Maree show in Chapter 9 in this collection, managers embrace limited forms of workplace-level decision-making which are yoked to their pre-existing plans for achieving competitiveness. Except in cases where unions are well organised and assertive, employers seek to restrict engagement to forms they believe to be functional to their overall agenda. Similarly, Webster and Macun in their contribution argue that – with few exceptions – existing forms of workplace representation amount to soft forms of consultation developed in response to firm-threatening crises. Such forums' powers are ambiguous and are seldom institutionalised. The existing cases, Webster and Macun report, fall well short of joint decision-making as, in the final instance, power rests with management, and come close to Pateman's (1971) famous description of 'pseudo participation'.

Thus, business has its own motivations for embracing forms of participation: to incorporate labour into their chosen strategies for increasing efficiency and competitiveness. To a great extent, this imperative is shared by the state. As Du Toit (1995) points out, the Minister of Labour, when launching the Draft Labour Relations Bill, described worker participation as 'more than a moral or ethical imperative' situated within 'parameters of equity and social justice'. However, the Act eventually passed by Parliament does not give precedence to this democratising and empowering intention, and prioritises instead that workplace forums 'must seek to enhance efficiency in the workplace' (LRA, Section 79(b)). 'Such an explicit directive,' Du Toit (1995) argues:

> will be binding on a court in a way that a general statement of intent by a minister is not. The implication is that economic efficiency must take precedence over the requirements of democracy and that, if 'efficiency' (as understood by a court) demands it, workers' rights to be involved in decision-making must be curtailed. An alternative approach … would be to seek a synthesis: a system of workplace governance designed to enhance democracy as well as efficiency, in mutually reinforcing ways …[17]

These orientations on the part of business and the state in turn activate labour's fears that engagement – despite certain advantages – will ensure their incorporation on unfavourable terms within capitalism and undermine their programmatic commitment to a socialist transformation. In this sense, engagement is perceived by labour as business's Trojan Horse.

Thus, in spite of advances that have created an unprecedented expansion of labour's potential power over decision-making, these opportunities have been met with considerable scepticism – even rejection – in the ranks of labour (see Buhlungu, 1996).

But the state's reservations about engagement do not coincide entirely with those of business. Without denying the attractions of bringing labour 'on board' a programme of increasing competitiveness, the state, too, has reasons to fear that engagement will indeed be a Trojan Horse for *both* labour and business. Engagement could well enable both to usurp the state's constitutional prerogatives by infringing on its sovereign right to make and implement laws. Where this infringement was inevitable during the transition to democracy (indeed, it may be argued, such power sharing was a necessary condition for transition), its attractions for a democratically-elected government are greatly reduced, particularly given that the new Parliament and other democratic institutions remain unconsolidated.[18]

Buttressed by a popular mandate and equipped with policy-making capacity, the ANC government has far less need than its predecessor to heed either business or labour (Friedman and Shaw, 2000). This does not mean that the state is free to ignore either, though with increasing frequency ministers and senior civil servants defend state autonomy in policy-making by invoking pluralist notions of parliamentary sovereignty. These notions could be the harbinger of a retreat from engagement. Indeed, as mentioned above, the government effectively blocked NEDLAC from considering macro-economic policy, though it must be stressed that such insulation was not aimed solely at labour, but extended to the ANC itself, as well as to civil society formations.[19]

The NALEDI research project thus arrived at an awkward conclusion. One can point to important trends towards engagement in the workplace, industry and at societal levels, but it is far more difficult to identify who is responsible for such innovations. None of the participants are unambiguous champions of engagement.

IMPEDIMENTS TO ENGAGEMENT

It is too early to conduct a proper assessment of engagement. Similar institutions have evolved over decades in western Europe and labour, business and the state have each taken considerable time to develop appropriate strategies for using them. However, it is possible to identify a range of obstacles that have emerged which could compromise engagement.

Legislative entrenchment

The statutory entrenchment of institutions is an important condition for the deepening of engagement. Certainly, entrenchment does not guarantee that the parties will take engagement seriously, but it does greatly increase the likelihood that the institutions themselves will continue and that agreements reached therein will be binding. As shown by Webster and Macun in Chapter 6, and Hirschsohn, Godfrey and Maree in Chapter 5, workplace and industry-level engagement were largely a crisis-driven response by powerful personalities on both sides who were converted to the wisdom of negotiated solutions. When the crisis waned, or individuals moved on, or firms changed direction, the institutions themselves tended to crumble. They make powerful arguments that, even if unions do not wish to use particular institutions for engagement, they should welcome their entrenchment in law since these options may become desirable when conditions change.

Capacity

All sides lack research, administrative and personnel capacity to engage effectively, but the problems are most extreme in the unions, and are increasingly acknowledged (COSATU, 1997 and 1997a). As Buhlungu shows in his contribution to this collection, a decline in servicing members is obvious, stemming largely from resource problems in many affiliates, and from excessive turnover and the rise of an ethic of self-interest and career advancement among union staff (see also Buhlungu, 1997). Some are unable to fund necessary functions, such as training for shop stewards and officials, and in many prominent cases, business has begun educating union factory representatives. These capacity problems are important because they directly affect union power. If management is training shop stewards – or, as bad, if no training is occurring – the unions risk compromising their power which is ultimately founded on the political sophistication, mobilisational ability and mandates of shop-floor workers and their shop stewards.

Union education efforts are weak, but their research capabilities are even more constrained, notwithstanding the development of NALEDI since 1993. The economic research capacity in even a single quasi-state institution – such as the Development Bank of Southern Africa – completely dwarfs the total research capacity at labour's disposal.

Unfortunately, multiple layers of engagement demand that education and research capacity be radically expanded. Without this, unions are likely to find themselves either blocking initiatives from business and the state or meekly agreeing out of ignorance or for want of alternatives. In this context, the silence in the LRA over the provision of appropriate funding for training members of workplace forums is cause for considerable concern. In many European countries, provision for funding of training by employers is an essential feature of 'second channel institutions'. The lack of similar arrangements here – where the impact of a racist education system heavily advantages business – threatens the viability of all forms of engagement.

Building organisation: Strong unions enable strong engagement and vice-versa

Gostner and Joffe report that labour has proven particularly effective at using NEDLAC in a defensive mode to block certain policies unpalatable to them. But defensive responses are only a small part of the potential gains to be had from engagement. The unions have not been able to realise fully the possibilities for building organisation by extending union membership. Such outcomes have been attained in Germany where unions have colonised supposedly non-union works councils and have brought their leaders and employees into union membership. While formally non-union structures, works councils tend to rely on unions to provide research and other support in their dealings with employers, and in this interaction councillors usually become converted to the cause of unionism. Further-more, unions have used rights of access to co-determined workplaces (for example, the right to attend works council meetings and the right to call for elections to establish a works council) to recruit new members. Given the symbiotic relationship between councils and unions, the election of a works council in practice amounts to a union recognition procedure (Streeck, 1992: 153; 1994a).

Much of the scepticism about workplace forums revolves around union fears that they will not only incorporate unions into capitalism, but will undercut the most important union structure: the shop stewards committee. The LRA's acceptance of a union-based workplace forum helps allay these fears. But it is also crucial to recall that 'second channel' institutions can operate through a multiplicity of forms. It is therefore necessary to reflect on ways to marry 'second channel'-type interventions with the traditional structures of shop stewards committees, combining bargaining with the more consensus-building practices associated with co-determination.

It is unclear at present exactly how union and workplace institutions can be combined. More research and debate, as well as well-chosen experiments on the ground can advance our understanding in this crucial area. This includes finding ways of functionally differentiating 'those issues which are too complex and detailed to be given proper consideration in the context of annual negations from those which are not' (Lagrange, 1995).

At the enterprise level, the unions' ideological hostility to co-management collide with their greatest capacity problems to block consideration of engagement. If for the time being unions are ignoring Chapter 5, neither do they appear to be debating ways of radically expanding the competencies of shop steward committees, as Satgar advocates in his chapter. However, if as some commentators feared, workplace forums were part of an employers' co-optive strategy, then owners seem profoundly uninterested in their own scheme. As Godfrey, Hirschsohn and Maree point out in Chapter 9 of this collection, employers have not developed strategies with respect to workplace forums, which they see as a union matter, and have passively waited for unions to approach them! This does not mean that employers have been reactive; their preferred route of union avoidance – where this is possible – is through tested models of 'employee involvement' which cannot be defined as co-determinist. Thus, enterprise-level engagement is stalemated, with important consequences for labour's ability to capitalise on gains made at industry and NEDLAC levels.

This inability to exploit the possibilities inherent in Chapter 5 signals a series of more profound problems related to union strategy.

New use of power and union strategy

The distinction between defensive blocking manoeuvres and proactive involvement in policy-making implies a subtle shift in notions of power embraced by all three parties. Friedman and Shaw (2000) argue that industrial relations in South Africa have been underpinned by 'realist' notions of power, defined as 'an actor's ability to impose its will, regardless of resistance'. By contrast, creative policy-making depends on the use of 'communicative action power' which is the ability to 'act in concert' with others. Power here rests on securing the voluntary consent of other actors. If 'realist power' concerns the division of existing capacities within society, 'communicative action,' they argue, 'is about creating new capacities' through co-operation between labour, business and the state.

Realist notions of power will continue to be important, not only because this is an inherited tradition, but because the oppressive conditions that generated such conflicts in the past will remain for the foreseeable future. Engagement – defensive and proactive – demands the use of both forms of power. However, Friedman and Shaw stress, 'the challenge of using the one while retaining the other is substantial and unions' experience equips them for it only partially at best'. Engagement demands of union leaders, Friedman and Shaw (2000) conclude,

> that they find both a strategic and a rhetorical balance between continued adversarialism and new forms of co-operation. If the balance is found at all, the quest will not be easy. And damaging failures to find it seem almost inevitable.[20]

If it is difficult to combine adversarialism with co-operation, the problem is made even more complicated for labour due to its strategic position. Where business is generally more comfortable with the status quo inherited from apartheid, labour's agenda depends on transformative action. Where business can retreat into the background in forums such as NEDLAC and play a blocking role, labour to a greater extent must play an active role, combining offensive and defensive strategies.

Given that the NEDLAC agenda has been set largely by government's legislative timetable, as Gostner and Joffe argue, labour often finds itself at odds not with business, but with a government intent on maintaining fiscal discipline and preserving its own prerogatives. In a process driven by White Papers and draft legislation often drawn up in relative isolation by government, labour frequently finds itself compelled either to oppose or to amend proposals at the edges. The first may lead to breakdown; the second to marginalisation, whereby labour accepts working within someone else's plan. Indeed, government not only tends to define what goes on the agenda but, as importantly, what is kept out of the forum.

Such a dynamic is made more complicated by the alliance between COSATU and the ANC. The alliance creates often self-imposed limitations on COSATU's freedom of action that would never have been contemplated in its conflicts with the apartheid state. More importantly, it also produces formal and informal channels of communication through which labour leaders at all levels can be quietly lobbied by a range of interests, outside the institutions and processes of engagement. Given this field of forces, labour faces more complex strategic challenges than the other parties to engagement, or than it faced during the fight against apartheid. The capacity problems described above serve only to intensify these difficulties, which are revealed in a number of areas.

A (partial!) list of commitments made at the 1997 COSATU Congress include campaigns for a living wage; paid maternity and family leave; restructuring of the Unemployment Insurance Fund; child-care facilities; a social security net for all; monetary and fiscal policies that enhance growth and employment creation; public sector restructuring; tariff reduction; a viable public works programme; fair regional labour standards; organisational renewal; changing the country's electoral system; transformation of the police and justice system; fighting globalisation (COSATU, 1998).

COSATU has made gains in many of these areas, and these goals are individually admirable. Taken together, however, they are well beyond any movement's capacity, particularly one with the problems mentioned above. In some respects labour has construed itself as a shadow government, developing policies in every conceivable area of interest to the working class.

This wide agenda is a symptom of deeper strategic problems. The labour movement has not decided which activities take precedence, nor ranked its involvement with any one campaign. If organisations cannot make these choices on a deliberate basis, they risk doing many things badly rather than a few things well. This is the opposite of strategic action. If they are unable to establish specific goals, differentiate short-, medium- and long-term objectives, and marshal scarce resources to achieve them, then unions risk lapsing into what the September Commission on the Future of the Unions labelled 'zig-zag' unionism: a reactive unionism, lurching from one issue to another as they pop up (COSATU, 1997).

Gostner and Joffe call instead for clarity in strategic vision as a prerequisite to the effective use of NEDLAC, though the same point can be made about engagement at the other two levels. Labour cannot maximise its opportunities because it is unsure how to deploy its scarce resources wisely, nor does it know how to link its efforts at NEDLAC with those at the other two levels. The huge and highly technical agenda of discussions in NEDLAC, combined with weakening links between leaders and members, means that issues cannot be debated throughout the organisation. With a relatively uninformed membership, how can the massive power of the unions be mobilised to achieve the organisation's goals?

Thus, the problem of strategic clarity has as its parallel the growth of what the South African Communist Party's Jeremy Cronin (1992) has called the tap theory of protest: turning the mobilisation off or on as determined by the ebb and flow of a very distant negotiation process. This development has serious implications for democracy. How can members possibly follow, let alone exercise democratic control over decisions, if these are made in far-away locations and are sealed by agreements brokered between top leaders? A membership that did not participate in agreements made at any of the three levels will be unlikely to feel bound by them. A labour movement that cannot make agreements stick will be unlikely to command the respect of either business or the state. These problems could result – as COSATU's secretariat acknowledged in its report to the 6th National Congress – in the 'strategic initiative passing into the hands of those opposed to fundamental transformation', and to the rollback of gains made during the apartheid era and since 1994 (COSATU, 1997a).

Transformation

Aside from labour's pragmatic concerns about engagement, and the complex strategic problems associated with it, lurking in the background is a very palpable principled objection. For many South African unionists, the historical reference point for both co-determination and corporatism is European social democracy, where they are seen to have contributed to labour's incorporation into capitalism. What is more often neglected is that both co-determination and corporatism have also come at a cost to business, that they continue to yield significant benefits for employed workers and union members, and that they have not meant the extinction of labour's independence.

Corporatism, in particular, has been associated with union success in weathering the storm of globalisation. According to Turner (1991: 12), in the period of heightened deregulation and global competition, union success or decline and the stability of industrial relations systems are largely determined by two critical variables:

> [First] the extent to which unions, as a broad national pattern, are integrated into processes of managerial decision-making, especially concerning work reorganisation; and second, the existence of laws or corporatist bargaining arrangements that regulate firm-level union participation from outside the firm.

The necessity of reaching agreement between management and workers helps ensure that even far-reaching restructuring programmes take into account *both* market imperatives and the representation of workers' interests. It also means that workers have an independent base from which to assess company needs, giving them the potential to develop a 'worker-oriented vision of the shape of new work organisation'. At the same time, the existence of corporatist bargaining arrangements outside the enterprise 'narrows managerial discretion' and ensures that 'both management and labour ... are pushed from without toward collaboration ...' (Turner, 1992: 12-13).

It is not coincidental that such integrated systems strongly correlate with those cases (for example, Sweden, Germany) where unions have succeeded in maintaining membership through the economic storms of the 1980s and 1990s. (Turner, 1991; Rogers and Streeck, 1994; Streeck, 1994) In an era in which unions are generally on the defensive, advantages which enable them to maintain their size and integrity are extremely important.

Moreover, Streeck (1992) argues that co-determination has resulted in a double incorporation. It has certainly increased labour's identification with management's goals, though it is important to stress that co-operation does not exclude serious conflict between labour and business. But it has also fundamentally changed the way firms deal with labour. Given the constraints co-determination imposes on human resources policy (for example, retrenchments and training), firms cannot easily take on or shed labour as market conditions would normally dictate. The organisational rigidities in co-determined firms have, in part, achieved the decommodification of labour:

> in effect reduc[ing] the dependence of employment on the product market and … turn[ing] labour, within limits, from a dependent into an independent or even constant factor. For many practical purposes, labour in co-determined enterprises is almost as difficult and costly to dispose of as fixed capital. In this sense, the status of capital and labour as factors of production has been made more similar. (Streeck, 1992: 159)

Thus co-determination has resulted in the subtle transformation of the nature of capitalist relations of production. Though the tendency may be strong for engagement to become an end-in-itself rather than a means towards transformation, it would be a mistake to see labour's incorporation as a one-way relationship entirely functional to business.

Still, the gains identified above have come within a capitalist framework. What remains unanswered is the extent to which engagement today can be translated into a means towards longer-term processes of transformation.

Engagement can bring about workers' empowerment by equipping them with skills beyond their specific knowledge, particularly regarding production, management and financial control in enterprises. Without these capabilities, workers will be less able to move beyond a traditionally narrow bargaining agenda as core functions of the firm will remain opaque, even in a context of thorough information disclosure. Furthermore, the opportunities provided by engagement would allow workers to intervene early in policy issues, and perhaps contribute to approaches that would avoid problems such as retrenchments. In such a fashion, workers could move beyond reactive and defensive responses to business's initiatives and mistakes. In the longer term, engagement contains the possibility, outlined above and in the chapter by Satgar, of usurping managerial functions, the Trojan Horse of co-determination most feared by business.

These arguments mesh well with COSATU's September Commission's recommendations for transforming the economy (1997). The Commission's economic vision portrays labour as both the major bearer of the public interest in industrial development, and the bearer of the majority interest in redistribution and social justice. The vision attempts to reconcile short-term defence of worker interests with a longer-term strategy of economic transformation that includes:

- restructuring the public sector to deliver better services; to serve as a source of productive investment in strategically important areas; and to serve as the cutting edge of workplace democratisation
- socialising the investment function through reintroducing prescribed assets – a requirement that enterprises invest in specified developmental areas
- using union investment companies to build 'a social sector' of co-operatives
- transforming the private sector into a 'stakeholder sector' where 'no longer only the rights of shareholders prevail, but also the needs of workers, communities and society'.

These goals in turn are unachievable, except through processes of engagement from the enterprise to the societal level. The Commission acknowledges this in its call for 'strategic engagement'. But the Commission did not fully perceive the multi-layered character of labour's engagement and the opportunities it provides for advancing in a more co-ordinated fashion the Commission's integrated development agenda.

It is worth registering a caveat: labour's aspirations to represent a broader constituency of the exploited need to be examined critically. Many assessments of engagement in South Africa have characterised it as a concern of the relatively well-off. Bird and Schreiner once argued for an inclusive multipartite version of corporate (collective) bargaining, also comprising 'civics, women's groups, associations of the unemployed and the aged, consumer and rural organisations . . .' (Bird and Schreiner 1992: 28-29 and 32).

To an extent, this problem is addressed in NEDLAC's development chamber which includes community-based organisations alongside labour, business and the state. But this sector is, at best, weakly represented at NEDLAC and does not provide an appropriate counterweight to the other groupings (see Webster, 1995). Engagement is weakened because 'there are large numbers of poor and oppressed South Africans whom the civics and trade unions do not represent and who are outside any significant radical popular initiative' (Harris, 1993: 95). By their absence, such groupings ensure that solutions to South Africa's problems of political and economic transition are less likely to meet their peculiar circumstances and needs.

In response, Jarvis and Sitas argue in their contribution to this collection for a more encompassing 'social co-determination' that goes beyond traditional shop-floor-based co-determination (as in western Europe) to include constituencies other than labour and business in processes integrating production and distribution decisions. While identifying a need for the state to co-ordinate and plan development, they call for new national, regional and local 'grids of decision-making'. Workplace co-determination mistakenly assumes that decisions can be isolated from broader societal interests. But who should 'co-determine' a firm's decision to open or close a plant in a particular region? Who has an interest in addressing possible environmental effects or the impact of hiring strategies on local labour markets? 'A plurality of interests', Jarvis and Sitas argue, 'needs to shape together the "co" side of our economic decisions':

> In other words we need to find a new *agency* for determination that is not 'univocal' but 'multivocal': a return to centrist, commandist and dictatorial forms of organisation is undesirable. A collapse of all determination into a reborn 'marketeerism' is also undesirable. Through social co-determination, we are signposting the need for an economic system that is accountable to social and civic needs. And this accountability demands new forms of 'co-decision'-making.

In this respect, arguments for engagement return full circle to the issue of deepening democracy. The forms of participation called for by Jarvis and Sitas cannot be accomplished through the formal institutions of representative democracy alone. Not only do these lack the power to regulate the economic system, in terms of Jarvis's and Sitas's argument, it would be undesirable for them to acquire such power. Rather, such participation depends on a creative mix between parliament (and regional and local legislative assemblies) and bodies that ensure the direct participation of civil society groups in economic decision-making, implementation and monitoring. The institutional forms through which this could be accomplished, their competencies, and the division of labour between them have not even begun to be theorised.

Such participation would have important implications for deepening South Africa's new democracy. Engagement helps ensure that workers can hold those in authority directly and immediately accountable; that such accountability can be extended to the sphere of private economic decision-making; and that it can be exerted before a decision is made, preventing or amending an objectionable policy prior to its implementation. Engagement may ensure that workers reap greater benefits from their labour, and thereby contribute to increased trust, in turn encouraging higher quality work effort. Engagement may increase the flow of information between all parties, which not only contributes to better – more informed – decision-making, but also to a climate of trust and reciprocity (Rogers and Streeck, 1994: 104-112). Agreement on goals helps bind all parties to a policy and ensures their joint responsibility in bringing it about (Gelb and Bethlehem, 1998: 17). In short, engagement may slow down decision-making, but it is likely to improve the quality of an outcome and vastly increase its legitimacy, while developing the participants' intellectual and technical competencies.

CONCLUSION

Engagement holds out the possibility – difficult as it may be to realise – of advancing workers' control over crucial economic decision-making, thereby deepening democracy and contributing to a transformative programme. The paradox is that such potential is realisable only through participation in, and risking incorporation into, the capitalist system.

Labour faces a tall order. It must develop strategic and feasible approaches to engagement at the workplace, industry and societal levels, and be in a position to synchronise these transformative initiatives. An approach that sees these as mutually reinforcing departures – rather than as a series of discontinuous encounters with the state and business – can help ensure that labour's limited capacities are better marshalled towards achieving its goals.

The South African labour movement, it has been said, has proven to be more adept at opening doors than walking through them. But the opportunities described in this chapter will not remain open for ever. The question posed above as to whether the institutions and processes of engagement are a passing fashion or enduring feature cannot yet be answered. But we will know – sooner rather than later – whether engagement has changed the relations between labour, business and the state, and – by extension – the nature of South Africa's new democracy.

In the meantime, the findings presented in this collection make but a first assessment of engagement. Further detailed work and debate is needed by all who share an interest in labour and democracy.

2

CO-DETERMINATION AND TRANSFORMATION

Co-option or alternative vision?

———— ◆ ————

David Jarvis and Ari Sitas

The chapter by Jarvis and Sitas is one of the most original theoretical treatments of the phenomenon of co-determination in South Africa. The authors situate current developments in long-standing debates on the possibilities of democratising work in capitalist economies, and show how thinking in the South African labour movement has, for decades, been intertwined with experiments in western Europe, socialist countries and the third world. They level a number of serious criticisms at the various possible institutional forms of expressing worker control, criticising participation schemes, including forms of co-determination, that seek to marshal workers' energies to management's goals. Moreover, they argue that co-determination as defined in the European experience is limited, and its adoption by the labour movement might mean the abandonment of a serious democratic challenge to the economy since workplace co-determination cannot address problems beyond the shop-floor. They argue instead for forms of what they describe as 'social co-determination' – 'means for integrating production and distribution decisions democratically' – involving not simply labour and business, but also a broad array of interest groups, delivery structures, urban and rural voices and NGOs.

INTRODUCTION

In the past, South African scholars as well as worker and community leaders have advocated various forms of co-operation, workplace democracy, worker control and participation in varying forms of intensity. In the nineties, since the debate on the new labour dispensation, the word that seems to have predominated is 'co-determination'.

For many who think that the word 'co-determination' implies a novel development in labour circles and a new trend in left thinking which pragmatically tones down its aspirations in a new world order, it would be a surprise to realise that co-determination was all the rage in the 1970s as an alternative to militant, adversarial and democratic trade unionism.

In fact, it was brought on to the agenda as an alternative both to the Trade Union Advisory Co-ordinating Committee's (TUACC) approach which argued for democratic shop-steward structures and class war, and to the co-operative communalism advocated by Black Consciousness. Loet Dowes-Dekker, for example, was one of the first to use the German model of co-determination (*mitbestimmung*) and, from the 1970s, spent his scholarship advocating more and more complex systems of local co-ordination. Much of this translated into the educational training resources of the Urban Training Project and Consultative Unions of South Africa (CUSA).

Does this rediscovery of 'co-determination' mean that the democratic left, COSATU and its intellectuals have finally understood the limitations of their vague notions of socialism and recanted? To answer this question, the first part of this chapter reviews local history and separates the indigenous flavours of South African traditions of participation and democracy. If we accept that co-determination is firmly placed within the tradition of European models, then these ideas are close to an argument for labour's accommodation of capitalist norms.[1]

The second part of this chapter deals with 'principles' – workplace democracy and social co-ordination. The third part discusses the levels of co-determination that we believe are necessary for a truly democratic society.

We propose a system of governance of economic institutions that goes beyond the dualistic European co-determination models where only labour and capital are represented. We argue that a broader 'co-determined' form of governance and co-ordination is the most necessary and most democratic form available to us in the late twentieth century and into the new millennium.

PART 1:
LOCAL TRADITIONS OF PARTICIPATION AND DEMOCRACY

In the 1950s, as part of the Congress Alliance, the South African Congress of Trade Unions (SACTU) subscribed to a two-stage theory of social transformation from apartheid to socialism (Lambert, 1988). The first stage, which was to be the result of a national democratic revolution, aimed to institute the democratic principles of the Freedom Charter. This stage implied a far-reaching democracy with a mixed economy but also with a state that intervened directly in the economy of the country. Within the Congress tradition, there were deeply embedded notions of social co-ordination, nationalisation and popular control. Even in its post-colonial democratic phase, the Congress shared these traditions with many anti-colonial movements, such as its namesake in India.

The idea of a first 'stage' involved a legacy of the Comintern's analysis that national democratic states would be transitional: neither capitalist nor socialist, but reflecting both the democratic aspirations of the oppressed in the colonies for self-determination and a state that nationalised the citadels of economic power. South Africa, of course, was seen as a 'colonialism of a special type' where its white masters were a settler population. It also involved a vision common to most third world anti-systemic movements – that the resources and wealth of the society belonged to the 'people'. All conceptions presupposed the emergence of strong states that would harness resources and the economy, control them in the interests of society and direct them for social development.

Indeed, the post-Second World War period was marked by major initiatives that included attempts to co-ordinate developing economies in the third world and to introduce democratic workplace practices. Assef Bayat (1991) traces how ideas around workers' control in the third world, or peripheral capitalism, were either inspired by the 'workers' state approach', hatched in the centrally-planned economies and influenced by the Soviet Union, or by populist ideas of building the nation through collaborative efforts. In both cases, the social determination of work was lodged within the state which represented either the interests of the working class (workers and peasants) or the 'nation'. Participation was consultative and usually involved enlisting workers into plans for raising output quotas.

Although SACTU was driven underground in the 1960s and the trade union movement was suffering serious setbacks, the experimentation that occurred in China, Cuba, Tanzania and Algeria, to name but a few countries, had some resonance. It led to the debates that informed the famous Morogoro declarations of 1969 that it was the *African* working class who was to lead the struggle for national liberation. The idea was strong that somehow the 'first stage' would set in place a democratic state that co-ordinated production in the interests of the oppressed and the majority.

But, by 1969, the 'golden years' of European social democracy (Hobsbawm, 1994) were also throwing up their own models of workplace democracy and economic co-determination. Bayat (1991), in his work on workers' control in the third world, describes these models as the 'corporatist' approach, the 'third world development' approach, the 'aggressive encroachment' approach and contrasts these to the 'workers' state' approach. Each approach had two levels of intervention to regulate the economy and the market: at the workplace and at a social level.

i)   The corporatist approach demanded peaceful co-operation between state (government), capital (management) and labour (workers' organi-sations). Within this context, a strategy of workers' participation at the level of the enterprise was envisaged where, in an atmosphere of co-operation, all parties were to benefit from improvement in individual companies and in the economy as a whole (Bayat, 1991: 27-29). Capital and labour were viewed as equal partners engaged in free agreements while the state, for its part, was to act as a neutral arbitrator between the two. This, Bayat notes, was the fruit of successful trade union movements in expanding, prosperous economies.

ii)   Within the third world, and enhanced by the Yugoslavian experience,[2] new ideas evolved that viewed workers' participation as a 'specific path of socio-economic development, a unique path that (was) different from those of the West and East' (ibid.: 30). In third world countries embedded within a populist ideology as a means of national economic development, and in Yugoslavia as an alternative to capitalism and statism, this general economic approach was centrally concerned with finding 'an alternative to the dehumanised economic systems of both private capitalism and statism' (ibid.: 31). As the Yugoslavian example highlighted, shop-floor democracy, state co-ordination and a market could be combined with remarkable effects.

(iii)   The aggressive encroachment approach was essentially a political approach. Workers' control was viewed as 'the means to a gradual but aggressive encroachment on the power of capital, both at the point of production and in society at large. It is, thus, a way of genuinely reforming capitalism' (ibid.: 33). This approach represented 'a socio-economic system in which workers' control from below was exercised not only at the level of the individual enterprises but also in all other social, political and cultural institutions in society' (ibid.: 34).

This saw the labour movement as a *political* movement and a vehicle for the transformation of the state. Inspired by widespread factory occupations and strikes in the late 1960s and the early 1970s, and by demands for direct democracy, proponents of this approach revived an interest in revolutionary 'councils' and sóviets. Workers were to overthrow the capitalist state and form a state based on the institution of workers' control.

By 1972, the idea that it was possible both to live and work in democratic institutions and in non-market or market-regulated societies was gaining currency. For example, it was the stories around the Chinese Cultural Revolution, the village socialism of *ujamaa*, and the workers' control movements around the Paris strikes of 1968, that influenced left thinking in South Africa, be it Rick Turner's ideas of a participatory democracy, Black Consciousness' communalism or Freireanism (a participatory approach to community empowerment politics). Turner spoke of 'a human model' where an individual would say: 'I need to be free from hidden conditioning processes, I need to be free to be open to other people. I need to be free from external social coercion; and I need meaningful and creative work, work that is an expression of my own autonomous being, and not something I do unwillingly and without understanding what my particular job is for.'

Thus, the social system required for the satisfaction of human needs must be one which (a) enables the individual to have the maximum control over his or her social and material environment, and (b) encourages him or her to interact creatively with other people. These two ideas are combined in the idea of *participatory democracy*. The first essential for democracy is that the worker should have power at his or her place of work, that is, that the enterprise should be controlled by those who work in it – only full workers' control can permit the realisation of human autonomy (Turner, 1978: 32-33).

The above ideas found a home in the democratic trade union movement that was developing after the Durban strikes of 1973. The belief that workers were more than just 'hands' operating at the whim of owners of factories was a fundamental founding principle of the South African trade union movement. It animated trade unionists and intellectuals of the left to argue and create democratic institutions that prefigured the future, that required relationships and refused to be bounded by employer and governmental demands. Furthermore, within the South African trade union movement, there has always been a belief that workers have rights within the factory that go beyond a safe working environment and a living wage. These were expressed not only in demands for participation and democratisation on the shop-floor, but also for a series of cultural rights. So, across the spectrum of unionism in South Africa, the ideas of social regulation and democratic control proliferated: voices were heard articulating the need for 'the workers' state approach', as well as the need for corporatism; other voices were heard arguing for an 'encroaching control' approach, as well as identifying with a Yugoslavian mix of democracy, regulation and markets. By the 1990s, utopian models of factory life had begun to be described (see Sitas, 1993).

By contrast, the arguments for workplace democracy that characterised the late 1960s and 1970s experienced new strains as monetarism took its toll. The dismantling of social welfare capitalism in Europe, as well as the failure of many nationalist regimes in the third world to generate tangible forms of development, turned the tide towards greater factory discipline and more vigorous forms of authoritarianism. One of the last remarkable calls for such forms of democracy was from UNESCO (1982). Its publication *Working Life and Culture*, the result of a six-country collaboration (both Eastern and Western bloc countries participated), argued that work had to be democratised and made more meaningful, and factory life had to be re-socialised and encultured. The study met a world which was deaf to such ideas; the subsequent collapse of Yugoslavia and the ferment in Eastern Europe during the late eighties sealed a period of labour retreats on a global scale.

For South Africans and for the local trade union movement, 1990 proved to be a watershed year. Up to 1989, most of the world's trade unions were caught between two competing 'dreams': a Western one which, in its most conservative strains, celebrated the American dream of consumerism; and an Eastern one, groomed through Moscow's promise to create a society without exploitation. After 1989, with the symbolic collapse of existing socialism after the Berlin Wall was dismantled, the second dream was in ruins. FW de Klerk's announcement in 1990 unbanning popular organisations was justified to his electorate as a consequence of the 'defeat of socialism': it allowed the unbanning of these organisations because they would not be able to survive as communist/ socialist entities.

A number of safe assumptions within socialist and communist movements began to be questioned too. Important here was Joe Slovo's article, 'Has socialism failed?' (1990) which, on the eve of the unbanning of popular organisations, called for a *new* socialist vision and a distinct shift from previous South African Communist Party (SACP) policy. Slovo reaffirmed that the future of 'humanity lies within a socialist framework' in which the 'all-round development of the individual and the creation of opportunities for every person to express his or her talents to the full can only find ultimate expression in a society which dedicates itself to people rather than profit' (1990: 28). But such a socialism had to be *democratic, pluralistic* and *participatory*.

This new socialist vision found a shadow in a new trade union language as well. Trade unions would have to accept that they were no longer *the* vanguard of struggle against an unjust state. Their role in the fight against apartheid was to be superseded by the ANC in its role as the political representative of the national democratic movement.

The response from COSATU was to shift its emphasis from a broad struggle for democratisation towards what has been termed 'strategic unionism' – a more corporatist approach, involving the government and employers at the macro level whilst, at the same time, insisting on democratisation on the shop-floor. In tandem, 'industrial strategy' proposals from the federation shifted towards a concern with human resource development. Through this, a number of training and National Qualification Frameworks (NQF) were mooted. There was a shift towards Swedish, Australian and German ideas of co-determination and discussions about tripartite economic forums. The early evidence of this shift was also to be found in the pages of the *South African Labour Bulletin (SALB)*. The March 1991 focus of the *SALB* examined the role of unions in the new South Africa – the edition was aptly titled 'From Resistance to Reconstruction'. The new role of the union would be a strategic one, entering into dialogue with both government and business, and committing itself to the delivery of a 'reconstruction and development programme' (RDP).

Even during the time of the adoption of the 'reconstruction accord' between COSATU and the ANC-led alliance (formulated at the time of the ANC's unbanning), people voiced both critical venom and assent. Voices emerged to criticise such a 'capitulation'. Words like 'co-option', 'transmission-belt' and 'reformism' proliferated and chastised the move to 'accommodation' with capital and the Government of National Unity (GNU). Unionists such as Etkind and Harvey (1991) spared no time in summing it up in a formula:

> Wage restraint + strict monetary policy + eternal co-operative partnership between capital and labour + achieve higher levels of profitability + government expenditure within existing constraints = the workers will pay.

However, participation in managerial structures and the new collaborative atmosphere were vigorously defended. In the words of Avril Joffe (1994), this had to be seen in the long term as a first step to the realisation of some fundamental social values:

> Democratic participation is a *learning process* for workers, worker representatives, trade union representatives, managers, directors, owners and governments. It is also a struggle. Once a certain level of power is attained, the desire for higher levels, other areas of power and *more effective and meaningful forms of participation* will grow. What is at stake in this struggle are the *fundamental values* inherent in the human right to participation – humanity, dignity, democracy, equity, social and economic efficiency and solidarity. *Democratic participation is a dynamic process* which has been constantly proposed, learned and defended – sometimes through struggle, and it must be constantly widened and adapted to new situations.

That the dominance of corporate priorities in society, in the polity and in the economy was increasing, there is no doubt (Sitas, 1992). That COSATU was pragmatically adjusting to the priorities of capital accumulation in the interests of a new social contract and sound industrial relations, there is no doubt too. The shifts in language and practice between 1991 and 1993 are easy to trace.

During COSATU's Fourth Congress and at its Economic Policy Conference in 1991, 'workers' control' was the demand from labour. Workers' control would afford workers the right to:

- inspect company books
- monitor production
- have time off for planning
- control investment
- veto retrenchments and factory closures
- sit on control committees.

On the shop-floor it was envisaged that there would be worker control over the production process, the products that were to be made, the use of profits and investment. Employee Share Ownership Schemes (ESOPs), which placed limited share capital of companies in the hands of employees were by and large rejected by unions as co-optation. This rejection was based, however, not on a principle that saw the ownership of capitalist companies as wrong, but on the basis that ESOPs offered too small a share of ownership to influence company decisions. It was envisaged that investment would be directed towards the goal of job creation rather than mere profit accumulation. Outside the shop-floor, nationalisation of conglomerates, of services and privatised institutions and the redistribution of land would ensure that the democratic state would be able to achieve its major goal – the redistribution of wealth and power and meeting the basic needs of the majority.

Three years later, in 1994, we witnessed COSATU calling for incentives for companies to encourage the increased training of workers. COSATU also proposed that companies with poor track records in industrial relations should have limited access to government contracts. COSATU's submission to the Department of Trade and Industry asserted that 'the South African economy must compete internationally on the basis of innovation, productivity and superior product quality: not on the basis of watering down worker rights' (COSATU, 1993). It also insisted that trade agreements should contain social clauses that bind South Africa's trading partners to upholding worker rights.

The major shift within COSATU's approach to human resource development (HRD) policies was the replacement of demands for worker control with demands for co-determination and HRD strategies compatible with a 'high road' of economic development. Authors characterised the shift during the early 1990s as one from 'resistance to reconstruction' (Von Holdt, 1991), from 'adversarialism to institutionalisation' (Sitas and Kruger, 1993: 29), from 'conflict to conflict *and* co-operation' (Maller, 1992). The unions' shift in strategy, on the whole, echoed the views of co-determination expert Wolfgang Streeck (1994: 96), who was the special guest for the *South African Labour Bulletin's* annual general meeting and workshop:

> In a capitalist society, in which the livelihood of workers depends on the prosperity of private enterprise, both unions and workers ... will recognise that if their industry or their company loses its competitive power then they, like the shareholders and bosses, will be negatively affected. That is a fact of life.

Therefore, co-determination offered the most empowering way of constraining the will of managerial agendas. Gwede Mantashe, Assistant General Secretary of the National Union of Mineworkers (NUM), a COSATU affiliate, warned that in this new era 'labour is being asked to put "national interests" before their "narrow constituency interests"' (Mantashe, 1994: 110). But he agreed, in the same breath, that co-determination was just one step closer to full workers' control. As Jeremy Baskin (1993: 3) forewarned: 'There is a trend towards co-determination in industrial relations. This doesn't mean the end of conflict between management and labour; merely the conflict is supplemented by the need for practical agreements to address common problems.'

The shift also reflected the acknowledgement of changing dynamics in the global economy and their increased influence on the South African economy. Michael Burawoy (1985: 150) warned that neo-liberalism had increasingly been empowered by 'the fear of capital flight, plant closure, transfer of operations and plant disinvestment'. Increasingly, business argued that workers and the governments they voted into power had the most to lose from falling profits; increasingly, businesspeople boasted that they could easily move to another more profitable site; that such views gave ground for the argument that the interests of capital were the interests of all – 'both in the present and future' (ibid.: 35). At the same time, South African intellectuals insisted on unique and different possibilities for our own trajectory. Time has conspired against such arguments. In the nineties, arguments about globalisation and neo-liberal injunctions seem commonplace and demand of us a climate of participation and co-determination.

The important point in this chapter is not to take sides on the immediate tactical and strategic questions. These concern other contributions in this project. Rather, the focus is on co-determination as a *principle* of organisational governance. It can be stated that any move towards making governance accountable in organisations is important new terrain for contestation. But we cannot fail to notice that the language of co-determination re-emerges precisely at the juncture of 'strategic' participation. Since then, we have been witnessing a trend towards co-determination and increased industrial democracy in South Africa.

It is in this context that Streeck's injunctions (1994: 87) became canonical:

> Co-determination presupposes that unions assume that somehow they have to come to terms with capital. On the other hand, co-determination presupposes the recognition on the part of capital that unions will be around for some time, and that one has to come to terms with a unionised workforce that makes its interests heard at the workplace.

Streeck offered five basic points to define exactly what co-determination is:

- It is the participation of workers in the actual management of the workplace.
- It is a limiting of managerial prerogative, introducing new onuses on management that require them to consult and reach consensus on issues.
- It allows workers representation on issues of production as well as distribution.
- It has legal backing or a legally-backed industrial agreement.
- Finally, co-determination normally takes place through works councils as opposed to trade unions.

Later contributions in this book focus on 'existing forms of workplace participation' in South Africa. What Streeck outlines is a far cry from actual South African shop-floor relations. It seems that most employer-employee relations during the nineties can be characterised as rudimentary, hostile and consultative (Ntshangase and Solomons, 1993; Jarvis, 1995).

Undoubtedly, the distance between promise and reality, theory and practice, proclamation and fact, can and will be great. The issue at hand, though, concerns two points: first that co-determination as defined in the European experience is limited, and its adoption by the labour movement, although understandable, might mean the abandonment of a serious democratic challenge to the economy as such; second, that co-determination has to be seen as a principle that covers realities broader than shop-floors.

PART II:
PRINCIPLES OF DEMOCRATIC REGULATION AND CO-DETERMINATION

As we have already pointed out, the South African trade union movement had embraced, if not a strong conviction, at least a constant reference to a democratic economy and state ownership of economic assets. Increasingly, from the 1970s onwards, it also embraced ideas of workplace democracy and shop-floor self-determination. Is the recent trend towards co-determination an abandonment of principle or a redefinition of goals?

Throughout the 1980s, debate ebbed and flowed around the limitations of the 'social co-ordination' clauses of the Freedom Charter. Critics of the mixed economy it prefigured argued for a stronger social *ownership* of the means of production and the extension of shop-steward structures into viable forms of factory control. Such critics also distanced themselves from the simple demand merely to *nationalise* economic assets and from third-world nationalists who wanted to *harness* resources through the state in the name of the 'people'. Rather, their criticisms were rooted in a more orthodox Marxist analysis.

Marx argued that the organisation of production in capitalist societies was a fetter on human emancipation. Organised for profit, using people's power as an expendable commodity, governed by an anarchic market, production under capitalism was the source of exploitation and alienation. For Marx and Engels, the seizure of state power by the working class, the nationalisation of economic assets and the destruction of private property formed a necessary first phase for genuine human development. The second phase, after the roots of exploitation had been destroyed, would lead to a communist society based on human equality – in the words of Lenin later, a *real* democracy. It was in this spirit that the Soviet Union, under the leadership of the Bolsheviks, attempted to create such an intervention in the territories of the old Russian empire.

The Soviet Union, though, got trapped in a highly distorted version of the first phase of Marx's and Engels' theory. Ideas of central planning were indeed developed by Soviet economists into tangible forms of governance: they pre-planned and calculated the production of goods, their input and output norms, and their technological parameters. The provision of basic services was also pre-planned. A managerial stratum emerged to run economic institutions within the broader macro-economic parameters of 'the' plan. And all this 'statism' organised to serve the interests of the working class, was put in place with the adoption of a policy of War Communism in 1918. Since then, Soviet workers have had very little control over their everyday lives. Without getting into a more complex historical account, the tragedy of Soviet development cannot be grasped in its totality. Suffice it to say that the twentieth century's lesson has been clear enough. The commandist economy failed to deliver the society of plenty it promised. Even if the 'model' was democratised, a centrally-planned economy had become unworkable. Its organisational apparatus failed to deliver economically or technologically, and it failed to create a motivated, satisfied and empowered working population.

There has been extensive criticism of the commandist model of social determination. Bad enough was the human cost of Stalin's reign and the repression of all those who did not respond to the central plan's dictates. For many, this was a profound aberration of a vision that saw centralisation of decision-making and plans as a means to a loftier goal. And here the critique of this divide between theory and practice has been well served by two generations of Trotsky-inspired intellectuals. What we would like to highlight further, though, is the highly problematic nature of the project itself. It is not possible to concentrate knowledge, technology inputs and outputs, plans, calculations, consumer demand and outcomes in the hands and heads of a few people. The complex division of labour in industrial societies makes this an unfeasible task. Although the first 20 years of Soviet industrialisation seemed to show success, its short-term (human) and long-term (economic and resource) costs proved to create serious problems.

Furthermore, it was a deeply *undemocratic* model. As many social philosophers and economic thinkers have argued, it proved to be a direct negation of the egalitarian and emancipatory promises of socialism (Bahro, 1978; Anderson, 1979; Marcuse, 1973). From a concept of the dictatorship *of* the proletariat, as the French Marxist Poulantzas (1980) argued, a system of a dictatorship *over* the proletariat emerged with very dire consequences. It was both the economic stagnation and undemocratic nature of the system that led to the Gorbachev bureaucratic revolution: through *perestroika* (restructuring) and *glasnost* (openness and democracy), the reform-wing of the Soviet intelligentsia sought to re-energise the country's productive forces and create socialism on a democratic basis. Gorbachev's administration conducted a revolution from 'above', trying to meet social movements from below to consolidate such a transition. Unfortunately for Gorbachev, the pent-up frustrations of the Russian population with the past swept the whole project of socialism off the historical stage.

The moment we abandon the idea of state ownership and *centralised* planning, what becomes necessary is to develop an adequate theory of *social* co-determination. The need for an alternative vision becomes pressing indeed. Although in this vision the state still has to co-ordinate the parameters of our development, and most certainly needs to plan as well, the form and nature of our economic relationships need new national, regional and local grids of decision-making. Furthermore, since work is also a material process that interacts with nature, with people, with the environment and communities, a plurality of interests needs to shape together the 'co' side of our economic decisions, no matter what the governmental arrangements of the state.

In other words, we need to find a new *agency* for determination that is not 'univocal' but 'multivocal': a return to centrist, commandist and dictatorial forms of organisation is undesirable. A collapse of all determination into a reborn 'marketeerism' is also undesirable. Through social co-determination, we are signposting the need for an economic system that is accountable to social and civic needs. And this accountability demands new forms of 'co-decision'-making. To echo Alec Nove (1981), we need a socialism that is democratic *and* feasible. Social co-determination should not be confused with proposals for shop-floor co-determination, or *mitbestimmung*, but should rather be seen as a means of integrating production and distribution decisions democratically.

By exploring the meaning of such an 'agency', we would like to see at least three currents of thought being brought to bear on the discussion:

- discussions around the meaning of human-centred development enunciated by African intellectuals who are rejecting the enforced marketisation of community structures;
- intellectual work that looks at the role of states and local governance in a globalising world – work that is defining the contribution of intellectuals in India, in the so-called 'Far East' and in California;
- last, but not least, the forms of public class knowledge and aspirations that have developed from the grassroots of South Africa's black working class: participation/accountability, equity and a utopian vision of 'community' based on deep communitarian beliefs.

The question confronting all intellectuals who agree on the need to create a just society without exploitation and oppression is the nature and composition of such a 'multi-vocal agency' and how it relates to governance structures. It is this multi-vocal agency of 'determination' that we would like to describe as social co-determination.

Similarly, forms of co-determination at the workplace are necessary. Such arrangements we would like to describe as forms of institutional co-determination: the experiments of worker control and of participation in economic institutions carried out in the last 70 years have taught us that the organisation of work under our most modern productive forces cannot yield total democratic self-determination.

At first, socialist intellectuals articulated the desire for workers' control and industrial democracy. But the rise of statism in the Soviet Union and its defence by the Communist movement stunted its growth. Lenin, originally a supporter of grassroots and soviet power, criticised the drive for workers' control and self-determination running through the factories during the first five years of the Russian revolution. For him, this would have created a new kind of 'anarchism' as each factory floor decided what it pleased, without caring about the next priority or indeed about the state's priorities. Furthermore, the ideas of factory councils enunciated by the young Antonio Gramsci were seen as too close to anarcho-syndicalism for comfort. Over the years, such ideas were muffled as the dictates of state plan and economic performance dictated to by centralised planning, scientific management and market dynamics in the West, rendered these ideas the talk of romantic idealists.

Yet, as Bayat (1991) has demonstrated, ideas of workers' self-management and workers' control proliferated further after the Second World War. As we also argued in the first part, such ideas have had a strong indigenous resonance since the 1970s. More and more people have become convinced that 'democracy', 'freedom' and 'self-determination' meant the possibility that workers could come to control the expenditure of their productive power and that work itself could be made more meaningful. The most desirable form of institutional and economic governance would be a democracy exercised directly by the immediate producers.

Here our argument takes an unpopular turn: we feel that such a direct, unmediated democracy is functionally impossible. As the division of labour advanced since the beginning of the twentieth century, it created new managerial *structures* alongside mass production, Taylorism and automation. At the heart of these structures was a new mental and manual division of labour and a new professional function. Those who co-ordinate the labour process, who articulate each of its moments and regulate the quality of its performance functions, constitute a new hierarchy that is separate and distinguishable from the direct producers. Even if each person occupying this hierarchy was elected democratically, he or she would still be in a *structurally* different position from the others.

Trade union pressure and a realisation by managements that labour, reduced to a 'cog' or a 'performance function', was not necessarily 'satisfied', 'productive' or 'functional' have opened up the possibility for more meaningful participation in management or, conversely, a more democratic shop-floor culture. New post-Fordist technologies further enhanced the possibilities of more worker autonomy and participation. Yet modern production processes cannot abolish the separation between those who co-ordinate and demand and those who are co-ordinated.

We would like to argue that the twentieth century, with its cruel laboratories of social engineering and control, has taught us that state ownership and centralised co-ordination of economic life is untenable and demands new forms of social co-ordination. It has also taught us that people will always be grouped together to produce use-values; that such groupings will always be co-ordinated so that they generate a surplus over and above what is necessary for their own reproduction. This, which under capitalism is translated into profit, may instead be a social good in some remote future. The co-ordinating function will always be separate from the performative one and, therefore, whether appointed or elected, it will demand new forms of co-determination.

In this sense, co-determination as an institutional principle must be distinguished from the concrete accommodationist forms of manager-ialism that it has been associated with. It can and must be seen as a necessary claim for co-decision-making, even in the most democratic of institutions.

Of course, capitalist managements, directorates of state departments and even co-operative leadership structures (and union executive committees) would rather do their expected work *unilaterally*. The principle of co-determination at once proscribes such a work ethic and guarantees a level of participation that respects different voices and aspirations.

Whether this leads to 'co-option', 'containment' or 'empowerment' immediately refers to 'power-balancing' in organisations rather than to questions of principle. Co-determined forms of decision-making could lead to any *one* of such directions. From our perspective, it is crucial to assert that as long as a trade union plays an active role in guarding workers' interests and rights, the debate cannot even arise: a principle of co-determination is far superior and closer to notions of industrial democracy and real control over working life and its effects than one which abandons the sphere of work to marketed windfalls and the whims of managements.

The nineties cynicism about 'co-determination' on shop-floors and in industry relates to the fact that managements are more interested in productivity increases, are busy 'right-sizing', are arguing for 'competitiveness', are demanding more flexibility from labour, and are talking of lean production and 'world class manufacturing/service'. It is only as an afterthought that a shift occurs towards an acceptance that some level of participation might expedite the above goals. The management approach to these issues often involves the introduction of new technology and the retrenchment of workers. From their perspective, managements realise that some union demands need to be addressed, and co-determination is seen as a 'soft' option by some of them because it does not involve large amounts of expenditure and most certainly sounds 'politically correct'.

Especially here in South Africa, where managers are attempting to undergo a transition from colonial, patriarchal, paternalist forms of management to a recognition of divergent interests and a commitment to reach consensus within established forums, trade union cynicism about such initiatives is understandable. Management may also be quite happy to engage in co-determination because they believe that unions will not have the capacity to challenge their corporate vision within enterprises.

We do not want to entertain here the 'participation' versus 'consultation' debate: all we can state is that co-determination cannot be mere consultation. In many cases, managements have attempted to consult with workers before a decision is implemented but, as Judy Maller has pointed out, this has always been 'pseudo-participation' and can never be a basis for co-determination. Although consultation is an essential element of any co-determined interaction between management and labour, it is not and cannot be anything more than an aspect of organisational 'decency'.

The most trenchant criticism of co-determined models by the trade unions is that they forge a partnership with managements within parameters set by the profitability of the firm and within broader capitalist macro-economic priorities. Co-option in this sense is real, tangible and effective. Staying out of any such arrangement and worrying about wages, conditions of service, health and safety in an industrial relations-based, *negotiated* sense does not free unions or workers from parameters set by the profitability of the firm or broader macro-economic priorities! Co-determination makes sure that those who are appointed, elected or ordered to decide for others are held in check.

The problem is not so much with institutional co-determination as a principle. Rather the problem is with the quality of the vision, the organisational practices and consistency of trade union and shop-steward initiatives in the long haul of positional democratic advances in any struggle for emancipation. In short, institutional co-determination has to interact with a variety of forms of social co-determination if it is to provide an *alternative* to capitalism's anti-social logic.

PART III:
LEVELS OF SOCIAL CO-DETERMINATION

The classic concept of the state as the node of power and decision-making, as the concentrate of force and popular will, and therefore the control-centre through which the regulation of society occurred, has given way to a humbler vision of an enabling, *facilitating* state which conducts its activities according to a social charter. Such a charter, or constitution, embodies a 'directionality': for example, it enshrines rights to shelter and housing, to gender equality, to equal access to resources and life-chances, and to jobs. In other words, it works within a parameter of social norms and principles that are human-centred and ecologically sound.

The classic concept of the state was shared by socialists, social democrats and the world's national liberation movements. Its simple message was to seize state power through revolution or incrementally through the ballot, and to determine socio-economic performance to meet human needs. By contrast, liberals of all hues argued that one needed a 'referee' state that looked after the rules of the economic games in civil society. Creating a *facilitating* and *human-centred* state is a departure and pre-condition for sensible forms of co-determination.

Political competition, then, would be about the various versions of 'human welfare', the new redefined 'commons', based on such a normative framework and not on the current corporate-sponsored electioneering. But such a state has still to be won and made so that new forms of social co-determination may flourish. Although Immanuel Wallerstein (1997) has argued that it is our task as scientists to study the 'possible' and the *utopistic*, such a task is beyond the confines of this chapter.

Any alternative, however, presupposes many sites of social and institutional co-determination: there have to be arrangements to govern socio-economic performance. As long as any alternative is rooted in our local experiences and enhances the capacity of people to take control over their life conditions as outlined in the first two parts of this chapter, it will be an element of our society's democratisation. In principle, therefore, there is nothing wrong with a NEDLAC-like institution at the national level and similar structures at regional levels that create frameworks and targets for economic performance and strive for consensus between social partners. Yet, the nature and meaning of economic performance has to be contested; indeed contested and broadened, perhaps beyond our borders, perhaps in a broader cluster of internationalised relations.

Then, there is the interface between the world of the economy and the 'community'. Social co-determination here can and must involve a broad array of interest groups, delivery structures, urban and rural voices and non-governmental organisations (NGOs). There are the possibilities, too, of local co-determination: since work is a material and physical process with qualitative implications for communities, the environment and the quality of life of citizens, a different nexus of power-blocs has to be involved. Also, if work is a nature-imposed necessity, it is also an intervention in environmental and social systems and, however much it is an input or a calculated digit, it qualitatively affects locals and communities. Within all these forums, however, the broadest definition of interest groups with representation has to be employed. For example, within industry, it cannot be just the employers, unions and government who have representation. Groups such as the unemployed, environmentalists, women and consumers all need to exercise their influence over production and distribution within the economy. Within such a context, the industr;y-wide and workplace-specific structures for co-determination make different sense. These forums would be more inclusive than sectoral-, micro- and meso-level accords proposed by Standing et al in the ILO's (International Labour Organisation) country review of South Africa (1996). The forums would allow active participation of citizens in the formulation of policies which impact on them in their everyday social and economic existence. They would be a means of extending democracy by exposing policy to a myriad of intervention possibilities. In effect, this would be an expansion of democracy away from politicians and would give labour two bites at the policy pie through its alliance partner in government and its forums of social co-determination.

Our basic premise within this chapter has been that work and society as presently organised place severe restrictions on the ability of people to influence decisions that impact on their lives. Democracy involves taking control of one's body, one's powers, one's environment, one's life. Co-determination is neither about co-option nor radical reform – it is a principle that guarantees a democratic voice and a democratised space so that those who work are not undone by processes beyond their reach or knowledge.

3

THE LRA OF 1995 AND WORKPLACE FORUMS

Legislative provisions, origins and transformative possibilities

———— ✦ ————

Vishwas Satgar

Satgar continues the themes developed by Jarvis and Sitas, but in a different context. He explores the development of the workplace forums provision of the Labour Relations Act of 1995 through an examination of the legislative drafting process and the negotiations that occurred in NEDLAC over the LRA. His rather startling conclusion is that none of the parties – most especially the legal experts who drafted the statute – had a clear understanding of their intentions in introducing this novel provision in South African labour law. Indeed, many of the stated intentions are themselves contradictory. Labour, he argues, was able to influence the process and to reshape the proposed legislation to develop a model of workplace participation more attuned to their own traditions and needs. Based on this review, Satgar makes an argument that trade unions – if they can clarify their own strategies and tactics – could use the opportunities created by new legislation and their adversaries' lack of strategic clarity to extend dramatically the possibilities for worker control in enterprises, especially in the public service.

It is in our interest to make the LRA work. We should not wait for employers ... we need to identify strategic industries and enterprises in order to establish union-centred workplace forums and, at the same time, clearly work out what can be achieved and what is required. (Sam Shilowa, General Secretary of COSATU, October 1996: interview)

Workplace forums are essentially co-operative bodies and, to work, you have to have real co-operation. If you end up with litigated workplace forums, and this is the danger with the union trigger, they are not going to work. This is an opportunity for parties to sit down and do straight talking … (Bokkie Botha, Business South Africa Negotiator in NEDLAC, February 1997: interview)

INTRODUCTION

Work in the modern South African economy – in a factory, on a mechanised farm or in a hi-tech office environment – has generally been characterised by exploitation, hierarchical work arrangements and managerial dominance. Industrial democracy, supposedly realisable through collective bargaining, has not, in the nineties, extended beyond a narrow bargaining agenda. Fundamental workplace issues, such as production planning, investment decisions and work organisation, have not featured prominently on the bargaining agenda. Nevertheless, for the first time in South Africa's industrial relations and labour law history, it is possible to change fundamentally decision-making and management within the workplace. This has resulted from the legal provision for a workplace democratisation institution, known as the workplace forum, in Chapter 5 of the Labour Relations Act (LRA) of 1995.

Although not blind to dangers in Chapter 5, both labour and business are clearly aware of the opportunities it holds for their different agendas. According to Sam Shilowa, union decisiveness and strategic engagement with Chapter 5 are essential to advance the interests of the labour movement while, for Bokkie Botha, it is essential to harness the co-operative thrust of workplace forums to make these institutions viable (see the quotations above). No matter where one sits in terms of the class divide, it is apparent that the LRA, in particular Chapter 5, has been legally crafted so that industrial relations and labour law reform are now at the threshold of a new frontier. This will become more apparent when the legislative provisions contained in Chapter 5 are unpacked. Such a descriptive overview is presented in the first section of this chapter.

The second section explores the potentialities that workplace forums hold for the labour movement to democratise the workplace by attempting to probe beyond the surface appearance of the law. For Karl Klare, this amounts to situating law in its social context to fully grasp its contingency: the impact of politics and power – in the ultimate sense – on law (Klare, 1990: 68). This entails an enquiry into these questions, among others: Where did Chapter 5 come from? Was it the result of a 'Newtonian' quantum leap in the collective mind of the legal drafting team or was it part of the new government's labour market policy? What were the underlying policy reasons for making legislative provision for workplace forums? How did the negotiations between the social partners contribute to defining the workplace forum concept?

Although much of the debate about workplace forums has amounted to defending and promoting the co-determinist philosophy of statutory workplace forums as the absolute horizon of democratisation, it is important to recognise the limitations of equating co-determination with democratisation. At the same time, given the historical commitment of the trade union movement to extending the frontiers of worker control beyond procedural and substantive checks on disciplinary issues, the general achievement of labour standards and the accountability of union leadership, it is essential to highlight the important challenges and pre-conditions that must be satisfied if worker control is to be used to redefine democratisation to extend beyond co-determination. This is discussed as the third aspect of this chapter.

Finally, stemming from this analytical exercise, is an attempt to define possibilities for worker-initiated workplace forums from a transformative viewpoint of democratisation that includes the possibility of these forums being designed as institutions of autonomous worker self-management.

LEGISLATIVE PROVISIONS:
CO-DETERMINATION AND THE LAW

After the complex and animated negotiations over the LRA in 1994 and 1995, it is reasonable to assert that Chapter 5, read with Schedule 2 of the Act, prompts a number of questions related to the realisation and establishment of workplace forums. The obvious questions are the following: What are the powers or competencies of workplace forums? What would be the agenda for information disclosure, consultation and joint decision-making? What are the practical steps that are necessary to establish a workplace forum? Can a workplace forum be voluntary or does it have to be statutory? Who would compose it? How would it operate on a day-to-day basis? Can it be established in the public service? How would disputes be resolved?

Theoretically, the workplace forum is an industrial relations institution intended to promote worker participation in workplace decision-making. It is envisaged as an institution that would be composed solely of workers which would open up a separate channel, distinct from collective bargaining, for information disclosure, consultation and joint decision-making. Since the South African workplace has long been dominated by managerial prerogative, providing workplace forums with such powers or competencies would make a fundamental inroad into managerial decision-making.

Fundamentally, joint decision-making or co-determination breaks with unilateral, hierarchical decision-making in the workplace because it allows workers to prevent management from deciding on a particular issue unless the consent of the workplace forum has been obtained. In general, for worker power in South Africa, this is a step beyond legally-sanctioned collective bargaining or 'soft' consultation regarding retrenchments, to a legal duty to co-manage. Consultation, as a power of the workplace forum, encroaches on managerial power to a slighter degree than joint decision-making. Essentially, consultation requires employers to present proposals before implementation to the workplace forum, with a view to reaching consensus.

Besides having the legal power to decide certain matters jointly and to consult over others, the actual effectiveness of workplace forums depends on what matters (or agenda items) fall within the ambit of the different powers. It is the conflict around the actual content of joint decision-making, consultation and information disclosure that would actually define the balance between worker and managerial power within the workplace. In Chapter 5 of the LRA, the matters for joint decision-making and consultation are not set in stone. They are open to variation – expansion or limitation – through a collective agreement between the representative union and the employer (which could include health and safety issues in terms of the applicable occupational health and safety legislation), a bargaining council and any other law that may confer additional matters.

This means that matters or agenda items, once dealt with through consultation, could be shifted to joint decision-making. Within the statutory make-up of Chapter 5, matters immediately subject to

consultation would include the following:
- restructuring of the workplace
- changes in the organisation of work
- partial or total plant closures
- mergers and transfers of ownership in so far as they have an impact on the employees
- the dismissal of employees based on operational requirements
- exemptions from any collective agreement or law
- job grading
- criteria for merit increases or discretionary bonuses
- education and training
- product development plans
- export promotion.

Joint decision-making in Chapter 5, if achieved in terms of the law, would immediately apply to:
- disciplinary codes and procedures
- rules related to the regulation of the workplace
- employment equity measures
- changes to rules regulating social benefit schemes.

Although, on the face of it, the statutory provision for joint decision-making matters might seem arbitrary, some of these items such as employment equity – if used correctly – could fundamentally alter the internal labour market of the particular enterprise. Rules relating to social benefit schemes could allow workers to influence the investment priorities of worker and pension funds, for example, to ensure that these are used to advance reconstruction and development.

The policy implications of jointly managing work rules cannot be underestimated. For instance, the reduction of working hours would not simply change the pace and rhythm of work, but would also contribute to employment creation, productivity enhancement and improved quality of life for workers. Added to this, the veil of secrecy around managerial prerogative would be raised through information disclosure provisions. These provisions require all relevant information that would facilitate effective engagement on consultation and joint decision-making to be disclosed to the workplace forum. Documented information would also have to be provided on request to the members of the forum.

If a workplace forum were to be initiated or triggered by a 'representative trade union', certain practical steps would have to be followed. First, an application would have to be made to the Commission for Conciliation, Mediation and Arbitration (CCMA) in the prescribed form. For the purposes of Chapter 5 of the LRA, a 'representative trade union' is defined as a registered trade union, or two or more registered trade unions acting jointly, that have as members the majority of the employees employed by an employer in a workplace.

The second step specifies the criteria in the light of which the CCMA must consider such application: (a) the employer employs 100 or more employees; (b) the applicant is a representative trade union; and (c) there is no functioning workplace forum established in terms of Chapter 5. Finally, the Commission must appoint a commissioner to assist the parties to establish a workplace forum by collective agreement or, failing that in terms of Chapter 5, with due regard to Schedule 2.

In the context of the public service, the establishment of workplace forums is to be regulated in terms of a Schedule promulgated by the Minister for Public Service and Administration in terms of Section 207(4) though this had not been done at the time of publication.[1] This would not preclude 'voluntarist' agreements outside the statutory framework for sectors within the public service.

What starkly emerges is that, although Chapter 5 tries to find a balance between legal regulation – or juridification – and voluntarism, with the ultimate thrust giving statutory backing to workplace forums, it nonetheless does not exclude the possibility of collective agreements outside the statutory framework to establish workplace forums. In the main, 'voluntary' or non-statutory workplace forums open up the possibility of redefining every aspect of the workplace forum fundamentally, including its powers (which could go beyond joint decision-making), agenda items, composition, level of operation, dispute resolution procedures and so on. However, this would require consensus and voluntary agreement by the parties, and could happen in a process overseen by the CCMA and finally embodied in a collective agreement. This option is sometimes referred to as the 'contracting out' option which essentially challenges the union movement to develop a 'model' collective agreement on the type of workplace forum that would be suitable for a given workplace. This would be similar to the recognition agreements that were developed to secure shop-steward structures.

However, if there were no agreement between the parties, then the CCMA should prescribe the statutory models in terms of the LRA. One variation of this statutory model would be in accordance with the features specified in Chapter 5, read with the 'Guidelines for establishing workplace forums' contained in Schedule 2 (S 80(10)). Alternatively, the competencies of workplace forums could be conferred on shop-steward structures. This is also a statutory model, referred to as a trade union-based workplace forum (S 81).

Even if workers in a particular workplace – for instance, in a factory, primary health care unit or retail outlet – wanted to establish a workplace forum, it would still be essential to determine whether they fall within the scope of the LRA. A cursory glance at the LRA suggests it has universal or global reach into the private and public sectors. However, in a strict legal sense this would depend on the definition of 'workplace' in the private and public sectors.

Within the LRA, the definition of workplace applicable to the private sector and public sector (which includes parastatals and quasi-governmental institutions) is defined by the physical location of where the employees of an employer work. Regarding the public service, the definition of workplace hinges, first, on consultation between the responsible minister and the bargaining council for a particular sector in the public service. Second, where there is no sectoral bargaining council, the Minister for Public Service and Administration determines this issue after consultation with the Public Service Co-ordinating Bargaining Council.

Another dimension to the scope of Chapter 5 is whether a workplace forum can be constituted to include several operational units. In other words, will the definition of 'workplace', as well as the statutory framework of Chapter 5, allow workplace forums to be established within different branches or plants of a company? In terms of the definition of 'workplace', this problem can be resolved by the following test: in a particular place where employees work, is the operation independent by size, function or organisation? If answered in the affirmative, then separate workplace forums with full competencies could be constituted for the different operational units. In addition, within the statutory framework of Chapter 5, read with Schedule 2, it would be possible to establish a co-ordinating structure for these workplace forums. Finally, also regarding scope, workplaces with less than 100 employees cannot establish a statutory workplace forum. This reflects an attempt by the legislature to promote workplace forums in large enterprises.

Chapter 5 excludes senior managerial employees from the workplace forum. It defines a senior managerial employee (S78(a)) as an employee whose contract of employment or status confers the authority to do any of the following in the workplace: (a) represent the employer in dealings with the workplace forum; (b) determine policy and take decisions on behalf of the employer that may be in conflict with the representation of employees in the workplace. As such, the workplace forum concept envisages an institution composed exclusively of workers which meets with management.

On closer scrutiny, the 'worker composition' of workplace forums holds out several possibilities. First, the legislative scheme, the composition could be determined by agreement hence anything is possible. Second, an 'all-comer' model could prevail, constituted of union and non-union members reflecting the occupational structure and physical location of the enterprise. Also, in numerical terms, a workplace forum of this type could be composed of five up to a maximum of 20 members. In terms of procedure, nominations for candidates for election could be provided by any registered trade union with members employed in the workplace or by a petition signed by not less than 20% of the employees in the workplace or 100 employees, whichever number of employees is the smaller (S 82(1)(h)). A trade union-based workplace forum would be composed of shop stewards in practice. Ultimately, the challenge to worker representation in a workplace forum is to ensure that the interests of all workers are represented.

The operations of both statutory and non-statutory workplace forums would be governed by a constitution which, among other consensual features, must specify: the procedures and substantive basis for recalling a member of a workplace forum, the procedures for filling vacancies, time off with pay for training and to perform functions, provisions for full-time members where there are more than 1 000 employees in the workplace, and provision for experts and trade union representatives to attend meetings of the workplace forum.

The training provisions referred to are necessary to contribute to the viability of workplace forums. However, it can be argued that workers have experience and knowledge within the division of labour and hence training is not necessary. But, given the structural deprivation under apartheid which has affected the literacy and numeracy capacity of many people, and the increasing use of sophisticated technology (such as computers) and automation in production, it is necessary for training and capacity building to be institutionalised within the workplace forums.

In addition, a workplace forum must meet regularly with employees to report on its activities, and with the employer regarding the financial and employment situation of the enterprise. Such a report must also be given annually by the employer to one of the meetings attended by all employees.

Finally, if the constitution of a workplace forum does not contain procedures to conciliate and arbitrate disagreements, then disputes about consultation may be resolved by industrial action. In terms of joint decision-making, disputes are to be resolved through arbitration. Information disclosure disputes must first be conciliated by the CCMA and, thereafter, be resolved through arbitration. If there is a breach of confidentiality, the commissioner may order the right to disclosure of information in that workplace to be withdrawn for a period specified in the arbitration award. Any disputes related to the interpretation and application of Chapter 5 would have to be conciliated and arbitrated by the CCMA.

SEARCHING FOR ORIGINS – THE POLITICS OF CO-DETERMINIST INDUSTRIAL RELATIONS

The eighties were the 'Wiehahn decade' of labour law reform, following the recommendations of the Wiehahn Commission of Enquiry of 1977 to 1981. Although racial dualism within the industrial relations system was abolished in a legal sense, the case law developed by the Industrial Court produced a power disequilibrium. It encouraged managerial unilateralism at a bargaining impasse,[2] as well as by curtailing and weakening the strike weapon.[3] In addition, the bargaining agenda[4] was narrowed, thus limiting the convergence of common interests. In the last instance, through legal regulation[5] – particularly to give legal efficacy to collective agreements – the state abandoned the 'outer ring' and became less of a neutral entity. The ideological prism of the Industrial Court – essentially pluralist industrial relations theory – failed to contribute to a labour law project that achieved industrial democracy.

Following the election of the first democratic government in April 1994, Tito Mboweni's Ministry of Labour produced a five-year plan which, in the main, proposed far-reaching labour law reform. A key element of this plan was the overhaul of the LRA of 1956, the statutory framework that governed collective and individual employment relations during the eighties. To give effect to this policy objective, in July 1994 the Cabinet approved the appointment of a Ministerial Legal Task Team with the principal brief to prepare a negotiating document in draft Bill form to initiate a process of public discussion and negotiation by organised labour and business and other interested parties (Department of Labour, 1995b: 1).

After consultation with employer and trade union representatives from the National Manpower Commission (NMC), the Minister of Labour appointed the Ministerial Legal Task Team[6] on 8 August 1994, under the convenorship of Professor Halton Cheadle, a lawyer long associated with the labour movement. Despite the trappings of political legitimacy enjoyed by the Legal Task Team, oppositional voices were also heard in the mainstream press against the drafting process. Both Brand and Brassey (an assistant to the Legal Task Team) argued that what the Minister required:

> was not a drafting committee of lawyers, but a commission of interested parties and expert assessors. In entertaining representations, gathering facts (not least about questions of feasibility) and drawing conclusions, the commissioners would do more than just educate themselves: they would stimulate a debate that would educate others and win for their ultimate proposals a broader measure of acceptance.
>
> (Satgar, 1995: 19)

What is evident from the intervention by Brassey and Brand is the assertion that the reform of the LRA was a top-down initiative. The state, notwithstanding its policy intentions and agenda, developed a Bill which set the parameters for debate, negotiation and public comment. In essence, all participatory responses to the Bill were incorporated into a legal framework and agenda set by the state.

This has serious implications for Chapter 5 of the LRA given that, ostensibly, the co-operative thrust of statutory workplace forums could integrate the labour movement into the formalism of a legislated industrial relations system. This is so because, unlike other countries (Germany, Sweden and Italy) where the co-determination channel is separated from collective bargaining, the LRA failed to provide legislated centralised bargaining across all sectors. At the same time, it provided an inherent duty to bargain over co-determination issues which were likely to blur the dividing lines between bargaining and co-determination.[7]

In addition, according to Munck, schemes promoting worker participation in other parts of the third world, in particular Benin, Madagascar, Congo, Algeria and Tanzania, have been strengthened by a co-optive intent on the part of capital and the state. More explicitly, Munck (1988: 150) concludes:

> in the post-colonial situation the state became the main agent of economic development and the organiser of 'human resources'. It is in this context that the state promoted a particular variant of workers' participation ... within quite specified limits while retaining full political power in its own hands.

This prompts the obvious question: is the co-determinist thrust of workplace forums an imposition by the emergent national democratic state in South Africa, to stabilise industrial relations and co-opt the labour movement? To answer this question, there is a need to probe the drafting and negotiations process related to Chapter 5 of the LRA.

The drafting process

The mystery surrounding the origins and motivations for Chapter 5 began with the mandating brief or letter of appointment of the legal drafting team. On close scrutiny of this document, it is apparent that workplace forums and co-determination are not explicitly mentioned. Except, the brief does make mention of the Reconstruction and Development Programme (RDP). It states that the draft negotiating Bill would 'have to give effect to government policy as reflected in the RDP'. Unpacking this reveals that the RDP chapter on labour and worker rights does propose worker empowerment. It even goes so far as to assert that legislation must facilitate 'worker participation and decision-making in the world of work'.

Thus, it would seem the origin of Chapter 5 is indisputable and, given that it originates from the RDP, it can be argued that COSATU's input into the development of the RDP as a tripartite alliance programme refutes any claim that Chapter 5 of the LRA was imposed by the government or the Minister of Labour,[8] on the labour movement. However, it is essential to recognise that the main thrust of the RDP was and is the promotion of workplace democratisation and, stemming from this, the possibility of negotiating workplace and industrial restructuring. This is very apparent in the RDP White Paper (Para 3 11 4) which asserts that:

> Industrial democracy will facilitate greater worker participation and decision-making in the workplace. The empowerment of workers will be enhanced through access to company information. Human resource development and education and training are key inputs into policies aimed at higher employment, the introduction of more advanced technologies, and reduced inequalities. Discrimination on the grounds of race and gender must end.

However, Chapter 5 was essentially drafted to promote South Africa's re-entry into international markets and to realise a more open economy (Department of Labour, 1995c: 35). In the explanatory memorandum which accompanied the original draft Bill, this is stated most explicitly as follows:

> South Africa's re-entry into international markets and the imperatives of a more open international economy demand that we produce value-added products and improve productivity levels. To achieve this, a major restructuring process is required.
>
> (Ministry of Labour, 1995b: 135)

In other words, the main policy rationale underlying the drafting of Chapter 5 was the provision of a labour market institution that would promote industrial restructuring and, ultimately, a new global competitiveness drive towards export-led industrialisation. Thus, the drafters' research – the study of South African best practice, overseas visits by the drafting team and advice obtained from international experts

– was informed by this policy thrust.[9] In the words of Amanda Armstrong, a member of the team, 'when we looked at other countries, the more successful way of restructuring entailed co-determination rather than adversarial relations and hence the main model for us was Germany'.[10]

Although the drafting of Chapter 5 in the negotiating Bill was constrained by the possible impact of the negotiations and largely informed by comparative experience, the drafting team developed a uniquely South African conception of co-determination. Thus, although the German model of works councils was used effectively to bring about industrial restructuring (Streek,1992), the drafters did not transplant it into South Africa. At the same time, there was no firm and clear intention to develop workplace forums into institutions that could fundamentally democratise the division of labour in South Africa and ultimately ensure that worker empowerment translated into worker control. In this sense, statutory co-determination (even with a union trigger) within the draft Bill represented an attempt by the government to allow unions and workers to participate in managerial decision-making to ensure stability and 'industrial peace' in the course of allowing the state to engineer the restructuring of the South African economy through 'free market' reforms and liberalisation.[11]

Hence, it can be argued that the legal drafting team blindly and uncritically imbibed the discourse of globalisation and its 'free market' policy prescriptions. However, the shift in public policy, in particular towards 'free market' export-led industrial development, has its origins in the retreat (Zita, 1997) of left intellectuals, particularly of the 1973 generation who were associated with the labour movement and the Industrial Strategy Project (Joffe et al., 1995).

Significantly, this policy thrust and agenda does not provide a basis for establishing workplace forums in the public service which could partially explain why this area of the draft negotiating Bill was not developed. The most that could have been read into the Bill was that its scope permitted workplace forums to be established in the public service. In an interview in February 1997, Cheadle explained that:

> A task team was established to look at industrial relations issues in the public service ... unfortunately, when the drafting was completed, the public service task team had not completed its work.

Negotiations in NEDLAC

On 2 February 1995, the negotiating document in draft Bill form was pre-sented at NEDLAC's Labour Market Chamber for consideration by government, labour and business. Negotiations commenced on 4 May 1995 and continued intermittently over three months. At the outset, main areas and issues of contention were isolated and prioritised for negotiations. One of these was Chapter 5 of the LRA.

In its opening comments on Chapter 5, government stressed its commitment to redesigning labour relations in South Africa to meet the challenges of this society. In other words, it stressed that 'economic growth can only be attained through a major restructuring process'. In this regard, it explicitly stated that it remained 'committed to the overall approach contained in the Bill, namely a statutory framework for the introduction of co-determination in the workplace'. In addition, government highlighted four areas it believed required more consideration. These included (Department of Labour, 1995c: 6-8):

- the proposal that a workplace forum, in terms of the Bill, can only be 'triggered' by a representative trade union
- the provision that neither management nor the trade union may disband a workplace forum once it is established
- the proposal that the model is employee-based, as opposed to being trade union-based
- those issues which are appropriate for consultation, and those issues which are appropriate for joint decision-making.

According to Wendy Dobson, the NEDLAC Labour Market Chamber convenor (1995: interview), the initial response from both labour and business was laced with caution. Labour initially asserted its demand for a union-based workplace forum. Underlying this was an argument that workplace forums, as conceived in the draft Bill, could undermine unions and established shop-steward structures. In addition, labour argued for a provision that would enable the dissolution of workplace forums (the draft Bill provided, that once established, workplace forums could not be disbanded: the so-called 'Catholic marriage'). In the main, business initially argued against the union trigger and for the law to allow employer-initiated workplace forums to be established as well.

Subsequently, the negotiations deadlocked with regard to workplace forums. The main issues of contention were the union trigger, the agenda items for consultation and joint decision-making, the information disclosure provisions and the relationship between workplace forums and collective bargaining (Dobson, interview). At this point, business proposed dropping Chapter 5 from the LRA. Dobson's perspective on this impasse suggests it was government that kept workplace forums on the negotiating agenda and introduced redrafts of Chapter 5 to facilitate the search for a middle ground and further negotiation. In her words, 'it was their baby and they did not want it to die'.

Nevertheless, with all the controversy around detail and the mechanics of Chapter 5, neither labour nor business discussed the policy reasons for establishing workplace forums. No questions were posed nor was debate initiated on democratisation of the workplace or even the 'globalisation challenge' of industrial restructuring. In addition, it seems unclear to what extent the multi-volume report on public submissions on the draft Bill was read by the negotiating parties. Furthermore, provisions for workplace forums in the public service were not seriously considered. Although there was recognition of the different setting within the public service, there was not much debate on the topic and the most that emerged from the negotiations were procedural provisions that could guide the initiation and establishment of workplace forums in the public service at a later date (S 80(12) and S 82(4)).

After the negotiations the Labour Relations Bill, Chapter 5 in particular, had a slightly different architecture and approach to workplace forums. From promoting statutory co-determination and, in a sense, inclining towards juridification[12] or state regulation in the draft Bill, the negotiations produced a regulatory framework that went beyond a state-driven model of workplace forums. Essentially, the balance developed between voluntarism and legal regulation not only accommodated labour's trade union-centred model within the statutory framework, but allowed for 'contracting out' whereby the parties themselves could define the type of workplace forum they wanted.

In short, statutory co-determination is just one thrust and impulse within Chapter 5 and, ultimately, workplace forums in terms of the LRA of 1995 cannot be construed as a state-imposed institution merely intended to co-opt labour.

BEYOND CO-DETERMINATION – CHALLENGES FOR WORKER CONTROL TO ADVANCE TRANSFORMATION FROM BELOW

With the collapse of authoritarian and centrally-planned Soviet socialism in 1989, most labour movements, in particular those on the periphery of the new 'global village' and aspiring to radically transform their societies, are now on the retreat. Western ideologues, such as Francis Fukuyama, have proclaimed the triumph of capitalism and, ultimately, the market. This articulation has attempted to reclaim history within a new hegemonic or supreme teleology which recasts and conflates democracy to the market. It has also gone further to assert multi-party competition within a liberal pluralist order as a dominant ideological construct, masquerading as a 'common sense' view of democracy and the climax of Western political thought.

However, for industrial relations theory (particularly pluralist theory) and labour law in South Africa, the political analogy of liberal democracy to industrial democracy has long been established (Rycroft and Jordaan, 1992: 119-125; Satgar, 1996). As mentioned above, the workplace, seen through the lens of liberal pluralist political theory and legal ideology, not only masked 'hierarchy and domination', but portrayed the workplace as a micro-level democratic order where the contending interests of workers and employers were mediated by the legal rules contained in the employment contract and, subsequently, also by collective labour law (Du Toit, 1994: 167). The state, through the juridifying edifice of labour law and pluralist legal ideology, was also given a neutral pre-eminence to maintain a balance of power in the conflict between workers and employers.

In South Africa today, the LRA of 1995, and mainly Chapter 5 on workplace forums, departs from the pluralist collective bargaining power equilibrium model by also attempting to institutionalise a power balance – but within a co-determinatist framework that allows hierarchy to be maintained through the direct inclusion of workers in management. Therefore neo-pluralism, if one were to describe the statutory co-determination paradigm of the LRA in these terms, is a power-sharing industrial relations framework. It does not confront the rationality of hierarchy in transformative terms and hence does not allow for an expansion of the frontiers of worker control.

Now, although worker control is a self-explanatory industrial relations term, it is important to clarify its wider political meaning at this point, to fully grasp the 'politics of labour law'. For Munck (1988: 151):

> workers' control is thus essentially a slogan in a political strategy which advocates a gradual role by workers in contesting management's 'right to manage'. Some of its forms may seem similar to co-management but it aims ultimately at workers' self-management and thus seeks to avoid integration within the industrial relations machinery.

Simply, worker control is a policy means, from below, to dislodge and supplant managerial prerogative in such a way that workers are collectively responsible for running and managing their workplaces. The transformative implications of this conception of worker control, for industrial relations theory and labour law reform, are profound and offer at least two challenges, *vis-à-vis* the statutory co-determination thrust that is deeply embedded in Chapter 5. In the first instance, the ideological and political boundaries that surround the statutory conception of co-determination have to be dismantled through critical engagement. This is not an exercise in 'verbal militancy', nor an attempt to dismiss co-determination. Instead, it is a realisation that co-determination is not the same as democratisation but is rather a determined form of hegemonic struggle.

Unpacking the notion of democratisation will further clarify this point. As part of transformative discourse, whether identified in the RDP as 'people-driven delivery' or 'democratisation of the state', the word 'democratisation' is imbued with an essentialist notion of ongoing societal change, laden with a host of transformative possibilities. In terms of the 'politics of labour law', it allows for a political subject, such as trade unions, to transform power and ownership relations within the workplace in such a way that industrial relations theory and labour law reform are essentially radicalised. In other words, the 'employer' and 'employee' relationship is transcended while, at the same time, workplace and community relations and workplace and state relations are transformed. This means that co-determination, in the context of democratisation, is one of many institutional expressions of worker power over management that ensures the substance of the employment relationship is no longer unilaterally determined by employers.

The second challenge posed to statutory co-determination by a policy of worker control is pinpointing it within a spectrum of transformative possibilities that exist in the course of workplace democratisation. At one end of the spectrum are 'soft options', including green areas and quality circles as part of world class management, control over grievance procedures, working hours and other basic shop-floor issues and processes. Alongside this, and moving into the opposite end of the spectrum where the power of employers is increasingly curtailed, are consultation, negotiations and co-determination (either through worker directors or joint decision-making through statutory workplace forums) which are all likely tranformative possibilities (Anstey, 1990: 6). But worker control also envisages a horizon for democratisation beyond co-determination in which autonomous worker self-management is realised, simultaneously, wherever possible.

In the main, however, numerous challenges stand in the way of realising autonomous worker self-management,[13] the ultimate goal of worker control:

> Increasingly the intervention capacity, reach and developmental role of the state is coming under attack within neo-liberal globalisation discourse. The neo-liberal prescriptions and proclamations of globalisation envisage a limited or minimalist state, which merely facilitates the trans-nationalisation and global mobility of capital. But, when the 'death of the state' proposition is questioned or the notion of rolling back the state, it is apparent that it is only a change in regulatory regime that is proposed.
>
> (Patnaik, 1995: 199-200)

Thus, to ensure that the new democratic state in South Africa is not trapped within a neo-liberal ideological conception, workers have to recognise the state as a site of contestation. Essentially, workers have to engage the state to ensure that, in its response to globalisation, it provides the necessary regulations, policy support and institutions to sustain and promote autonomous worker self-management. For instance, training institutions such as Ditsela would have to be re-oriented to ensure that they empower workers beyond the ABCs of the LRA, but also provide them with the relevant skills to manage enterprises. In addition, the financial system would have to be regulated to ensure that the necessary financial support and viability of worker-run and worker-owned enterprises are achieved.[14]

Achieving autonomous self-management in a factory or public sector unit could amount to a mere island of workplace democratisation unless the trade union movement, when embracing a transformative union strategy, advances in concert. In other words, a policy for worker control and ultimately autonomous worker self-management has to be part of an ongoing process, driven by a united labour movement. The COSATU Congress in 1997 took a first step in this direction when it rejected co-determination as the sole thrust towards advancing worker control. Instead, COSATU opted for a transformative resolution which sets as a challenge the realisation of 'new socialist forms of work organisation and management which advance worker control'. At the same time, advancing autonomous self-management as a united labour movement enables international experience to be drawn on most effectively. For instance, the Corporate Plan developed by British shop stewards at Lucas Aerospace (Wainwright, 1994: 162-163) to ensure worker management and control, or the takeover and renewal of Kamani Tubes (Srinivas, 1993) in India by workers, or the experiment by a women's movement in Sweden (Wainwright, 1994: 115-143) which self-managed a school, can be closely studied and experimented with as part of the worker control movement to achieve a democratised economy.

Clearly, democratisation envisages workplace change that ultimately transforms the division of labour. This recognises that capitalist forms of workplace organisation and methods of production, whether Taylorist or Fordist in terms of the detailed division of labour for mass production or for 'flexible specialisation', are not consistent with worker control and the de-alienation of work. In fact, most of the technological innovation within these methods of production has undermined worker control and enhanced the dominance of capital. Within the context of third world industrialisation, this is complicated by the uneven diffusion of technology and methods of production (Bayat, 1991: 184-186, 202-207).

Hence, the challenge for worker control and, in the main, for autonomous self-management is to define a new concept of work. This should not reject technology but rather recognise that technological development and innovation are neither neutral nor natural developments intrinsic to economies. In fact, employers and states have played a conscious role in developing technologies. However, if technology is to be democratised and transformed through worker control, then workers have to take the planning and design of technology seriously, with a view to meeting social needs. At the same time, it is essential to change decision-making fundamentally so that the intellectual and manual divide between workers is overcome. Ultimately, labour power has to be liberated from the law of value so it is no longer merely a factor or input into production for profit maximisation but, instead, is an outcome of socialised production.

However, what does this mean for Chapter 5 of the LRA and workplace forums? In other words, can workplace forums become organs of worker control that advance autonomous worker self-management? Essentially, these questions enable a departure from theory into the realm of the practical in an attempt to define workplace forums as a worker control model.

WORKPLACE FORUMS AS A WORKER CONTROL MODEL: CO-DETERMINATION AND AUTONOMOUS SELF-MANAGEMENT

The emergence of a new democratisation institution in the workplace is bound to be embroiled in struggle. Employers are most certainly going to resist inroads into managerial prerogative. Besides trying to thwart these initiatives, concerted attempts would be made to institutionalise workplace forums within a co-optive framework. Without a clear perspective on what should be achieved by the union movement, this could end in disaster, with flawed institutions that are controlled by employers.

Since Chapter 5 of the LRA is trying to strike a balance between legal regulation and voluntarism, several models could emerge. The first is a statutory model with two variations, developed as follows:

- through prescription, if the parties fail to reach a 'voluntarist' agreement which requires the CCMA to establish and define a workplace forum in terms of Chapter 5, read together with the 'Guidelines for establishing workplace forums' contained in Schedule 2
- through the statutory provisions for trade union-based workplace forums, which would allow the competencies of workplace forums to be conferred on shop-steward structures.

According to Halton Cheadle (1997: interview), 'first prize should be a thousand voluntary workplace forums rather than statutory forums'. This is the second model permitted by the LRA which allows for collective agreements outside the statutory framework. It is this model that holds out the prospect of going beyond legislated co-determination and ultimately subverting the rationality of hierarchical management in both the private and public sectors. Essentially, it would allow parties to define a workplace forum that is trade union-centred, but which allows for autonomous self-management.

In practice, autonomous worker self-management can broadly have two voluntarist variations. The first is a completely autonomous self-management workplace forum which would allow skilled and unskilled workers to run an enterprise, public service unit or co-operative. For example, in the public service, an autonomously self-managed workplace forum can be established in a school. This would bring together skilled and unskilled workers in the managerial realm of the school. Besides this collective forum deciding on work schedules and education policy issues relevant to the school, it could also work out accountable, transparent and participatory ways of managing the administration of the school. Similarly, in a primary health care unit or even a police station, workers can self-manage their work.

Essentially, the devolution of managerial power in the public sector holds out the prospect of transcending individual-centred and authoritarian forms of management. To achieve this, an 'Autonomous Self-management Workplace Agreement', for instance, can be negotiated in the public service co-ordinating bargaining council. This would not only delineate and separate collective bargaining from autonomous self-management, but would also contribute to identifying those base institutions of the public service – such as schools and primary health care units – that can establish autonomous self-management workplace forums.

Another variation of an autonomous self-management workplace forum is one which allows for co-determination over certain issues and, at the same time, has an autonomous self-management competency and agenda for workers. For example, in a parastatal or large conglomerate such as Anglo American Corporation, an autonomous self-management workplace forum could exist alongside the board and include competencies such as information disclosure, consultation, joint decision-making and autonomous self-management. In terms of the agenda, there could be – at least in the short term – co-determination on investment decisions, production planning, work re-organisation and technology use, but autonomous self-management on affirmative action policy, training, and health and safety issues. The challenge of this variation of autonomous self-management is to achieve a full and complete self-management agenda that eventually transcends the co-determination competency. This would become likely if workers also address the ownership dimension of the enterprise.

CONCLUSION

It would seem that the future of workplace forums within the industrial relations and labour law system in South Africa has still to be decided by debate, policy reflection and serious strategic decision-making. Although spawned through policy provided for in the RDP, a point often missed in labour movement ranks, the regulatory framework and institutional make-up of workplace forums have been fundamentally shaped by the negotiations on the LRA of 1995, in the National Economic Development and Labour Council (NEDLAC). Although the outcome of these negotiations does not provide a comprehensive legal framework for workplace forums in the public sector, the statutory provisions do allow for private sector forums that could be trade union-centred (that is, accommodating shop steward-structures) or composed in terms of Schedule 2 of the LRA.

However, if the labour movement in South Africa were to engage purposively with the opportunities that workplace forums hold out for democratisation of the employment relationship, worker control is bound to extend its frontiers into a radical zone. In this regard, 'contracting out' of the LRA could enable unions to transcend the limits of statutory co-determination and, ultimately, attempt autonomous worker self-management.

There are no guarantees of success, either with co-determination or autonomous worker self-management. Nonetheless, experiments, initiative and creative innovation by workers are required now and over time. It is the knowledge and experience gained from this process that would allow workers to deal with neo-liberal restructuring and, most importantly, contribute to redefining legal ideology and industrial relations theory through transformative practice.

4

NEGOTIATING THE FUTURE

Labour's role in NEDLAC

———— ✦ ————

Karl Gostner and Avril Joffe

Gostner and Joffe assess the development of NEDLAC, the national negotiating forum that gives labour and other groups broad rights of consultation on proposed government legislation and policy. In addition to describing NEDLAC's powers and internal structures – including the unofficial consultative processes that have developed within it, the chapter assesses labour's gains and losses, as well as the problems created by participation. The most important problem is a straining of resources as top policy-makers and leaders are drawn into numerous NEDLAC activities. In turn, this has contributed to an increasing gap between leadership – who have less time to devote to their union responsibilities – and members, many of whom have limited knowledge of decisions taken at NEDLAC. As a consequence, agreements reached in NEDLAC may not be shaped by the wishes of members who, in turn, may not abide by their leaders' commitments. The authors argue that the resource and representational problems are exacerbated by labour's deeper confusion about how to use NEDLAC effectively and how to fit engagement with this institution into its other activities.

INTRODUCTION

The history of the South African labour movement has been one of a struggle to limit the power to act autonomously of both business and government. Since 1990, the labour movement has become increasingly involved in processes of multipartite policy formulation as it attempts to ensure that state policy does not compromise the interests of working people. The National Economic Development and Labour Council (NED-LAC) is the key statutory body which institutionalises this mode of policy-making.

This chapter is about labour's role in the processes of policy formulation that occur under the auspices of NEDLAC. Our specific concern is to assess the gains that labour has made from its participation in NEDLAC, as well as to analyse the difficulties experienced by labour in its engagement with the NEDLAC process. The chapter is divided into five sections. First, we discuss the formation of NEDLAC and its structure. Second, we identify the aggregate gains that accrue to society as a whole because of NEDLAC, before proceeding, third, to discuss the gains that labour has made from NEDLAC. Fourth, we analyse the difficulties experienced by labour in NEDLAC and the implications of these problems for its effective participation. The final section draws some conclusions about labour's involvement in NEDLAC.

THE FORMATION OF NEDLAC

At the time of South Africa's transition to political democracy, not only did the South African trade union movement have a high degree of numerical strength but it was able to wield this power strategically to make significant inroads into the power of the apartheid state (Adler and Webster, 1995). By 1994, union density in South Africa stood at 50% (Macun, 1997). While this union membership was dispersed across eight federations, 67% of membership was concentrated within three federations: COSATU, NACTU (National Council of Trade Unions), and FEDSAL (Federation of South African Labour Unions).[1] These three federations made up the labour grouping represented in NEDLAC.

During the late 1980s and early 1990s, COSATU's and NACTU's strategic use of power resulted in the restructuring and transformation of the National Manpower Commission (NMC) and the establishment of the National Economic Forum (NEF). The NMC and NEF became the forerunners of NEDLAC.

The NMC was restructured from a 'toothless advisory body' (Baskin, 1996: 30) into a tripartite negotiating body which compelled the state to consult before changing labour legislation. The NEF resulted from conflict over the introduction of the new Value Added Tax system in 1991. It represented an attempt to parallel the political negotiation process within

CODESA (Convention for a Democratic South Africa) by compelling the apartheid state to negotiate on economic restructuring and policy direction.

The changes in the NMC and the creation of the NEF were testimony to both the strength and strategic capabilities of the South African labour movement. However, labour's performance inside these institutions was by no means an unequivocal success. A number of labour analysts and labour negotiators have identified problems with the unions' engagement in these structures (see Friedman and Shaw, 2000; Adler and Webster, 1995).

In the first instance, while unions were able to put issues onto the agenda, they lacked the technical capabilities to impact significantly on the outcomes of these negotiations. In addition, there was a loss of internal union democracy. Consequently, negotiating positions were rarely mandated, and did not always reach the union's membership. The conclusion some analysts draw was that the NEF, in particular, did not deliver much in the way of significant outcomes. However, the primary concern of the NEF was to prevent unilateral restructuring by an illegitimate government and not to formulate new policies. As Christian Sellars (1997: interview) formerly of the Chemical Workers' Industrial Union argued: 'The National Economic Forum did not accomplish much, but then its purpose was to block unilateral reform by the National Party, rather than to develop new policy'. This contrasted sharply with the central objective of NEDLAC which is to actively consider and influence policy through consensual agreements on social and economic matters before they are tabled in Parliament.

Notwithstanding this primary objective, Friedman and Shaw (2000: 349) have argued that the process of blocking government restructuring within the NEF 'inhibited the unions' attempt to pursue an alternative social policy agenda', thus reducing them to adopting a reactive role within tripartite institutions.

Thus the history of labour's engagement in tripartite structures is somewhat mixed. On the one hand, labour had the political power to prevent the unilateral restructuring of policy yet, on the other hand, it lacked the capacity and internal communication structures to deal fully with engagement in these forums. This history is further complicated by the experience of tripartite structures as mechanisms for blocking government initiatives rather than actively shaping policy.

In February 1995, the NMC and NEF were integrated into NEDLAC by an Act of Parliament (35 of 1994). This statutory body both consolidated and extended the powers of the NEF and NMC, although it was substantially different from these institutions (Baskin, 1996: 30).

Perhaps self-evidently, the fact that NEDLAC is a statutory body means that it has substantially more power and stability than the tripartite consultative forums that existed before, or which exist elsewhere in the world. The NEDLAC Act recognises four groups as being eligible for membership. These are representatives of organised business (at present, business is represented by Business South Africa (BSA) and the National African Federated Chambers of Commerce (NAFCOC)); representatives of organised labour, comprising COSATU, FEDSAL and NACTU; representatives of community and development organisations; and representatives of government.

The Act establishes the objectives of NEDLAC, as well as delineates its structure. According to Section 5(1) of the Act, the Council shall:

- strive to promote the goals of economic growth, participation in economic decision-making and social equity
- seek to reach consensus and conclude agreements on matters pertaining to economic and social policy
- consider all proposed labour legislation relating to labour market policy before it is introduced in Parliament
- consider all significant changes to social and economic policy before it is implemented or introduced in Parliament
- encourage and promote the formulation of co-ordinated policy on social and economic matters.

The provision of the Act for consultation on all proposed labour legislation and social and economic policy provides considerable formal space for labour to shape government policy, as well as places strong limits on the policy areas in which government has autonomy. As Adler and Webster (1996: 16) point out: 'Although Parliament is sovereign and NEDLAC is an advisory body, a potential consensus between the social partners would be difficult for parliamentarians to disregard.'

However, the extent to which the space that the Act provides is realised is contingent on the power relations between the social partners and the ability of labour to contest the policy process within NEDLAC, and thereby shape the outcomes.

The question that this chapter tries to answer is twofold: first, to what extent has labour managed to use that legislative space to win real gains for its membership, either through influencing the content of policy proposals and outcomes or through blocking undesirable policy proposals? Second, what are the reasons for its success or lack of it in using this space?

THE STRUCTURE OF NEDLAC

Constitutional structures

To achieve its objectives, the NEDLAC Act makes provision for three structures. The Executive Council is the most senior structure. It receives report-backs from the chambers and concludes agreements which are then taken through the parliamentary process. The Management Committee is in charge of co-ordinating the work of the chambers (NEDLAC, 1996: iii). The chambers are the formal negotiating structures of NEDLAC.

There are a total of four chambers, each dealing with a different policy area. The Trade and Industry Chamber deals with issues related to the 'economic and social dimensions of trade, industrial, mining, agricultural and services policies and the associated institutions of delivery'. The Development Chamber's area of focus is 'all matters pertaining to development, both urban and rural implementation strategies, financing of development programmes, campaigns to mobilise the nation behind the RDP, and associated institutions of delivery'. The Labour Market Chamber deals with all issues 'pertaining to the world of work and the associated institutions of delivery'. Finally, the brief of the Public Finance and Monetary Policy Chamber is to reach agreement on all issues 'pertaining to the framework within which financial, fiscal, monetary and exchange-rate policies are formulated: the co-ordination of fiscal and monetary policy, and related elements of macro-economic policy; and the associated institutions of delivery' (NEDLAC, 1996: 12-24).

Since the chambers are constitutional NEDLAC structures, they operate according to a set of formal procedures which include the taping of debates and the tabling and endorsement of minutes from previous meetings (Kettledas, Botha and Du Plessis, 1997: interviews). Adrian du Plessis, BSA negotiator in the Labour Market Chamber, notes that the formalism of the chambers sometimes constrains the process of negotiations: 'Especially in the chambers where you sit there with a tape recorder and there are minutes, people are going to argue about whether they said "shall" or "may"' (Botha and Du Plessis, 1997: interview).

Les Kettledas (1997: interview), Deputy Director-General of the Department of Labour, makes a similar point when he notes that '[in] the chamber you go on record and people may not want to bind themselves'. Thus, the formal nature of chamber meetings means that people are reluctant, at times, to engage in hard negotiations in case they find themselves tied to a position that may have shifted between chamber meetings.

Extra-constitutional structures

In an attempt to 'achieve the spirit of NEDLAC rather than the letter', a number of extra-constitutional bodies now exist within the NEDLAC process (Botha and Du Plessis, interview). The first and most senior of these bodies is the Committee of Principals which was established during negotiations over the Labour Relations Act of 1995 to explore ways to further the negotiation process (Kettledas, interview). These meetings are attended by the overall convenors of the social partners, and discussions are aimed at facilitating the NEDLAC process rather than at concluding agreements.[2]

The second form of extra-constitutional structure is the conveners' meetings which take place both at a management committee level and at a chamber level (Wolmarans, Bethlehem and Lekwane, 1997: interviews). These meetings are attended by the conveners of each of the social partners in the chamber or management committee. Their function is to set the agenda for the chamber by deciding which issues should be placed on the agenda. In addition they prioritise issues for discussion within the particular structure that they convene (Lekwane, 1997: interview). In short, they give a strategic focus to the workload that faces NEDLAC and each of the individual chambers.

The third and final kind of extra-constitutional structure is the working groups or negotiations committees. These structures are set up by the social partners in the chamber and report to the chamber. Aubrey Lekwane (interview), convener of the Development Chamber, notes that '[most] of the chamber's work would be dealt with in sub-committees. The chamber acts as a ratifying body for the sub-committees'. Kettledas (interview) elaborates of the role on the negotiations committees:

> It has always been felt that you cannot negotiate in a full chamber, so we set up sub-committees which then allow the partners to bring in specific expertise on issues. You must distinguish between the negotiation committees and the chamber. The negotiation committee is about a process of negotiation, it allows for a process of exploring settlement.

Thus, the working groups fulfil a dual purpose. First, they allow the social partners the opportunity to bring in expertise on a specific issue, competencies that their chamber delegates may not have. Second, they allow negotiators to explore various options for settlement without the concern of being bound to a position that was a tentative rather than a final offer, aimed at facilitating the reaching of agreement.

While the extra-constitutional structures represent an innovative response to the challenges of multipartite policy formulation, they also hold the potential for undermining the structure of NEDLAC as agreements get shaped in the crevices of the organisation and the constitutional structures become no more than rubber-stamps for less-than-transparent negotiations.

Notwithstanding the dangers that the extra-constitutional structures hold, they do point to a vigorous and growing institution. However, it is essential to channel and consolidate this growth so that the lines of authority and responsibility between the different structures are clear. This multiplicity of structures creates the potential for a multi-layered negotiation process in which an agreement is shaped at numerous levels within NEDLAC. In turn, this signifies that labour's internal mechanisms need to be functioning well to ensure that all its negotiators are fully apprised of the state of negotiations in various NEDLAC structures.

Placing issues on the agenda

NEDLAC's agenda is drawn principally from the legislative programme of government although, as Sellars (1997: interview) points out, there are some important exceptions to this. In order for an issue to pass through all the structures, it first needs to be tabled for discussion by one of the social partners. Issues cannot, as Jayendra Naidoo, former Executive Director of NEDLAC (1997: interview) points out, come from nowhere.

When NEDLAC was created, an issue of concern could be tabled by any of the social partners at any level within the Council (Bethlehem, 1997: interview). However, this approach resulted in some of the chambers becoming reactive to debates in the public realm, instead of focusing on meeting goals established by a strategic agenda. This was particularly the case in the Public Finance and Monetary Policy Chamber during 1996, where discussions were largely driven by debates in the press or by the tabling of items from the Finance Ministry (Wolmarans, interview). While this worked to the advantage of the labour movement in terms of obtaining access to information, many of these issues were not raised for negotiation which meant that very few agreements were reached in that chamber.

The management committee and the conveners' meetings of each chamber now play a greater role in determining the agenda for the chamber, as well as in prioritising issues on that agenda. A central concern behind this strategic focusing of the agenda is to ensure that the work of the chambers becomes more results-oriented and therefore more able to influence the policy process.

Labour's representation in NEDLAC

As noted above, the NEDLAC labour caucus is comprised of three federations: COSATU, FEDSAL and NACTU. Each of the federations has representatives on all of NEDLAC's constitutional structures, the exception being the conveners' meetings that are attended by the convener of the labour caucus who, in all cases, is a COSATU representative (by virtue of the federation's greater size). The number of representatives from each federation in each NEDLAC structure is determined by a 4:1:1 ratio, in proportion to the respective organisation's membership.

In dealing with the demands of NEDLAC, NACTU and FEDSAL have internal NEDLAC-specific structures that develop the positions on issues related to NEDLAC. NACTU has a NEDLAC caucus that meets on a fortnightly basis and, together with the central committee, forms the mandating structure for NACTU in NEDLAC (Ngcukana, 1997: interview). FEDSAL has a total of five NEDLAC caucus meetings a year which together with the FEDSAL executive, develop the organisation's mandates for NEDLAC (Van der Merwe, 1997: interview). COSATU does not have a formal structure solely dedicated to the consideration of NEDLAC issues. Instead, its executive committee acts as the mandating structure for COSATU's position in the labour caucus (Nhlapo, 1997: interview).

The positions of the three federations then have to be amalgamated into the position of the NEDLAC labour caucus. This is done through three structures: a biannual negotiation school; a quarterly labour caucus meeting; and labour caucus meetings before each NEDLAC chamber meeting. The first negotiation school was held in early 1995 to discuss the strategies which labour would adopt and the objectives it hoped to meet in NEDLAC. The school developed a detailed programme of caucuses and seminars to build capacity and to ensure that representatives were properly co-ordinated and accountable (Sellars, 1997: interview). The quarterly labour caucus meeting develops mandates for labour's NEDLAC negotiators. During 1996, a NEDLAC labour co-ordinating office was established to co-ordinate report-backs from negotiators, as well as to ensure the presence of negotiators at NEDLAC meetings. The successes and weaknesses of these structures are discussed below.

LABOUR'S PARTICIPATION IN NEDLAC

In analysing labour's role in NEDLAC, we need to differentiate between the outcomes of the institution and the process through which those outcomes are realised. The former indicates the extent to which labour has realised its goals in NEDLAC. An assessment of the latter provides us with an understanding of the extent to which outcomes positive to labour will be sustained.

The outcomes

Expanding influence
The NEDLAC Act provides broad ranging rights of consultation on proposed government legislation and policy and, in so doing, provides labour with considerable access to the ways in which policy is formulated. As such, one of the most clearly identifiable outcomes of NEDLAC is access for labour into the policy-making process.

As Cunningham Ngcukana (1997: interview), General Secretary of NACTU and labour representative on the NEDLAC Management Committee, notes, 'NEDLAC is a line to put an alternative vision into government'. Lucky Monnokgotla (1997: interview), General Secretary of BIFAWU (Banking Insurance Finance and Assurance Workers' Union) and labour representative on the Public Finance and Monetary Chamber, makes a similar point, 'NEDLAC is good for labour in the sense that we are able to participate. We can have our views heard around issues that affect our class'.

Of particular importance is the fact that this is a right entrenched in legislation. Thus, labour already has a guaranteed voice in the policy-making process and as such, it needs only mobilise when negotiations deadlock and no longer has to expend considerable resources on getting a place at the table. In some instances, labour has used NEDLAC to put in place structures and processes that expand its area of influence over government policy and actions. The most significant of these is the Technical Sectoral Liaison Committee, established as a result of labour's insistence that its views be taken into account in the conclusion of trade agreements. This committee provides a forum in which government officials consult the social partners on trade negotiations, thereby giving labour the opportunity to shape trade negotiations.

Other achievements have included gaining representation on the government contingents to UNCTAD IX and the ministerial meeting of the World Trade Organisation (Ramburuth, 1997: interview). Thus, NEDLAC provides labour with the legislative right to influence the policy process and therefore the kinds of policy that government adopts. The scope of this potential is described by Jayendra Naidoo (interview), when he says that 'NEDLAC has given labour a far bigger bite than any other system (in the world). From a union point of view it is a much desired outcome'.

New legislation
The labour movement has managed to use the space provided by NEDLAC to intervene successfully in the area of labour legislation. This has resulted in the Labour Market Chamber being the site of slow, painstaking, but ultimately conclusive negotiations. Obviously a key victory for labour in this chamber was the new Labour Relations Act of 1995. Aspects of the Act were the specific result of labour's intervention, including the entrenchment of organisational rights, the facilitation of participation in industry restructuring and the right to the disclosure of information (Kettledas, interview).

Power on the streets

The LRA negotiations constitute a good example of how labour has both utilised the space within NEDLAC to influence the policy process, as well as employed power to ensure that its interests are represented. Labour has maintained its capacity to mobilise to break deadlocks on issues of importance to its membership. This dual process of engagement inside the institution and mobilisation on the streets is a continuation of COSATU's strategic involvement in struggle from the mid-eighties to the mid-nineties. The ability of the movement to translate mass power into an institutional voice both on the factory floor and in the policy arena has been the hallmark of the South African labour movement, and continues to be of importance in ensuring that labour's interests are clearly represented in NEDLAC outcomes. Jayendra Naidoo (interview) noted that 'labour has successfully retained the right of action'.

Shaping international relations

The labour caucus also succeeded in putting human rights on South Africa's trade agenda in the form of a side-letter on human rights. While labour had to retreat from its initial position of a strict link between market access and a country's ratification of the core International Labour Organisation (ILO) conventions, it nonetheless compelled the government to concede a side-letter. This requires those countries with which South Africa has trade agreements to sign a non-binding agreement to respect human rights and to work towards the ratification of core ILO conventions (Gostner, 1997). The social clause framework agreement is also a symbolic victory because it has shifted the dominant vision of trade from one in which trade is represented as a purely economic phenomenon to one in which trade is seen to have a social dimension. In so doing, the social clause process has enabled labour to challenge the ideological terrain in which the policy process is embedded, thereby opening space for the insertion of a greater social orientation into the policy process.

The partial victory of the social clause also set other processes in motion within NEDLAC, that furthered labour's agenda. Because labour was able to compel the government to sign the Social Clause Framework Agreement, the government had to embark on the ratification of core ILO conventions (Rosenthal and Gostner, 1996). Thus, through NEDLAC, labour has not only been able to win concessions from government to improve the domestic context in which it operates, but it has also been able to set in place a number of mechanisms and processes through which it can attempt to influence the policies adopted by international bodies.

Shaping government policy

Labour has also managed to win a commitment from government that the reduction of the budget deficit will not take place at the expense of social expenditure (Monnokgotla, interview). This commitment was ratified in the 1997-1998 Budget where social spending as a percentage of GDP remained constant, while total social spending increased by R8 billion (*Business Day*, 13 March 1997: 8). Joshua Wolmarans (interview), convener of the NEDLAC Public Finance and Monetary Chamber, acknowledged labour's ability to shape policy:

> I can definitely say that if they [labour] hadn't been there, the discussions would have gone in a very different direction. Government and business are often just concerned with the pure economic issues, whereas labour has a social focus. So labour definitely brings more of a social dimension to the chamber's discussions.

The above are just a few of the legislative and policy gains that labour has made through NEDLAC. However, what this review of some of labour's gains through NEDLAC has demonstrated are the ways in which labour has been able to optimally utilise its existing power base and history of mobilisation, in combination with the rights entrenched through the NEDLAC Act, to further an agenda that is favourable to its interests.

Problems and challenges for labour

If at first you don't succeed

Labour has also successfully used NEDLAC as a way of a getting 'a second bite at the cherry'. Perhaps the clearest example of this is the negotiations surrounding the Compensation for Occupational Injury and Diseases Act (COIDA). COIDA was initially negotiated through the multipartite Compensation Board, and then was passed on to NEDLAC for what was meant to be a formal process of ratification (Government and labour sources, 1997: confidential interviews). However, labour felt there was inadequate representation of its interests in the Compensation Board outcome and used NEDLAC as a forum for renegotiating aspects of COIDA.

Yet, while this strategy has been a relatively successful one for labour, it does pose questions about the status of other stakeholder bodies *vis-à-vis* NEDLAC. Using NEDLAC in this way could undermine the work of other forums, as well as create a duplication of activities and slow down the decision-making process. In addition, it establishes a precedent for an opportunistic approach to influencing the policy process where labour avails itself of any opportunity to 'renegotiate' a prior agreement. While such an approach does provide 'a second bite at the cherry', labour runs the risk of being criticised for slowing down government's delivery and undermining the integrity of agreements forged in tripartite forums. As such, it seems imperative that the nature of the relationship between different tripartite structures be clarified. It would be ideal if the substance of negotiations could take place on what Jayendra Naidoo (interview) calls 'preliminary bases' so that final agreement in NEDLAC becomes a formality.

Labour and the alliance

Despite the successes of NEDLAC, on occasion COSATU has chosen to pursue certain issues through its alliance with the African National Congress (ANC) and the South African Communist Party (SACP). This decision has been a tactical move generally with the intention of trying to minimise the influence of business over the negotiation process. Vusi Nhlapo (interview) elaborates:

> One very obvious example was the restructuring of state assets. In this instance, we felt that business should not be involved as they would want to buy up the sold-off state assets. It is those issues where labour feels that if business had an equal say we will be perpetuating problems of the apartheid era – the underdevelopment of workers, structural unemployment – forever. So if business would gain an advantage that they wouldn't otherwise have, those issues can't go to NEDLAC. NEDLAC and the alliance are not mutually exclusive. Labour knows very well what to take to NEDLAC and what to take to the alliance.

Thus, for COSATU, the Alliance does not replace NEDLAC. Instead, the two operate in tandem, on occasion giving labour a double opportunity to shape the outcome of policy. Also, the use of the Alliance needs to be balanced with the fact that it does not offer the same degree of structured and formally guaranteed influence that NEDLAC does. In particular, it is not possible to make detailed agreements at the Alliance level. Rather, it is a platform for acceptance or adoption of broad principle. More importantly, from a labour point of view, the Alliance is a more complicated forum than NEDLAC because of the myriad of different interests represented there (Naidoo, interview). The Alliance is a supplementary process to NEDLAC but, because of its loosely structured nature and, more importantly, the fact that it does not give labour any legislatively guaranteed rights, it is unlikely to replace NEDLAC as the primary focus of struggle over policy.

Notwithstanding the benefits that using the Alliance provides to COSATU, some commentators have remarked that a preference for the 'Alliance route' reflects a lack of commitment from labour leadership to NEDLAC. Such a perception was strengthened by the fact that in September/October 1997, when the institution was under attack from critics, there was not clear public support for NEDLAC from labour. That said, at the second annual NEDLAC Summit, John Gomomo, President of COSATU, made the following comment: 'We remain committed to NEDLAC and pledge to defend the existence of the institution.'

While the possibility of lobbying its Alliance partners does strengthen COSATU's position, it also serves to diminish the status of NEDLAC. In fact, the federation needs to evaluate the relative merits of these two routes and decide to back one or the other. Vacillating between the two serves both to stretch resources and to dissipate strategic focus.

'Non-negotiables'

Although labour has managed to exert influence within NEDLAC and thus shape a number of the policies and laws adopted by government, it has wielded progressively less influence over the shaping of macro-economic policy. This is perturbing, given the centrality of this area for future legislative and policy developments. In particular, the Growth, Employment and Redistribution (GEAR) strategy articulates a doctrine of economic rationalism in a global context that considerably constrains the policy options which are seen as feasible.

As one respondent put it, 'GEAR is now the orienting framework for NEDLAC, for the country, for all of us' (NEDLAC source, 1997: confidential interview). The effect of the non-negotiable nature of the GEAR policy has been most stark in the Public Finance and Monetary Policy Chamber. One participant in the chamber argued that:

> The whole GEAR thing meant that the chamber had to redefine what it was doing as it couldn't talk about the big issue ... this has resulted in a strange whittling away of issues to try and reach something that we could discuss constructively within the chamber.

Thus, while labour has generally been able to exercise a fair degree of influence in NEDLAC, the fact that it has been unable to contest GEAR may have negative implications for the extent to which it is able to impact on policy in the future.

That said, NEDLAC is a product of labour's struggle to limit government's power to introduce policy unilaterally. Accordingly, it will remain an important site in which to contest the implementation of some of the more conservative elements of GEAR. As Vusi Nhlapo (interview) put it: 'NEDLAC plays a critical role in ensuring that government does not have unfettered power, so it is a necessary thing'.

Lost opportunities

The above discussion has established that labour has made considerable gains through NEDLAC, both in terms of a scorecard and in terms of processes. Labour has been able to make a significant impact on a number of key legislative mechanisms and policy developments, as well as to increase its access to the policy-making process. However, these successes have been compromised by a variety of problems which have limited labour's ability to use effectively all the space that it has won for itself. Accordingly, a number of actors in NEDLAC have argued that labour has been unable to use NEDLAC optimally. One trade unionist close to labour's caucus in NEDLAC (cited in Gostner, 1997: 134) asserted that:

> ... these are real opportunities; the fact that labour isn't taking them up is a different question. Government is offering us [labour] a place at the table which we aren't taking up. We've

been knocking at the door for all these years, now it is open
and there is a feeling that we can't go through.

The discussion now turns to identifying those problems and the ways in
which they have affected labour's participation in NEDLAC. By virtue of
its broad focus – according to the Act, 'all significant changes to economic
and social policy' – NEDLAC poses unique challenges for each of the
social partners. As Kettledas (interview) notes, 'there are capacity problems
in business, there are capacity problems in government, there are capacity
problems in labour'. The problems of capacity relate both to the amount
of meetings generated by the NEDLAC process, as well as the complexity
of issues, many of which the labour movement had not needed to engage
with until the formation of NEDLAC.

Martin Nicol, a former labour representative in the Trade and Industry
Chamber, estimated that NEDLAC took up approximately 20% of his time.
Likewise, Dannhauser van der Merwe (1997: interview), General Secretary
of FEDSAL and labour representative on the Management Committee,
estimated that if he attended all NEDLAC-related meetings, he would
have to attend 48 meetings a year. This workload is then added on to the
unionists' normal responsibilities, with the result that they are often unable
to attend adequately to either. These time commitments do not only affect
labour. Business South Africa argues that their representatives spend
considerable time on NEDLAC work and added that this was all voluntary
(Botha and Du Plessis, interview).

Perhaps the most striking example of the implications of labour's
inability to attend all meetings was around UNCTAD IX in April 1996. As
noted above, labour had managed to obtain access to the conference by
inclusion in the government's team. However, labour leadership was
simultaneously involved in organising a stayaway to protest the attempt
by business to include a lockout right in the Constitution. Despite the fact
that labour had access to UNCTAD IX to lobby developing countries to
support its position on the social clause, it failed to attend any of the
meetings (Ramburuth, interview)!

Labour, therefore, has been able to use NEDLAC to increase the space
available to it to influence policy. However, it does not always have
sufficient capacity to use the opportunities that it has created. As a result,
labour has not always been able to influence the formulation of policy to
the full extent possible.

The second area of the capacity problem relates to the technical expertise and negotiating ability necessary to deal with the issues on NEDLAC's agenda. As discussed above, although labour has added a social dimension to the discussions in the Public Finance and Monetary Policy Chamber, it has been unable to make significant inroads (Labour and NEDLAC sources, 1997: interviews). This stems from the relative distance of these issues from the usual concerns of labour, as well as from the lack of skills within labour to deal with these issues. One of our respondents contended that 'on tax, COSATU has been making a lot of noise for some time but, at the end of the day, they haven't had the capacity to deliver a clear package' (Labour source, 1997: confidential interview). This observation is affirmed by the comments of Monnokgotla (interview), one of labour's representatives in the Public Finance and Monetary Chamber:

> On income tax and the restructuring of tax, initially labour didn't have a very coherent policy position. The social equity document is one attempt to address that. But we have lost battles. For instance there is now a tax on pension benefits which we were unable to stop.

Thus, in some instances, labour's lack of capacity and skills has limited the impact it has been able to make on some of the policies that have passed through NEDLAC. However, some of labour's representatives have improved their knowledge of the issues over time and, therefore, are able to engage constructively in debates and to assist in shaping the outcome of the policy process. While this is an important step forward, the knowledge base is restricted to a few key individuals who, should they leave, would inflict a severe blow to labour's capacity to engage in the policy process. As a confidential respondent linked to the NEDLAC labour caucus argues, 'there is a failure to build the capacity of negotiators so the knowledge, the information remains very secure in that small group of people'.

Government in the driving seat?

This combination of too many meetings to attend with insufficient skills to deal with all the issues has resulted in labour 'being more reactive than proactive' (Monnokgotla, interview). Where labour has put policy proposals on the table – various noteworthy instances include the social clause, the Labour Relations Act and the social plan – it has managed to influence the outcome of the process substantially.

To a large extent, however, it is government's legislative programme that drives the NEDLAC agenda. The consequence is that government, notwithstanding the provisions of the Act, has considerable power over what comes to NEDLAC. This is witnessed in the Labour Market Chamber where 'the Department of Labour's five-year plan drives the work programme of the chamber' (Business source, 1997: confidential interview). The Public Finance and Monetary Policy Chamber experiences similar constraints: 'Government does not directly define what is discussed in the chamber, what it does is define what can't be discussed in the chamber' (ibid.).

Although it is largely government's agenda driving NEDLAC, labour has developed an independent approach to the formulation of policy which is articulated in the labour caucus's social equity document. Yet, despite this document, the experience of NEDLAC suggests that, with the exception of a few cases, the policy framework is largely that of government while labour has exercised some influence over the details.

Because government is largely setting the agenda, the potential for labour to define an alternative approach to policy-making has been significantly constrained. For this reason, it is critical that labour develop the capacity to take a more proactive approach in contesting the policy arena. In so doing, it will be able to shape the framework within which discussions occur and thereby increase the potential for the adoption of policies that challenge dominant government thinking. The formation of the NEDLAC Labour Co-ordinating Office in 1996 was subsequently strengthened by the appointment of an experienced unionist from SACTWU. This held great promise for providing a nucleus around which a proactive labour caucus could grow.

Dysfunctional structures
The lack of person power has also made a significant impact on the extent to which the three federations are able to caucus and get mandates. While, as discussed above, there are very clear structures for mandating, it is not at all clear that they are operating effectively. One respondent argued that 'structures are dysfunctional, no-one can say that there is even a semblance of functionality' (Labour source, 1997: confidential interview).

The failure of structures to function effectively is also identified by Dannhauser van der Merwe (interview), who says:

> We are meant to meet for a labour caucus before each chamber meeting and each management committee meeting, but in reality we only managed between 10% and 20% of the time for the chambers and between 30% and 40% for the management committee.

Dysfunctional structures pose a serious threat to labour's engagement in NEDLAC. This is especially true in the context of a plethora of constitutional and extra-constitutional structures within NEDLAC, all of which impact on the negotiation process. It was noted above that if labour did not have clear and functional structures, the multiplicity of structures could undermine the extent to which the union's negotiating position is reflective of a broad consensus. Instead, the NEDLAC labour caucus position runs the risk of being reduced to one or two people in a side-meeting. Thus, the apparent lack of functional structures results in situations in which even the NEDLAC labour representatives are not sure of exactly how and where deals get brokered. Martin Nicol (cited in Gostner 1997: 138), labour's negotiator in the Trade and Industry Chamber, noted this problem in relation to the social clause process: 'Look, when you go into negotiations you expect to go backwards, the problem is that we don't know how it happened'.

Loose mandates but tight leadership

A second consequence of the failure of structures to operate consistently is that 'in practice our [labour's] mandate is very loose, mainly because the NEDLAC labour caucus doesn't meet more often'. Another said: 'mandating is often a process that is controlled by a very few individuals, about three to five depending on the issue' (Labour sources, 1997: confidential interviews). Tony Ehrenreich, then of NUMSA (cited in Gostner, 1997: 137) makes a similar point:[3]

> Most of the time as labour we hold a caucus meeting before each NEDLAC meeting and that is informed by the principles underpinning the social equity document. [But] because there are so many things on the go at NEDLAC, there is not enough

time to always go back for a mandate, so you operate within broad parameters.

However, the problem of mandating exists not only between the federations, but also within each federation, as the links between the federation and each of the affiliates are unclear. As Enoch Godongwana (Gostner, 1997: 138-139), formerly General Secretary of NUMSA, put it:

> Most of these decisions take place at the level of senior negotiators and then it goes to COSATU EXCO [Executive Committee] to be mandated. The capacity of the affiliates to absorb all that is churned out of NEDLAC is very limited. I don't want to try and give this a semblance of democracy, most of the discussion is at an executive level. This is not an intentional thing, but it has to be that way in order to be expedient.

Where there are no specific mandates, labour can always fall back on congress resolutions, such as occurred during the employment standards negotiations. Operating within broad policy directives agreed upon at union congresses is not problematic in itself since these constitute a mandated position. However, NEDLAC negotiations often cover areas that are not addressed at congresses and, as such, there need to be regular meetings of the structures that provide for the formulation of mandates and policy positions within NEDLAC.

The fact that mandating appears not to happen in any consistent or coherent way is borne out by the experience of negotiations within NEDLAC, where agreements reached at one level are often overturned by leadership at the level of the management committee (Labour source, 1997: confidential interview). In some instances, such as the social clause process, it would seem that the decision to reject decisions rests in the hands of the labour caucus convenor[4] (Gostner, 1997). As one labour negotiator noted in a confidential interview: 'Look, you need to understand something about NEDLAC. The leadership lets us play in the sandpit and then they arrive in fire engines. They do what they want and ride into the sunset.'

The role of labour leadership in giving strategic direction to the negotiations process, as well as in ensuring that the outcome of this process fits into labour's overall agenda, is a critical one and should not be dismissed. However, this role should happen through a process of continual mandating and evaluation, not as a crisis intervention at the eleventh hour which serves to undermine labour's frontline negotiators, as well as to slow down the negotiation process.

The lack of consultation and mandating between the different levels in NEDLAC and the affiliates has two implications. First, labour's negotiators are often compelled to negotiate in a situation in which they are uncertain of the official mandated position on the particular issue that they are negotiating. This insecurity can undermine the negotiating team since they may be unsure whether or not they have their organisation's backing on a particular issue. In this context, the ability of labour's representatives to negotiate with confidence becomes contingent on their own standing and power within labour, rather than following from the power of a mandated collective decision.

This problem has not affected the functioning of all chambers because some labour movement representatives have relatively senior standing, but the operation of some chambers has been slowed down as negotiators do not have the organisational power to access senior leadership for approval (Naidoo, interview). This results in labour's participation in NEDLAC resting on the veto power of a few senior leaders which undermines the essence of the democratic labour movement: that of collective and mandated positions.

The criticism of the form that labour leadership's interventions take is not limited to the labour caucus, but is also expressed by the other constituencies within NEDLAC. As one government representative (1997: confidential interview) stressed, 'there is nothing wrong with leadership intervention, especially if it is creative, innovative and has vision: [the problem] is the manner or the process of that intervention'. A consequence of this seemingly ad hoc process of intervention is the perception from other social partners that there is an 'A-team' and a 'B-team' within labour. This perception then translates into a wish to deal only with the 'decision-makers' within labour, which undoubtedly militates against the image of labour as a collective agent.

Thus, while the role of leadership is critical, it is essential that the interventions of leaders take place in a structured way that makes them accountable to a broader section of the labour movement. In general – as the history of the South African labour movement demonstrates –

organisational structures and processes are longer-lasting than the presence of key leaders.

Second, lack of communication and consultation within labour decreases the rate at which NEDLAC can reach decisions, thereby making labour vulnerable to criticisms of preventing government from delivering reforms to the workplace. A response from a confidential labour source describes this situation:

> The fact that there is not clear communication between labour in the different structures within NEDLAC complicates issues. The result is that you find that an issue has been discussed comprehensively in the chamber, but when it goes to higher level structures you have to sell it from the beginning because senior level leadership knows nothing about it. So the lack of communication really slows down the decision-making process.

Difficulties of mobilisation

A substantial part of labour's influence within the NEDLAC process is derived from the rights granted to it in the NEDLAC Act, and from its ability to mobilise members in support of a particular issue. While it may be easy to mobilise members around the LRA or a 40-hour working week – both deeply entrenched in the history of the South African workers' struggle – the reality is that a considerable proportion of issues negotiated in NEDLAC are not of that nature. Tony Ehrenreich (cited in Gostner, 1997: 139-140), then labour's representative in the Trade and Industry Chamber, captures this aspect of the NEDLAC process:

> The LRA has a history in South Africa, so in workers' minds it is seen as an important issue, there were many historic struggles fought over the LRA and that is in people's minds. When you choose an issue to fight it has to be winnable and people are not going to go onto the streets for a social clause.

Undoubtedly, issues such as the LRA and employment standards are close to the shop floor and to workers' hearts and are therefore easy to mobilise around. However, these issues have also been the subject of a number of well-orchestrated campaigns that have helped to put them high on workers' agendas. If information about NEDLAC negotiations was not being dispersed to union membership nor even to union officials not directly involved in NEDLAC, it is difficult to imagine that any of these new issues would become sites of struggle to expand labour's rights through NEDLAC.

The present lack of information dispersal in the federations was captured by one respondent who exclaimed, 'You don't have a filter at the top of COSATU, you have a ... plug' (Labour source, 1997: confidential interview). Another confidential source made the same point somewhat more subtly: 'At the moment an issue gets plugged into COSATU and it gets stuck. That is the biggest capacity problem. You need mechanisms that facilitate participation'. Although these quotations refer directly to COSATU, the other federations – FEDUSA and NACTU – are also characterised by a failure to disperse information within their structures. That said, NEDLAC is a fairly new institution to which labour is slowly showing signs of adapting in that, increasingly, it is a subject for discussion on the agendas of the executive committees of some of the affiliates.

This failure to disperse information creates the potential for a situation in which labour will have progressively less influence over an increasing range of issues. The issues tabled at NEDLAC will become more and more removed from the power-base of the unions – the rank-and-file membership. It must be recognised that campaigns are not simply the spontaneous outpouring of workers' objective interests but events requiring a considerable amount of information dispersal and mobilisation. If labour is to maintain an influence over the policy process within NEDLAC, it needs to address this problem.

CONCLUSIONS AND RECOMMENDATIONS

This chapter has explored the implications of the legislative rights, articulated through NEDLAC, that labour has won as a consequence of its struggle to limit the state's control over policy-making. In addition, it has explored the ways in which labour has used these rights within the context of the challenges posed by its engagement in a complex institution with an ambitious mandate.

Labour's success in obtaining the legislated right that all proposed changes to labour legislation and economic and social policy have to be negotiated through NEDLAC has ensured that its role in policy-making is firmly entrenched. The NEDLAC labour caucus has managed to use those rights successfully, both to influence significantly policy outcomes and the policy process, and to stall government departments in their functioning where the interests of labour were being undermined, thereby compelling government to make some sort of concession. As Jayendra Naidoo (interview) outlined: 'Labour has already got a lot out of NEDLAC, such as the LRA, the details of changes to regulations, institutions and other minor actors, the ILO conventions, access to WTO, the Workplace Challenge ... the scale is a million times more than that which was achieved before'.

Notwithstanding labour's gains, our investigation has revealed a number of weaknesses in the nature of labour's engagement in NEDLAC which raise a question mark over the efficacy of its involvement in negotiated policy-making. The question, put simply, is whether these weaknesses are a result of labour's ambivalence about this new institution, and indeed about the relatively new government, or whether they have to do purely with capacity and leadership problems associated with a union movement that is struggling to develop the competencies necessary to engage with a wide range of technical issues. This is not a question which we have managed to answer conclusively through our research. That said, our interviews revealed broad support for NEDLAC within labour. As such, it may be possible to conclude that the problems facing labour have more to do with coming to grips with the complexity and scope of the demands of NEDLAC than an antagonism to or disinterest in the institution.

However, labour has yet to develop a clear strategy of how to use NEDLAC, what issues to bring to the table, what policy directions and strategic parameters must be agreed to up front, and which battles should be fought and why. The capacity and leadership problems are reflected in the host of problems identified in this chapter, including time constraints, skill shortages, and dysfunctional structures. There is no doubt, however, that if labour fails to develop a strategic response to and programme for its involvement in NEDLAC, then the capacity and leadership problems will simply grow. At present, the failure to build up a team, appoint dedicated officials to NEDLAC and address capacity issues, would seem to predict the possibility of labour having an increasingly tenuous hold on the policy process.

An unintended consequence of the lack of functioning structures is that information about NEDLAC negotiations is not forthcoming. This effectively stalls the mobilisation of campaigns to put pressure on government and business within NEDLAC or to expand the rights won through NEDLAC. Clearly, not all issues are 'strikable', but the effective dispersal of information may form the basis for a creative campaign. For instance, consumer boycotts have a long and successful history in South Africa. In addition, they have been used successfully by northern consumers to put pressure on multi-national companies to respect labour rights in their foreign subsidiaries. A well-organised consumer boycott of goods manufactured in countries that fail to respect labour rights would form a strong support of labour's position in the Social Clause Framework Agreement.

The lack of functioning structures also raises concerns about the extent to which labour's engagement can be said to be democratic and broadly representative of the labour movement. This has raised the serious possibility of the emergence of a small group of individuals who control labour's engagement in NEDLAC, instead of decision-making power being the responsibility of the elected leadership and senior officials of those unions engaged in NEDLAC through the three federations. However, the formal framework of structures exists, so all that is required is the use of these structures in a regular and consistent manner. This would ensure that labour's negotiators are aware of the official position and that position is broadly reflective of labour's interests. In addition, it would enable a wider range of activists to shape labour's engagement in NEDLAC, thereby providing a larger pool of knowledge, skills and expertise for the negotiators to draw on.

Certainly labour has made significant inroads into key areas of labour market and trade and industry policy, achieving gains for its membership. However, the *modus operandi* is generally one of reaction. Accordingly, it is largely government's frame of reference that drives the NEDLAC process, and sets the limits on what is possible. In certain instances, labour has been able to make significant gains within that framework; however, it is not so clearly advancing a labour-friendly approach to the formulation of policy.

This is due, in part, to the approach of government to drafting policy in isolation from the social partners, then tabling it at NEDLAC as a *fait accompli*. Government's approach to policy formulation has also meant that NEDLAC is drawn into the policy process only after a considerable amount of development has taken place. This creates a situation where considerable time is spent debating the policy basics once it gets to NEDLAC, in turn slowing down the process of implementation. If government were to develop a more consultative procedure for developing policy, it would allow the social partners the space to shape the framework within which policy is formulated, as well as facilitate the process of consensus-seeking. This could mean that NEDLAC becomes a site to formulate briefs for policy development rather than to debate the final product. The labour movement may wish to consider raising this demand within NEDLAC.

The credibility and effectiveness of institutions such as NEDLAC will be a product of stakeholder ownership of the outcomes. The first task must surely be to challenge and debate the 'big picture issues'. Here the presentation of GEAR by government as a non-negotiable seriously undermines the principles and vision of NEDLAC. If the parties (and this includes government) are serious about seeking consensus in economic and social management, then the very essence of NEDLAC that everything is negotiable, both in principle and in legislation, needs to be affirmed.

If labour is to optimise its utilisation of NEDLAC, it is essential that it devote time and resources to the development both of a comprehensive vision for South African society, as well as to the revival of structures to drive and struggle for that vision, both within NEDLAC and on the streets. Without such a strategic focus for NEDLAC as a whole, and for the various chambers, labour will be relegated to a role of tinkering with government's legislative programme or arguing over the details. As one of our confidential respondents noted: 'Labour can't be careless: it must use NEDLAC strategically. No other labour movement comes close to the influence labour can wield though NEDLAC, but if you use it badly it will swallow you up.'

The agenda for labour, then, is to develop the necessary strategic focus to effectively use the space it has won through NEDLAC. If it fails to do so, the problems of capacity and of leadership will not be addressed and labour will find itself reacting – or adapting by default – to government's proposals and policy rather than significantly shaping and influencing policy directions in its own right.

5

INDUSTRIAL POLICY-MAKING IN THE AUTOMOBILE AND THE TEXTILE AND CLOTHING SECTORS

Labour's strategic ambivalence [1]

—————— ✦ ——————

Philip Hirschsohn, Shane Godfrey and Johann Maree

While Gostner and Joffe examine engagement at the national level, Hirschsohn, Godfrey and Maree explore engagement by assessing the two manufacturing sectors where major attempts have been made to formulate industrial policy on a tripartite basis in the 1990s. After decades of protectionism favouring import substitution industrialisation, the textile and clothing and automobile industries are increasingly facing global competition in domestic markets as the government progressively reduces tariff protection. The strength of COSATU prior to, and during, South Africa's political transition in the early nineties created a unique opportunity to lever the National Party government and business to develop and implement consensus-based policies to restructure these sectors. In both industries, the three parties agreed to reduce progressively tariffs and integrate South African industry into the global economy. In return, both labour and business sought numerous supply-side inputs, including retraining and trade incentives, to offset the likely shocks of adjustment. In addition, they sought the creation of industry authorities to implement these measures and to monitor progress. In principle these agreements provided workers with substantial powers to restructure their industries according to their own agendas, rather than responding reactively to adjustment imposed from without. However, the institutions through which the engagement occurred were not statutorily based, but depended on the goodwill of the participants. The parties – most especially government – were not bound by the agreements produced. Indeed, once in power, the ANC government 'cherry-picked' both the textile and clothing and automobile agreements, endorsing those aspects consistent with the policies of the Department of Trade and Industry, such as tariff reduction, while rejecting those that meant increased state expenditure or the creation of multipartite implementation and monitoring authorities which could usurp state functions. While COSATU could impose tripartite industrial policy-making on the weakened National Party government, it could not achieve the same result with a legitimate government, even one headed by its alliance partner!

INTRODUCTION

Globalisation and the move for international competitiveness have become the defining characteristics of the forces driving change in manufacturing sectors worldwide. Governments appear to be increasingly unable to protect national markets from international competition and neo-liberal forces demanding trade liberalisation in the interests of economic freedom, organisational efficiency and competitive rationality. After decades of protectionism and a policy favouring import substitution industrialisation, South Africa's manufacturing industries are progressively being exposed to increasing foreign competition as a result of a major shift in state policy to promote open markets, export orientation and international competitiveness.

The automobile and the textile and clothing industries are no exception to this general pattern. In accordance with the country's commitments under the General Agreement on Tariffs and Trade (GATT), tariff reductions are being phased in over a number of years. As intended, the South African government's policy is precipitating industrial restructuring in both industries and competition between domestic producers is being replaced by 'real' competition as imported products, particularly from low-wage Asian economies, challenge two long-protected and relatively uncompetitive South African manufacturing sectors.

In the absence of an alternative politically acceptable policy paradigm, the state's approach has been framed to facilitate the country's re-integration into the world economy and to re-establish the attractiveness of South Africa as a destination for foreign investment. As an approach to industrial policy, trade liberalisation and limited generic supply-side support for industry appears to run contrary to the experience of the fastest-growing, late industrialising countries. These countries combine comprehensive sector-specific supply-side measures and export incentives to help develop internationally competitive industries while protecting domestic markets from foreign competition (Amsden, 1992).

Unlike other late industrialising countries, where unions have typically been made ineffective by state repression, the labour movement led by COSATU grew from strength to strength in the late 1980s. During the political transition and social and political upheaval in the early 1990s, an aggressive and ascendant labour movement exploited the inability of a weakened state and an uncertain business community to change policy unilaterally or jointly, and opened up opportunities to assert a role for itself in socio-economic policy-making. As a result, for the first time, industrial policy was developed on a consensual basis by government, business and organised labour. The political transition thus created a unique opportunity for the social partners to develop and implement consensus-based industrial policies in these two sectors in order to restructure them to ensure their long-term viability.

Of three attempts at tripartite industrial policy-making in the early and mid-1990s, the auto and textile and clothing industries represent the only two manufacturing sectors in which enduring attempts have been made to formulate industrial policy on a corporatist or multipartite basis in the 1990s. An attempt by the National Union of Mineworkers (NUM) to establish a tripartite process to plan the future of the gold-mining industry in the face of substantial downsizing lacked commitment from government and business and slowly disintegrated with little impact on policy, other than in the area of health and safety (Urquhart, 1996).[2] Subsequently, however, NUM's persistence partially succeeded with the establishment of a tripartite social plan to cope with industrial restructuring.

Because unionisation rates are over 80% and a powerful affiliate of COSATU is the major representative of organised labour in each sector, these industries represent the 'best case' examples for assessing (a) how close the social partners come to meeting the demands of corporatist industrial policy-making; and (b) the potential for organised labour to play a meaningful role in tripartite industrial policy-making in South

Africa. If unions fail to make an impact on policy-making in these sectors where they are strong and well-represented, the prospects for unions in other sectors are not encouraging.

The involvement of organised labour in economic and industrial policy-making began in the early 1990s. At the macro-level, organised labour succeeded in its demand for the formation of the National Economic Forum, a tripartite economic policy-making forum to prevent unilateral economic restructuring during the political transition. SACTWU (Southern African Clothing and Textile Workers' Union) and NUMSA (National Union of Metalworkers of South Africa) were the first manufacturing unions to participate in policy-making at industry level. In both industries, the state established comprehensive industrial policy / strategy reviews in 1992. As part of these reviews, these two unions and the labour movement as a whole formulated South Africa's GATT proposals with business and government, and agreed to the progressive reduction of tariffs in order to reintegrate South African industry into the global economy. These two industries provide a useful opportunity to observe, compare and assess two extended examples of tripartite industrial policy-making.

During the political transition, COSATU imposed corporatism on a weakened state. However, since the first democratic elections in 1994, the state is leading the policy-making process and has adopted a clearer trade policy by boldly implementing tariff reform. But, the ability and commitment of the state to provide the resources required to fund a comprehensive industrial policy remains unclear and it is extremely slow in delivering supply-side measures.

While the state has demonstrated a willingness to open up opportunities for unions to participate in industrial policy-making, this door may not remain perpetually open if labour fails to take advantage of the current opportunities. Given the state's ambivalence, this chapter seeks to identify some of the key questions that face the labour movement when assessing its strategic role and continued participation in the industrial policy arena.

The research is primarily based on an extensive series of open-ended interviews which were conducted with key role-players from organised business, the trade unions, and government in the second half of 1996. The research was intended to help identify options for organised labour.[3] The purpose of that investigation and this chapter is not to evaluate the merits of the industrial policies per se. Rather it is aimed at assessing how the policy-making process has evolved and what challenges this poses for the labour movement in these sectors and others.

The structure of the chapter is as follows. We begin by outlining the characteristics that define industry-level or meso-corporatist policy-making as an ideal type. We then discuss the cases of industrial policy-making in the auto and textile and clothing sectors, emphasising how they measure up against our ideal. Before concluding, we assess how well equipped the social partners are to engage effectively in corporatist policy-making.

CONDITIONS FOR MESO-LEVEL CORPORATISM

This analysis of the efficacy of industrial policy-making at meso-level in the auto and textile and clothing sectors is framed against the background of the following criteria which represent a corporatist ideal type. While this ideal type does not necessarily represent a standard to which the interest groups should aspire, it provides us with a helpful analytical framework.

Following Schmitter and Cawson (cited in Maree, 1993: 25), corporatism can be defined as 'the process of negotiation and implementation of agreements between sectors of the state and powerful monopolistic interest organisations whose co-operation is indispensable if desired policies are to be implemented'. In specifying the characteristics of this ideal type, it is useful to distinguish between the general requirements for effective corporatism and the specific requirements for meso-level corporatist industrial policy-making.

At all levels, the effectiveness of corporatist policy-making depends on interest groups, such as business associations and unions, that:

- are highly representative of their constituency and able to bind them to agreements
- have an independent capacity or resources to engage in policy-making and the ability to implement any agreement reached between them
- recognise the legitimate participation and contribution of other interest organisations and their respective capacities to contribute
- agree with other 'social partners'[4] on the participatory framework, and the functioning and scope of the consensus-based policy-making process.

In addition to these general requirements, Atkinson and Coleman (1985) argue that the successful development and implementation of corporatist industrial policy depends on:

- the existence of a state strong enough to develop and defend a conception of the public/national interest that is autonomous of sectoral interests
- the development of a centralised, sectoral bureaucracy or independent industry authority that can co-ordinate a range of sector-specific policy instruments of various government departments and tripartite agencies, commit the requisite financial and other state resources, and exercise the powers required for effective implementation.

The corporatist institutions of co-operation that were established after the Second World War to rebuild national economies endure today as the foundation of policy-making in many European countries. In contrast, South African industry must now restructure rapidly to survive an enforced baptism into an increasingly competitive global marketplace.[5] Consequently, in addition to the above criteria identified by Atkinson and Coleman, we suggest that effective corporatist industrial policy-making requires organised industry, the state and labour to succeed in formulating an industrial strategy which complements firm strategies, is responsive to changing patterns of international competition and ensures the long-term viability of the industry.

While the corporatist ideal type remains a useful standard against which to evaluate recent industrial policy-making, it is helpful to introduce the concept of tripartism to adequately describe a policy-making dispensation that is less rigorous than corporatism. Grant (1985, cited in Maree, 1993), for example, regards tripartism as a weak form of corporatism in which business, government and labour engage in policy discussions which guide policy, but neither impose firm obligations on them to implement agreements, nor are articulated with further policy discussions at different levels.

The strength of the South African labour movement during the political transition in the early 1990s provided the initial thrust behind the establishment of corporatist policy-making structures. However, it remains unclear whether corporatist policy-making was solely a contingent development brought about by the combination of a strong union movement and the political transition, or if the post-apartheid government will continue to promote corporatism or tripartism as an enduring dimension of our political economy. We begin to address this question by outlining the policy-making experiences of the auto and textile and clothing industries before applying the analytical framework outlined above to these cases.

AUTO INDUSTRY

Approximately 85 000 people are employed in the auto assembly and component sectors which constitute the major sectors of the auto manufacturing industry. Like many other areas of South African society, the industry is characterised by an alphabet soup of acronyms which can be bewildering to the uninitiated. The firms are organised into two industry associations – NAAMSA (National Association of Automobile Manufacturers of South Africa) and NAACAM (National Association of Automotive Component and Allied Manufacturers), while NUMSA represents over 80% of workers in the industry. Collective bargaining in the auto assembly sector is centralised in the National Bargaining Forum (NBF) where employers are represented by AMEO (Automobile Manufacturers' Employers' Association).[6] NUMSA and AMEO jointly established the Automobile Manufacturing Industry Education and Training Board (AMIETB). In the industrial policy arena, the state established the Motor Industry Task Group (MITG) to develop an industrial policy or strategy for the industry which culminated in the Motor Industry Development Programme (MIDP) and the establishment of the tripartite Motor Industry Development Council (MIDC) to monitor the implementation of the MIDP. The relationship between these organisations is represented in Figure 5.1 below.

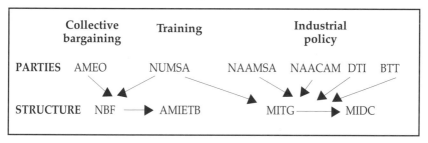

Figure 5.1: Collective bargaining, training and industrial policy structures

Industrial policy context

As was the case in many other developing countries, South Africa introduced an import substitution policy to facilitate the local manufacture of components and vehicles, rather than the assembly of imported components. While auto plants in other developing countries became increasingly integrated into the global operations of multinational firms from the 1970s, the South African industry remained internationally isolated and developed behind a protective tariff wall. Because both sectors produce a wide range of products in low volumes for the domestic market, their cost structures are not competitive with international mass producers.

In the late 1980s, government began to place greater emphasis on the need for export-oriented manufacturing (Oberhauser, 1993). To enhance international competitiveness, encourage exports and save foreign exchange, the state introduced Phase Six which increased local content requirements. This could be achieved by sourcing components locally or by exporting vehicles or components to secure duty-free imports. This policy had little impact on productivity, exports or the improvement of manufacturing efficiency. If anything, the policy had perverse results. Car firms increased unproductive overheads to meet the Phase Six local content requirements, while the components sector underwent major restructuring.

Following the report of the MITG in 1994, the government ushered in a new phase of restructuring. The state hopes this strategy of steadily reducing tariff protection and progressively infusing more intense international competition will improve efficiency, productivity and competitiveness. Tariff protection, which was reduced from 115% to 80% in 1994 to 54% in 1998, will decline to 40% by 2002 – a lower level at a faster rate than that required under South Africa's GATT commitments. Although assemblers still remain highly protected from international competition, the progressive reduction in tariffs has already resulted in increased sales of imported vehicles and intensified competition, particularly for component suppliers.

In order to compete internationally and domestically, South African firms will have to restructure their production techniques, work organisation and human resources policies to compete with 'lean production', the Japanese-style production system that emphasises flexibility in technology and the organisation of production (Womack et al, 1990). In addition to multiple skills, workers will need a conceptual grasp of the production process, as well as the analytical skills to identify and solve problems on- and off-line. To face these challenges, the NBF and AMIETB have developed a human resource development strategy to provide operators with the incentives and training required to develop the necessary skills to undertake quality control routine maintenance and problem-solving.

In analysing the industry's response to the challenges of increasing international competition, our discussion of the industrial policy-making process takes cognisance of the sectoral policy-making process leading to tariff reform, the training and human resource development initiatives of NUMSA and employers in the NBF and AMIETB, and the interaction between these domains of policy formulation and implementation.

Industrial policy reform –
the Motor Industry Task Group (MITG)

In October 1992, Trade and Industry Minister, Derek Keys, established the MITG to develop a long-term strategy for the industry based on the consensus of key stakeholders. Keys appointed representatives from the trade unions, assemblers, components suppliers and government to the MITG to develop a strategy that would (a) ensure the industry's growth, develop human resources and create employment opportunities; (b) minimise the use of foreign exchange; (c) encourage the industry to become more productive and increasingly internationally competitive; and (d) reduce tariffs to meet South Africa's commitments under the 1993 GATT. While it may have been a break from the past to invite NUMSA, the establishment of the MITG could best be considered a holding action during a period of political uncertainty, rather than a new state vision for industry policy-making.[7] (Black, 1996: interview)

In early 1994 the MITG presented a delicately balanced consensus-based programme that focused on tariff reduction and incentives to discourage the local production of low volume models. By proposing that tariffs be reduced even faster than the rate required under GATT, the MITG argued that increased competition from imported vehicles and parts would force improvements in efficiency and competitiveness. To implement and monitor the industry development programme, the MITG also proposed that the Minister establish a statutory Motor Industry Authority, with interest groups represented in an advisory capacity. Despite NUMSA's attempts to keep the supply-side issue as an MITG priority, it was given relatively little attention. The recommendations focused on tariffs which have long been the core of South Africa's industrial policy.

The MITG report was submitted to the Board of Tariffs and Trade (BTT) which is responsible for making recommendations on trade and industrial policy to the Minister. The BTT, a nominally independent statutory body, agreed with the MITG's long-term aim to develop an internationally competitive industry that would become integrated into the international market, but rejected the MITG proposals on model rationalisation as interventionist and inconsistent with GATT. On the BTT's recommendation, the Minister initiated an accelerated tariff reduction process in August 1994, cutting tariffs from 115% to 80% in the midst of an industry strike. A year later, the government finalised the MIDP which led to the further reduction of import duties on vehicles from 80% to 65% and a planned phase-down to 40% by 2002. Local manufacturers are allowed to import some components duty-free and may reduce import duties on other components by exporting cars or components. According to the assembly firms, the impact of the MIDP will be to:

> progressively, but in a gradual and balanced way, expose the domestic vehicle and component manufacturers to the pressures of international competition and the need for efficiency improvements, thereby facilitating greater affordability in the domestic market. Moreover, the programme will reinforce the industry's export momentum, thereby providing a better balance between the industry's forex usage and earnings.
>
> (NAAMSA, 1996: 9)

As a result of the MIDP's export incentives, the industry is becoming increasingly integrated into global production chains of the major multinational car companies, and both components firms and assemblers are restructuring their production strategies and product ranges to secure export business. However, because of falling tariffs, imports of components have also risen markedly.

The Department of Trade and Industry (DTI) did not establish a statutory tripartite industry authority but instead appointed Anthony Black, a former NUMSA advisor, as a consultant to monitor the implementation of the MIDP. In recognition of the need to listen to the views of all stakeholders and to develop common goals for the industry, an informal Motor Industry Development Council (MIDC) was established to represent the major interest groups – NUMSA, NAACAM (component industry) , NAAMSA and DTI. The MIDC monitors the implementation and effects of the MIDP and provides a discussion forum in which all players can make policy proposals for the benefit of the industry as a whole.

Black (interview), who chairs the MIDC, suggested that the MIDC is not intended as a policy-making body since this role resides with the government which leads the process and determines the parameters of policy formulation. A critical function of the MIDC has been to draw on the resources of the DTI, NAAMSA and NAACAM to develop a reliable database on all aspects of industry performance in order to monitor the effects of the MIDP. At the same time, the DTI has been restructured along sectoral lines and has established an auto industry directorate which is intended to be primarily responsible for tariff policy administration rather than policy development.

Progress in the National Bargaining Forum (NBF)

In 1989, NUMSA used its shop-floor militancy and organisational strength to force the seven assembly firms to establish a National Bargaining Forum (NBF). NUMSA soon initiated discussions on restructuring to enhance the industry's international competitiveness and to formulate a comprehensive human resource development strategy. The first milestone in this process was marked by the NBF agreement of 1991 in which the parties committed themselves to the long-term growth and viability of the industry, the protection of employment, the improvement of quality, and the negotiation of work reorganisation to ensure international and local competitiveness (Bethlehem and Von Holdt, 1991). At the time, however, because of economic isolation and tariff protection, management largely ignored international competitive developments and remained locked into a siege mentality, focused on domestic political and labour problems (Smith, interview: 1995).

Because NUMSA took the initiative while management's attention was focused elsewhere, the union provided the vision and framework for the assembly sector's human resource development strategy. NUMSA (1993: 4) recognised that the industry had to become world class and capable of meeting the changing demands of the domestic market while maintaining a high export profile in order to provide employment growth. Performance benchmarks, based on issues such as export growth, skill formation and quality measures, should be put in place in order to determine the rate of reduction in tariff protection. Incentives should be available in order to assist companies and regions to restructure and adjust to changing patterns of location and employment.

To achieve these objectives, NUMSA developed a systemic bundle of human resource development principles on which the 1993 and 1995 NBF agreements were based. NUMSA adopted key elements of the lean production framework, coupled with progressive ideas based on developments in the Australian metal industry and the German auto industry. Vocational training was seen as an integral part of an approach to restructuring that focused on job reorganisation to facilitate productivity improvement and greater union participation. According to Kraak (1992: 404), this strategy:

> entails the introduction of more participatory forms of work organisation and the use of new technologies which bring benefits to both capital and labour. This economic growth path is premised on a strong trade union movement participating in the process of industrial restructuring. Multi-skilling, active labour market [policies] and lifelong job security are some of the human resource benefits which accrue to workers in this new accord between capital and labour.

The NBF agreements provide for competency-based training by individual firms that will be recognised across the industry and offer workers career paths from general to specialised skills. Training is linked to the broad-banding of grades and aims to lay the basis for career-long learning so that workers can acquire workplace skills and keep pace with technological change. Training is to be provided in modules and is competency-based to accommodate employers' need for flexibility in combining workers' skills. To encourage workers to continue learning, they progress through the first four grades based on the completion of certified competencies, irrespective of whether the skills are utilised on the shop floor.

Automobile Manufacturing Industry Education and Training Board (AMIETB)

In 1991 NUMSA and AMEO, which represents the auto assembly firms in the NBF, decided to establish a jointly-controlled, employer-funded, Automobile Manufacturing Industry Education and Training Board (AMIETB) to determine the detailed content of the education and training principles concluded by the NBF. While the NBF provided a conceptual framework, the principles of education and training left significant room for disagreement and dispute when AMIETB had to design and implement the training system in detail. On paper, the parties had common aims. However, it took training management, who had not been party to the NBF negotiations, a long time to understand the meaning and implications of the agreement that had been concluded (De Klerk, interview: §1996). Furthermore, Volkswagen management admits that the industry was unprepared for the major cultural shift required to move from a low-wage strategy towards a system founded on equity and a skilled workforce (Smith, interview: 1995).

The critical factor that underlies this process is the acknowledgement by management that the human resource development agreements in the NBF were conceptualised and structured by union leaders. It was they who provided the vision of the industry requirements to become internationally competitive and who created a blueprint at the intellectual level. In the NBF, employers were in a weak position because the industrial relations managers who represented them in negotiations had a limited understanding of training issues and were primarily in a reactive mode. Training managers, who do not participate in the NBF, were effectively marginalised from the design of the framework. However, when it came to interpretation and implementation of the agreed principles in AMIETB, Volkswagen's De Klerk (interview) argued that training management had to adopt a proactive mode to ensure that the training meets employer needs as well as NUMSA's stringent requirements.

AMIETB operates on the basis of joint labour-management control and thus needs to reconcile the often conflicting objectives of employers who are primarily concerned with improving productivity, and NUMSA which is primarily interested in uplifting its members (De Klerk, interview). The slow progress in AMIETB reflected NUMSA's failure to secure precise financial commitments from employers in the NBF and highlighted the ongoing tensions between firm and industry strategic choices. Initially AMIETB was operated purely by a part-time training specialist and a shop steward from each plant. These plant-level training specialists and shop stewards were later employed full-time and AMIETB is now staffed by a small secretariat.

Employers did not enter AMIETB enthusiastically and were conceptually and organisationally ill-prepared for the challenges it posed. While AMEO exists on paper, it still commands no resources of its own as employer attitudes are dominated by a competitive culture and employers lack the desire to make it work (Gazendam, 1996: interview). This attitude was also evident in AMIETB as employers initially failed to realise the importance of standing together. Each firm believed that they could 'go their own way' and impose their own approach to training on all other firms in the industry (Best, 1996: interview).

Employers also had great difficulty in harmonising and synergising their collective efforts because they were bound together only by the threat of the union (De Klerk, interview). Competing car firms were not accustomed to working co-operatively with one another or with NUMSA in an industry-wide initiative, particularly to provide training, a field that had traditionally been regarded as one of firm-level competitive advantage and exclusive managerial prerogative. Some firms believed that their competitive advantage rested on human resource development and remained reluctant to reveal details of their training programmes.

It took a long time for the parties to agree that AMIETB would not design training modules but would ratify industry standards and the competency outcomes of each module, and regulate the provision of training. AMIETB began by developing the training structure for grades below artisan level. The syllabus covered modules in adult basic education (ABE), core business and technical skills for each wage band. Progress was extremely slow because both sides had conflicting, but educationally valid, arguments (Handlinger, 1996: interview).

Following the MITG tour to Australia, the UK and Germany (described below), Australian employers and unions were invited to share their recent experience in developing and implementing a multi-skilling training structure on an industry-wide basis.[7] Exposure to the Australian experience provided a breakthrough for NUMSA and employer representatives at AMIETB because their approach matched the broad vision embodied in the NBF agreements and provided both sides with a working understanding of the relationship between national standards and competencies that are central to the training system. The detailed manuals from the Australian system then provided a template to adapt and develop local standards that would be internationally competitive.

As an equal partner with unequal resources, NUMSA is clearly under enormous pressure to monitor training implementation since shop stewards are also required to complete their regular tasks. In 1996, joint union-management teams across the industry engaged in a Recognition of Prior Learning (RPL) exercise to assess the technical competencies of every operator in his or her present and past jobs. Initial projections of the failure of almost all workers to progress up the skills hierarchy as a result of this assessment threatened the entire RPL process. It also exposed the industry's neglect of human resource development and indicated the massive investment in training required to become globally competitive.

Interface between industrial policy and training

An ongoing challenge lies with integrating the policy-making processes being driven by DTI and the negotiations between NUMSA and the employer association AMEO in the NBF and AMIETB. In its final report, the MITG recognised the progress made by the NBF in addressing training and related issues, and emphasised the need for government assistance to facilitate the skills development and training required to prepare the industry for integration into global markets. Subsequently, the MITG sent 25 delegates on a tour of automobile plants in Australia, the United Kingdom and Germany to examine the process of change in industrial relations and work organisation. The industry hoped to replicate a similar process which the Australian union movement had initiated in the mid-1980s to prepare for the challenges of international competition. This tour exposed a large group of key players – human resource and production managers, union officials and shop stewards, and government officials – to overseas developments, as well as to the magnitude of the challenge posed by restructuring and catching up with a moving target of improving quality and productivity.

The key recommendation of the delegation was that the 'restructuring of the industry should not be piecemeal but proceed from a coherent package of tariff reductions, supply-side measures and labour market adjustment programmes'. Thus far, however, implementation has been piecemeal. The tariff reduction programme was introduced in 1994 and 1995 but, as in the case of all other industries, DTI and other state departments failed to develop or deliver the sector-specific supply-side measures required to facilitate restructuring. Despite this failure, employers and NUMSA are addressing the key supply-side issue of human resource development in AMIETB.

Following the MITG visit, Australian unionists and employers were invited by AMIETB to run extensive workshops on their auto industry's competency-based training system that had been developed since the 1980s. The workshops were critical to breaking the log-jam in AMIETB which had made minimal progress in two years. The mode of engagement at AMIETB shifted from a debating forum to a problem-solving workshop and, literally overnight, AMIETB was able to develop a new training framework by building directly on the Australian experience.

We move now to discussing developments in the textile and clothing industry before comparing the progress of the two industries in jointly developing and implementing industrial policy.

TEXTILE AND CLOTHING INDUSTRY

The South African textile sector primarily produces a wide range of fabrics for the clothing, household and automobile sectors. It is dominated by a few large companies, many of which are vertically integrated. The clothing sector is made up of a large number of mainly small firms and is extremely competitive. It produces a wide range of garments but is focused primarily on the middle and upper ends of the clothing market. Both sectors are relatively labour intensive and have been susceptible to the threat of low-wage competition, and consequently were protected by high tariff barriers. As a result, most manufacturers produce for the domestic market.

Historically, the sectors were deeply divided on the question of tariffs. Textile firms favoured high tariffs on fabric to protect the local market. Clothing firms demanded lower textile tariffs so they could source fabric more cheaply, but sought high tariffs on the finished product. The firms lobbied for continued tariff protection through their industry associations

– TEXFED (Textile Federation of South Africa) and CLOFED (Clothing Federation of South Africa). SACTWU represents over 80% of workers in the industry. Collective bargaining is centralised at sectoral level, with a single national bargaining chamber in clothing and nine such chambers in textiles. Although initially established by employers, the Clothing Industry Training Board (CITB) and the Textile Industry Training Board (TITB) are now under joint labour-management control.

A recessionary economy, as well as the liberalisation of global trade and the intensification of international competition placed the two sectors under increasing pressure during the late 1980s. In response, the government introduced a structural adjustment programme (SAP), phasing down tariffs and aiming to promote exports by providing marketable duty-free import permits based on the achievement of very modest exports. While the SAP significantly increased exports and generally benefitted the clothing sector, it accelerated plant closures and job losses in the textiles sector. As a result, the two sectors continued their bitter feud and lobbied the government over appropriate tariff protection (Mollett, 1995: 110, 124; Maree and Godfrey, 1995: 129).

Debating and developing industrial policy

In this context, corporatist industrial policy formulation emerged in response to labour's concern about the sharp declines in textile employment. At its 1991 national congress, SACTWU adopted a resolution on industrial restructuring. It then sought to engage government and business in developing an industrial policy to facilitate restructuring. At the time, SACTWU was excluded from policy formulation because the Board of Tariffs and Trade (BTT), which developed industrial policy, mainly consulted the major firms and the industry associations (CLOFED and TEXFED) and excluded unions from this process. SACTWU made an important intervention when assistant general secretary, Ebrahim Patel, addressed a CLOFED conference on labour's role in promoting international competitiveness. Patel threatened that the union would take the industry out on a strike if the government failed to involve SACTWU in formulating a new industrial policy.

After failing in its call for a conference of all stakeholders to initiate the process of developing a growth strategy for the industry, SACTWU agreed to participate in the Hatty Committee initiated by the Minister of Trade and Industry to address the industry's problems. In Hatty, SACTWU failed to get support for its proposals of a broad restructuring programme comprising a growth strategy, an investment programme, a productivity training and technology policy, and an industrial relations policy. The Hatty Committee focused exclusively on tariffs and import quotas. Hatty's proposals collapsed within six months, mainly because of opposition from small clothing manufacturers who had been marginalised during the committee's deliberations (Maree and Godfrey, 1995).

The government introduced a new tariff regime which led to another bout of lobbying by CLOFED and TEXFED. SACTWU tried to reconcile the two sectors and pressured the government to launch a long-term development plan for the industry. In September 1992, Trade and Industry Minister Keys established the Panel and Task Group for the Textile and Clothing Industries (the 'Swart Commission') to formulate achievable strategies to improve international competitiveness. The Commission included representatives from SACTWU, the textile and clothing sectors, raw material suppliers and retailers, DTI, the BTT and the Industrial Development Corporation (IDC). The government representatives were not mandated. Thus, they participated but could not bind the government to any agreements reached by the Panel (Swart, interview).

The Swart Commission's recommendations intended to counter the impact of tariff reductions with various supply-side measures to support restructuring and enable the two sectors to compete internationally. Various measures, including public support, employer support and union capacity-building, aimed to address the social dimension of restructuring. The most important supply-side proposals included:

- a strategy for training and skills development which stipulated that employers should spend 4% of their payroll on training
- the promotion of participative management to improve productivity
- the investment of R2.7 billion in new technology over eight years, supported by an interest subsidy of about R258 million
- a wool beneficiation programme
- additional financial support measures for small businesses
- the development of an up-to-date industry data base.

The Commission could not reach agreement on the phase-down of tariffs. While South Africa was committed to a 12 year phase-down period under

GATT, CLOFED, TEXFED and SACTWU proposed an accelerated phase-down over ten years to a level equal to or below the GATT tariffs. The retailers and small clothing manufacturers proposed a period of five years for fabric and seven years for clothing, with end rates well below the GATT offer (see Swart Commission, 1994: vi).

The Commission also proposed the establishment of an independent Textile and Clothing Authority (TCA) to further develop and implement their recommendations, and to monitor and evaluate their impact. It would report regularly to the Minister on progress made towards achieving industrial policy objectives and would conduct a comprehensive review of the industries at the midpoint of the tariff phase-down period, i.e. 1998/99. Once established, all lobbying activities at government level would be prohibited: the TCA would be the only place where the parties could address their problems (see Swart Commission, 1994: 170-171).

Minister Keys rejected the Commission's ambitious restructuring proposals, labelling the supply-side measures and state subsidies as unaffordable. Similar sentiments were expressed by his successor, Trevor Manuel, the first Minister of Trade and Industry under the ANC government. Instead, the new government's provisional strategic plan focused on phasing down tariffs. It accepted the Commission's tariff end rates, but proposed that the phase-down period be reduced from ten to eight years. Other recommendations included:

- a three-year extension of the Duty Credit Certificate (DCC) Scheme which allows a manufacturer to offset exports against import duties, on condition that the firm, together with an outside consultant and SACTWU, develops and implements a training programme and a plan to improve productivity
- a 50% subsidy of management consultancy fees for five years
- the provision of finance by the IDC or other external institutions to upgrade technology
- the referral of training issues to the Department of Labour and the establishment of a forum to develop a training programme and address the social dimension of restructuring
- that an independent TCA not be established; instead DTI, assisted by outside consultants, would monitor the industries
- that no support be given for stabilising the cotton price or for wool export marketing assistance (DTI would investigate wool separately).

(Ministry of Trade and Industry, 1995a)

The government's response suggests that the Swart Commission's non-tariff recommendations were either unaffordable or not a priority. SACTWU disputed the alleged unaffordability and proposed that the supply-side measures be financed by scrapping the General Export Incentive Scheme (GEIS).

Tariff reform as industrial policy

In August 1995, the government's final plan for the industry introduced an eight-year phase-down of tariffs. While it reiterated that sector-specific supply-side measures were unaffordable, the plan stated that the industries would qualify for the general supply-side measures being developed by the government, and accepted a proposal to appoint a small working group to pursue supply-side issues (Ministry of Trade and Industry, 1995b). However, the development and implementation of these general supply-side measures lagged behind the tariff phase-down which was implemented immediately. Without the protection afforded to local manufacturers by the devaluation of the Rand in the nineties, this lag could have resulted in many more job losses.

Since the Swart Commission's proposal to establish an industrial authority was quashed, the collection and monitoring of data has instead been contracted out to a consultant. DTI has been reorganised to establish a Textile and Clothing Directorate, but it remains unclear whether it has the staff to perform the functions that had been envisaged for the TCA. Consequently, no permanent structure supports tripartite engagement over the development path of the industry and engagement takes place on an ad hoc basis.

Freddie Magugu of SACTWU argued that the union had not relinquished the idea of an industry authority, but it did not have the capacity to contribute to set up such a body and preferred to focus on campaigns (such as the Project Jobs Campaign) to deal with immediate problems in the industry. Hennie van Zyl, former Executive Director of CLOFED, also regretted that the TCA was not set up since it would need little funding, would stop much of the current lobbying and would help to build understanding and co-operation between the main players. In contrast, Eben Marais of the DTI argued that an industry authority is not necessary as all parties are consulted on an ad hoc basis whenever adjustments are made to industrial policy. A good example of ad hoc tripartism was the re-negotiation of the Zimbabwe Trade Agreement in 1996 when newly appointed Trade and Industry Minister, Alec Erwin, brought SACTWU, CLOFED and TEXFED into the South African government's team which negotiated with the Zimbabwean government. All parties were involved in a multi-party forum to assist the Department of Customs and Excise to plug the numerous holes in the customs system.

Addressing training needs

Unlike the AMIETB, which was jointly established by employers and NUMSA to develop a training framework for the auto industry, the Textile and Clothing Industry Training Boards, TITB and CITB, were initially formed by employers. Both training boards had shifted their focus from operator training to training supervisors, technicians and management. However, the boards operate quite distinctively. The CITB is older, larger and provides direct training, while the TITB facilitates training, developing curricula for distance learning. Consequently, the task faced by SACTWU in restructuring training in these two sectors is significantly different from that faced by NUMSA.

SACTWU began an initiative to secure representation on the training boards in the early 1990s, but only succeeded in 1994. At the same time that the national education and training framework was being restructured, the training boards had to bring a new partner, with a quite distinctive agenda, on board. Asserting joint union control over the training boards was necessarily the first phase of SACTWU's approach to implementing a strongly centralised national plan. Although SACTWU included the principles of a national, centralised skills-based training plan among its demands in 1996, no agreement was reached as wages dominated the national bargaining agenda (Goldman, 1996: interview).

In both sectors, significant differences remain between the union and employers on the vision for an industry training framework. While SACTWU envisages a national plan to develop a multi-skilled workforce, employers favour an incremental approach of training operators when the need arises. Many textile firms remain unconvinced of the need for a new training strategy as, historically, they have relied on imported technical skills (Clark, 1996: interview). The union has encountered significant resistance to its proposals. Employers fear SACTWU's pay-for-skills approach is not focused on improving performance but is a way of pushing up wages. In a labour intensive industry, this fear may be justified if employers do not share labour's vision of the future organisation of production. Given the conservatism of the industry and the lack of a single world-class production paradigm in the clothing sector, SACTWU's plans may be too ambitious.

ANALYSIS OF THE CASE STUDIES

Before reflecting on these cases in terms of our framework, it is useful to reiterate the common elements of the two cases described above. In 1992, in response to pressures from various quarters, Trade and Industry Minister Derek Keys established multi-party commissions to formulate strategies for the auto and textiles and clothing industries to enhance their international competitiveness. By 1994 both commissions recommended:
- a tariff reduction policy that was more aggressive than South Africa's commitments under the 1993 GATT Agreement
- a package of sector-specific supply-side measures to facilitate restructuring
- the establishment of a statutory industry authority to monitor and manage the restructuring process.

In 1994/95, after hearing industry and union inputs to its draft policies, the post-apartheid government with Trevor Manual as Minister:
- introduced a more aggressive tariff reduction policy than required under GATT or than either commission recommended
- promised the future delivery of generic supply-side measures
- appointed consultants and informal multi-party structures to monitor policy implementation.

A key difference between the two industries lies in bilateral labour-management initiatives on training in the auto assembly sector. The existence of a jointly-developed industry training framework through the NBF and AMIETB represents a critical element of supply-side capacity-building. The slow pace of delivery highlights the difficulty of formulating and implementing consensus-based industrial policy instruments.

It is useful, at this stage, to review briefly our ideal requirements of effective corporatist industrial policy-making against which we will evaluate these cases.

- Organised business and labour must be representative of their constituencies, be able to bind them to agreements, have the capacity or resources to engage in policy-making, and be prepared to recognise the legitimacy and contribution of one another.
- They must agree with the state on the policy framework, and on the scope and functioning of consensus-based policy-making and implementation.
- The state must be sufficiently autonomous of sectoral interests to develop and defend a policy perspective that reflects a public / national interest.
- A centralised, sectoral bureaucracy or industry authority is required to co-ordinate sector-specific policy instruments and to commit the financial and other state resources required for effective implementation.
- Most importantly, business associations, the state and labour must formulate an industrial strategy which complements firm strategies, is responsive to changing patterns of global competition and ensures the long-term viability of the industry.

In the sections below, we do not rigorously evaluate the policy-making processes against the ideal type but use it as a reference point to assess the approaches of the state, business and unions towards industrial policy-making and their capacities to engage effectively in this process.

Does trade liberalisation constitute an industrial policy?

The tariff reforms introduced in the mid-1990s reflect a distinct shift in government policy away from import-substitution industrialisation, where industries are developed to satisfy local markets behind high tariff barriers. Under this more liberalised trading environment, domestic manufacturers are progressively being exposed to international competition in domestic markets and are now encouraged to export. This open-market policy is in line with South Africa's commitments under GATT. However, tariff reform alone does not constitute an export-oriented industrial policy, as the term is conventionally used, until the state implements complementary export incentives and sector-specific supply-side measures.

As Amsden (1992) has convincingly argued, the industrial policy successes of the fastest-growing, late industrialising countries – South Korea, Taiwan, Malaysia and Thailand – can be attributed to extensive government intervention to subsidise factor prices and to 'discipline business'. In these countries, the state 'disciplines business' by operating according to reciprocity principles, providing domestic market protection and various subsidies in exchange for the achievement of concrete performance standards with respect to output, exports, product quality, investment in training, and research and development. Achievement of these performance standards raises productivity levels and increases cost competitiveness and efficiency levels which then leads to lower subsidies.

While there is extensive debate about the pace at which trade liberalisation should take place, and about the extent to which South African industry should produce for a mass domestic market rather than for niche export markets, there can be little argument that increased exposure to international competition is an essential ingredient in forcing local industry to improve its productivity levels. Amsden recommends that industrialising countries respond pragmatically to the campaign by the United States to eradicate industrial policy regimes in world markets. In contrast to South Africa's practice of being 'holier than GATT', Amsden (1992: 80) would argue that industries should only be weaned off subsidies 'when major trading partners won't tolerate it a minute longer'.

State policy direction and capacity

The industrial policy reviews of the auto and textile and clothing industries were initiated by Minister Keys during a phase in the political transition when the apartheid state was politically incapacitated and unable to drive policy. While government policy had been slowly shifting away from import substitution and protectionism towards export promotion and trade liberalisation, neither attempt to develop a long-term strategy was conducted with clearcut guidelines from the state. Consequently, both policy-making processes were compromised because of this lack of firm government commitment to the process and the knowledge that the government was soon to end its term of office.

While the state previously lacked a concrete policy, Minister Erwin (interview) has argued that the trade liberalisation policy direction is now clearly established. The state is committed to a policy of involving all parties in policy-making and strategy-developing processes, as was the case with the Swart Commission and the MITG. It is also committed to strengthening labour's capacity to engage in policy-making on an informed basis, but is not as firmly committed to the principle that labour's involvement should necessarily extend to policy implementation. However, the state will not be held back if labour is unwilling or fails to make the most of the opportunities provided (Erwin, interview).

The state's limited capacity to fully develop sectoral industrial policies is partially attributable to the legacy of an import substitution policy that focused primarily on tariffs rather than supply-side measures. Under the old policy regime, the DTI was structured to implement policy rather than as a policy think-tank. Consequently, the experience of staff in these directorates is limited to implementing tariffs, and does not include developing industrial policy. For this reason, the DTI could provide little more than secretarial services to the Swart Commission and MITG and most of the research work had to be contracted to outside consultants or the Industrial Development Corporation. Where there was in-house research, it was assigned to senior members of the BTT, most of whom have retired or are near retirement age.

To address these deficiencies, the DTI has been restructured into sectoral directorates, including one which specialises in the auto sector and another in clothing, textiles and footwear. Erwin (interview) expects an increasing flow of personnel between the DTI and the private sector. This concentration of expertise and cross-fertilisation of ideas will, no doubt, have long-term benefits for the development of industrial policy. However, if the DTI comes to rely on the inputs of seconded personnel, the state runs the risk of losing its autonomy and becoming a captive of industry interests.

In the fastest-growing late industrialising countries the state has provided strong leadership to direct industrial policy. Erwin (interview) envisages that sectoral directorates in the DTI will play a more facilitating role, along the lines of Japan's Ministry of International Trade and Industry (MITI). With the state defining the broad policy parameters, the Minister believes that responsibility for determining the 'nitty-gritty' must lie with negotiations between business and labour.

Problems with this approach will continue if the delivery of resources depends on a reticent or under-resourced DTI. The policy-making debacle of the Swart Commission may be repeated – while business and labour reach agreement on the necessary supply-side policy instruments, the state is unable or unwilling to deliver. It remains unclear whether the state is prepared to commit the resources required to develop industrial policy, as successfully practised in East Asia and envisaged by organised labour. Current practice suggests that the state will not develop a strategic package of sectoral mechanisms to incentivise and 'discipline business', but that it will rely primarily on the forces of global competition to drive restructuring and enhance efficiency.

The corporatist model suggests that effective industrial policy requires the state to have the capacity (i.e. resources) to co-ordinate the sector-specific activities and policy instruments, particularly supply-side measures, of various government agencies. However, the DTI is currently focusing on providing generic, rather than sector-specific, supply-side support measures to facilitate restructuring. Consequently, there is little evidence to suggest that the DTI recognises that effective industrial policy requires the capacity to formulate and co-ordinate sector-specific instruments to become a core competency of each sectoral directorate.

Business capacity and commitment

The capacity of business to engage effectively in industrial policy formulation and implementation also remains questionable. Business associations are relatively inadequately staffed and rely extensively on their largest members to provide expertise. Consequently, they are rarely prepared to take policy positions on behalf of their industry if the consequences seriously challenge the interests of their largest members. Poor resourcing of business associations by their members reflects an ambivalence about the degree to which firms should co-operate with their competitors, as well as their commitment to relying on their associations, rather than private lobbying, to represent their interests in the policy-making process. The mandating process within business associations also remains problematic, particularly with respect to the limited voting power of small business. The ability of associations to bind their members to agreements is limited by the readiness with which big players lobby the government directly when policy changes may go against their immediate interests, even if they have been party to those decisions.

The weakness of business associations is exacerbated by the long history of antagonism between the components sector and the car assemblers, and the textile and clothing manufacturers respectively. While this antagonism has resulted from their conflicting interests around tariff reform, it undermines the potential to develop co-operative relations between suppliers and their customers. Co-operation between industries and their key suppliers is essential if South African industries are to become players in international markets, where a key to competitive advantage lies in the ability to add value at all steps in the supply chain. In many situations the unions, which have members in both sectors, have been observed to play the role of broker between these conflicting interests.

Interface between bargaining, training and industrial policy

The agreements reached by labour and employers to establish a jointly-controlled sectoral training authority and to implement a human resource development framework in the auto assembly sector suggest how bilateral agreements can effectively complement a corporatist industrial policy-making process. The devolution of responsibility for the development of certain supply-side measures to those interest groups which are directly involved may speed up the decision-making process. It may also be preferable to solutions that rely on state intervention or the provision of subsidies from the state.

Despite this complementarity, no formal interface exists between the NBF and AMIETB on the one hand, and the MIDC on the other, to facilitate the co-ordination of the supply-side elements of industrial policy. This lack of co-ordination reflects the traditional focus of business and government, and hence the MIDC, on tariff issues and the relatively low priority that they place on supply-side measures. While the same union officials and shop stewards may be involved in all the forums, business is represented by different organisations in these two domains – the employer association and the industry association – and by different functional specialists.[8]

While AMIETB was jointly established by an NBF agreement, the training boards in the clothing and textile sectors were initially established by employers. Even though they are now under joint control, SACTWU had great difficulty in transforming their agenda. In trying to restructure the training boards, to reform who is trained, how training is provided, and what principles should inform and guide the training provided, SACTWU had to contend with the vested interests of the training board staff in addition to those of employers.

The case of training highlights the difficulty of developing and co-ordinating a comprehensive package of industrial policy measures that integrate the activities of different state departments, DTI and the Department of Labour, bilateral institutions such as training boards and bargaining forums, and the key interest groups themselves. Progress with a joint initiative involving the clothing and textile directorate at DTI and the Department of Labour to establish a pilot training project with SACTWU reflects the need for labour to keep up pressure on the state to deliver the sector-specific supply-side measures essential to effective industrial policy.

CONCLUSION

In the 1980s, COSATU utilised its powerful shop-floor organisation, militancy and alliances with civil society to challenge the state. The early 1990s posed a completely new set of challenges as the extended political transition and the inability of the apartheid state to act unilaterally created many opportunities for labour. Instead of wielding power against the state and employers 'from the outside', COSATU shifted strategy and pursued its ambitious agenda for social and economic transformation by demanding, and securing an institutionalised role in tripartite policy-making to exercise influence 'from within the power structure' (Patel, 1993).

Unions then began to engage in many new domains – economic policy, tariff reform and industrial restructuring, training and human resource development. One of the greatest challenges was the need to craft new institutional arrangements in which organised interests could formulate policy. In the turbulence of the transition, when the old order was not quite dead and the new era was yet to be born, the institutional foundations for participatory policy-making were not agreed to – the state had no clear policy direction, the social partners were neither 'social' nor 'partners' in their interaction, and all sides lacked the underlying commitment to compromise on which stable corporatist systems must necessarily be founded.

The state has clarified many policies in the democratic era since 1994, and tripartism has been institutionalised statutorily with the establishment of the National Economic Development and Labour Council (NEDLAC). However, corporatist policy-making has not yet taken firm root and an institutional framework for tripartite industrial policy-making has yet to be put in place. A prerequisite for effective corporatist policy-making is mutual recognition of the legitimacy of other interest groups to engage in the process. However, the state and business remain ambiguous towards the role of labour in industrial policy-making. While their practice suggests that business leaders may be coming to terms with the need to negotiate with labour on a wide range of policy issues, their rhetoric suggests that they have yet to convince the majority of their constituency about this need.

For its part, the state provides the opportunity for labour to participate, but actual participation depends on whether labour organises itself effectively. If labour wants an ongoing role it has to assert itself continually, particularly in the policy implementation phase. The failure to establish an industry authority, consultative forum or development council in any industry other than auto, suggests a lack of state commitment towards consensus-based industrial policy and the low priority that unions have placed on involvement in this type of institution. This also inhibits the development of a shared database and an ongoing opportunity to monitor the impact of the new industrial policy regime systematically. Furthermore, it forces all parties to address issues on an ad hoc basis which limits the possibility of adopting a long-term perspective on the challenges facing the industry.

With this unsettled constellation of interest groups and institutions, it is not surprising that COSATU and its affiliates remain ambivalent about engagement in corporatist policy-making structures 'as an agent of social integration'. Labour must now decide whether continuing dialogue over policy formulation and implementation is preferable to marginalisation from decision-making processes that will otherwise continue without them. Unions appear to face three choices.

The first involves a withdrawal from the industrial policy-making arena because of a lack of capacity and a reversion to what Chris Allen (1990: 270n) calls 'oppositional militance' – 'a traditional, defensive, anti-capitalist militance, unable (or unwilling) to formulate an alternative to the status quo'. While unions clearly helped to set the policy agenda, persistent failure to make use of opportunities to participate in industry-level structures is likely to lead to progressive marginalisation. Withdrawal or abstinence from the industrial policy arena will signify labour's retreat from 'radical reform' that has characterised COSATU and its affiliates (see Adler and Webster, 1995). It would also mark the abandonment of the movement's objective to restructure consiously the economy in the interests of labour. Withdrawal will leave unions without ready access to, and influence on, a ministry in which Minister Erwin (interview) believes labour has an important role to play in influencing thinking 'because in the DTI there's a lack of appreciation for IR [industrial relations] matters'. Most importantly, abstention exposes unions to the risk of the DTI becoming captured by, or exclusively responsive to, the interests of business.

The second option involves an incremental approach of 'muddling through', developing policy step-by-step in a process in which one chooses a policy to attain certain objectives and at the same time chooses one's objectives.

Muddling through appears consistent with the observed patterns of passive or ad hoc participation by NUMSA and SACTWU. This reflects the perceived constraints faced by these unions. Not only do senior union officials have enormous demands on their time but the 'brain drain' to the civil service and politics – particularly from the leadership cadre – has placed enormous pressure on their capacity to engage effectively in NEDLAC and industrial policy-making forums. As long as unions believe that they cannot afford the luxury of dedicating resources to set up tripartite institutions (Goldman, interview), they must continually rely on the mobilisation of power to ensure their participation with business and government in policy formulation.

Muddling through is also vulnerable to changes in the style or approach of the Minister of Trade and Industry. Despite his neo-liberal approach, it was Derek Keys who first involved COSATU affiliates in industrial policy-making because he valued ongoing dialogue between the 'golden triangle' of business, labour and the state to exchange opinions and ensure shared responsibility for the economy. Business and labour have found Alec Erwin to be much more accessible than Trevor Manuel. The aggressive trade liberalisation policies implemented during Manuel's term (1994-1996) highlight the need for labour to ensure equitable access through formal participatory structures.

Through continued participation in tripartite structures, such as the MIDC, unions can secure an ongoing role in monitoring policy implementation and its impact. Labour can thus (a) keep in touch with the complexities of policy implementation; (b) ensure that its perspective and interests are adequately represented as policies are adjusted on an ongoing basis; and (c) gain access to information about the industry that can be distributed broadly in the sector.

This brings us to the third option, and potentially the most attractive, which involves an offensive incursion by unions into policy-making arenas that remain dominated by employers and the state. With a policy of 'innovative militance' – 'the use of union mobilisation that points to a strategy and tactics that can be used for more potentially transformative processes' (Allen, 1990: 270n) – unions can begin by forcing the establishment of permanent industry-level corporatist structures. By accepting the logic of change to the competitive environment and by dedicating substantial resources to research capacity, unions can seek to transform the industrial policy agenda, rather than merely react to imposed change.

The important roles played by NUMSA and SACTWU in the MITG and the Swart Commission suggest that this option is not beyond the capabilities of the labour movement, particularly given the relatively limited policy capacities of the state and industry associations. However, proactive participation in policy-making requires the continuous involvement and support of the rank-and-file. In addition to developing research capacity, unions will have to dedicate sufficient resources – financial and human – to disseminate information, and to provide education and training to keep officials, shop-floor leadership and study groups up to date and informed about policy debates.

Given the opportunities that the second and third options offer to advance labour's agenda, it seems surprising that unions have demonstrated such limited commitment to ensuring the establishment and success of tripartite and corporatist structures. This can be understood by recognising that, although unions were instrumental in driving the establishment of corporatist structures, COSATU remains at heart a social movement. It is ambivalent about the risks associated with becoming involved in corporatist policy-making; ambivalent about the risks of being compromised by participation in processes over which it has little control and may have little expertise to offer; ambivalent because it is struggling organisationally to remain true to its roots and underlying philosophy of worker control.

Like the 'tempered radical', labour wants to pursue an ambitious agenda, but does not want to get so enmeshed in the game that it violates or abandons its own organisational principles and beliefs (Meyerson and

Scully, 1995). While Patel (1993) argued that labour wanted to exercise influence 'from within the power structure', it may be more accurate to describe COSATU's radical reform strategy – combining negotiation inside with mass mobilisation outside – as indicative of 'living on the edge'. This, Meyerson and Scully (1995) suggest, provides access to the insight of the insider with the associated opportunities to change the system, while retaining the detachment and independence of an outsider. While union leaders may be forced to adopt the language of insiders to gain legitimacy in the policy arena, they risk losing their outsider language and identity. By staying on the edge, they may be most effective if they can communicate with each audience in their own language.

Given the hesitancy of the state and business to commit fully to tripartite institutions and processes at industry level, and labour's social movement character, it can be stated that labour has not adopted 'innovative militance' but a type of 'muddling through' that we label *strategic ambivalence*. In making this choice, labour has retained strategic flexibility and has not been subjected to 'interest intermediation' whereby collective interests are shaped and union members are subject to a range of social controls in exchange for union influence (Schmitter, 1981). This is strongly associated with integration into corporatist institutions and fits uncomfortably with labour's social movement character and independent ethos. Instead, labour retains its private voice in the corridors of power and decision-making, but remains as sceptical as business and government about the benefits of, and its commitment to, tripartite institutions. Labour stands with one foot inside and one outside; it picks its battles and choose its allies, inside and outside. Whenever necessary, it utilises mass mobilisation as a resource to drive institutional reform, while avoiding the risk of becoming a governing party.

It remains to be seen, however, whether COSATU can continue down this ambivalent path as the forces of globalisation and the drive for international competitiveness could compel it to go one way or the other. Furthermore, strategic ambivalence still requires labour to develop the independent research capabilities to explore policy alternatives and the organisational capacity to take a proactive stance to transform industrial policy in pursuit of its strategic interests. If it fails to do this, the most likely scenario is a return to 'oppositional militance'.

6

A TREND TOWARDS CO-DETERMINATION?

Case studies of South African enterprises

───────── ✦ ─────────

Eddie Webster and Ian Macun [1]

The chapter by Webster and Macun pushes the analysis of engagement down to the shop-floor. Since few statutory workplace forums have been established, they investigate companies that are at the cutting edge of introducing new co-operative processes. Their results indicate that such processes were introduced at 'breakpoints' when business and political conditions changed dramatically, and usually in the aftermath of a major strike that resulted in stalemate. In reaching for co-operative solutions, management often seized the initiative from unions: policies to increase 'worker participation' accompanied management's pre-existing plans to devolve power to line managers, to redefine line workers' tasks (such as increasing job content) and to retrench. While some companies have formal agreements covering the powers and functions of workplace institutions, most do not, introducing a risk that forums will have a limited lifespan, and will be sacrificed to more urgent priorities when companies enter difficult times. Their powers are ambiguous and are not institutionalised in any way, and there are no binding mechanisms on the parties as few formal agreements establishing the structures are in place. Webster and Macun conclude that the new forums do not promote joint decision-making, but are based on a form of partial participation where power ultimately rests with management alone. Thus, many unionists feel that shop stewards are being drawn into management strategies, a development that may create cleavages between shop stewards and rank-and-file workers and among shop stewards themselves. Unless unions develop effective strategies for countering these problems, the new forums open up the risk of serious conflicts within unions.

INTRODUCTION

For the first time in South Africa's industrial relations history, European-style co-determination has been brought into our labour legislation through the introduction of workplace forums in Chapter 5 of the Labour Relations Act (LRA) of 1995. The rationale for introducing a system of workplace representation is stated clearly in the explanatory memorandum of the Legal Task Team set up in 1994 to review the labour relations system.

> South Africa's re-entry into international markets and the imperatives of a more open economy demand that we produce value-added products and improve productivity levels. To achieve this, major restructuring is required. In those countries, such as the United Kingdom, where the adversarial labour relations system was not supplemented by workplace-based institutions for worker representation and labour/manage-ment communication – 'a second channel' of industrial relations – this process fared badly. Workplace restructuring has been most successful in those countries where participatory structures exist: for example, Japan, Germany and Sweden. If we are to have any hope of successfully restructuring our industries and economy, then management and labour must find new ways of dealing with each other.
>
> (Ministry of Labour, 1995: 35)

The Legal Task Team argued that the old system of industrial relations, designed in the 1920s, was not suitable for this task. This Act provides for workplace forums to be established by the Commission for Conciliation, Mediation and Arbitration (CCMA) on application by a representative union. This is designed to reassure unions that forums will not be used, as works and liaison committees were used in the past, to supplant unions. Instead, they are designed to compel employers to co-operate by providing workers with statutory rights of consultation and joint decision-making in the workplace. Specifically (ibid.):

they are designed to perform functions that collective bargaining cannot easily achieve: the joint solution of problems and the resolution of conflicts over production. Their purpose is not to undermine collective bargaining but to supplement it.

In the light of the new form of participation offered by workplace forums, the aim of this chapter is to identify the changing forms of workplace representation that have been emerging in South Africa. The chapter does this by reviewing recent survey evidence of the extent to which new forms of workplace representation have been emerging. The bulk of the chapter is devoted to presenting the findings of a number of preliminary case studies of selected companies where new forms of workplace representation were introduced prior to the new legislation in 1995. In our interviews we explored how these forums[2] were established, how they function and what their main characteristics are.

CONCEPTUAL FRAMEWORK

Two clarificatory conceptual points are necessary before proceeding. First, the existing forms of worker participation in South Africa have not constituted a legally supported system, as in a number of European countries. In Germany, for instance, one finds a union movement that has had '(a) a consuming preoccupation with *mitbestimmung*; the equal sharing of control over economic decisions between capital and labour at all levels, including the enterprise' (Streeck, in Rogers and Streeck, 1995: 319). Underlying this system is a different theory of the firm. Firms are public institutions, not just the property of their shareholders, and are required to take account of the interests of employees. Thus, the law provides for representation at workplace level (through works councils) and representation at enterprise level through a worker representative on the management board and equal representation of employees and shareholders on supervisory boards in enterprises with more than 2 000 employees. This strong political and legislative support for co-determination has ensured that it has become the cornerstone of the industrial relations system.

Under this system, managers of large firms face capital and labour markets that are highly organised, enabling both capital and labour to participate directly in the everyday operation of the firm and requiring decisions to be negotiated continuously. Thus, decisions take longer, but are also easier to implement. Furthermore, by giving the workforce a legal right to co-decision-making, it becomes more difficult to dismiss workers. The result is that the average employment spell in a German firm (10,4 years) is almost as long as Japan (10,9) and much longer than the United States (6,7) (Streeck, 1995: Table 5). Importantly, by turning labour into more of a fixed cost, high investment in skills is encouraged. To understand co-determination, then, it is necessary to understand that a different kind of capitalism emerged in Germany after the Second World War, what Michel Albert calls the Rhine model, as distinct from the American model (Albert, 1992).

In South Africa the opposite is the case. Workplace representation evolved in an adversarial fashion, with black workers and their representatives maintaining a strategic distance from areas of responsibility and decision-making. An important reason for this orientation was the historically hostile stance of the state towards unions, particularly black trade unions. Thus, South African legislation until 1995 repeatedly tried to introduce mechanisms for employee representation that were intended to supplant trade unionism. The first instance of such legislation was the Native Labour (Settlement of Disputes) Act of 1953 which provided for the establishment of works committees to represent black workers. These structures were limited to an essentially advisory role *vis-à-vis* management, and were meant to supplant unions for black workers. This Act was amended in 1973 to provide for the establishment of liaison committees where works committees did not exist. The new version of the Act, called the Bantu Labour Relations Regulation Act, constituted the liaison committees as consultative bodies, composed of equal numbers of management and worker representatives and, as in terms of the 1953 Act, to be chaired by an appointee of the employer.

Both the works and liaison committees discredited workplace representation in the eyes of trade unionists, although works committees were used strategically by certain unions in certain areas because these bodies could be constituted through worker election of representatives. The Wiehahn Commission revisited these mechanisms and introduced major changes to the Industrial Conciliation Act, later renamed the Labour Relations Act (LRA), the most important feature of which was the recognition of black trade unions. But the Commission also recommended the retention of a weak form of workplace representation in the form of works councils which were to replace the works and liaison committees. In practice, very few works councils were established. Bendix (1991: 428) reported that 'the experience is that works councils are soon overtaken by trade unions and, even where this does not happen, conflict arises between the plant-level union and the works committee / council'.

In contrast to state- and management-initiated workplace representation and employee involvement, shop steward committees emerged in the 1980s as the central communication channel between workers and management on the shop floor. Shop steward committees perform a dual function: they engage in collective bargaining and participate in joint problem-solving where problems arise in production. Thus, unlike Germany where the works councils are institutionally separated from collective bargaining which takes place at industry level, in South Africa a form of union-linked workplace representation emerged that engages in both problem-solving and collective bargaining.

However, during the early 1990s, a number of companies began to separate these two functions institutionally by establishing joint forums with unions within which information-sharing, consultation and, in some cases, joint decision-making occurs. These innovative structures formed a point of departure for the Legal Task Team's recommendations that work-place forums be introduced. In exploring these structures, the Legal Task Team also drew on the legislation governing the German works council system.

The second conceptual point relates to the distinction between workplace representation and employee involvement. Employee involvement is a much broader phenomenon than that of workplace representation and incorporates a variety of schemes aimed at enhancing quality, productivity and motivation amongst the workforce. It is a form of direct involvement in the immediate work environment and constitutes an example of what Pateman (1971) calls 'pseudo participation', or techniques which persuade employees to accept decisions that have already been made by management.

Workplace representation, however, involves formal mechanisms of management-worker interaction that seek to 'institutionalise rights of collective worker participation, including rights to information and consultation on the organisation of production and, in some cases, formal co-determination in decision-making' (Rogers and Streeck, 1995: 98). In the South African context, co-determination can be taken to refer to joint decision-making, where decisions can be made only if they are agreed to by both parties. Co-determination as a form of decision-making can be usefully distinguished from consultation, which involves obligations, usually from management, to inform workers before taking a decision, to wait for a response or counter-proposal, and to take any response or counter-proposal into consideration when deciding the issue (ibid.: 149-150).

Workplace representation, then, takes place through structured interaction between management and workers. Such interaction, however, may vary in the form it takes, the frequency of interaction and the powers ascribed to representative institutions, and it may combine consultative and representative functions (ibid.:11).

FROM EMPLOYEE INVOLVEMENT TO WORKPLACE REPRESENTATION?

Instead of workplace representation, management in the 1980s began introducing forms of employee involvement, such as briefing groups, communication schemes, quality circles, 'green areas' and suggestion schemes. Almost all of these structures were limited to the immediate work environment and concentrated on increasing productivity (Maller, 1992). These findings have been confirmed in more recent research.

First, in both rounds of the South African Labour Flexibility Survey (SALFS) conducted in over 300 establishments in the manufacturing sector during 1995-1996, over 50% of establishments reported having joint committees, with the number increasing slightly from 51% to 56% between 1995 and 1996 (Macun, 1997: 5). The SALFS sample was weighted to include a larger number of smaller firms (employing between 1 and 50 persons) and it is interesting to note that roughly 46% of firms which reported having joint committees were in this small-size grouping. Postal surveys conducted in 1992 and 1995 also found a significant number of companies embarking on employee involvement initiatives (Veldsman and Harilall, 1996). Interestingly, Veldsman and Harilall found that in 1995 most companies (91%) had initiated employee involvement to prepare for future environmental changes and to make it easier to introduce changes in the functioning of their organisations. This contrasted with their 1992 finding where most organisations had cited improvement in quality, productivity and worker motivation as the main reasons for initiating employee involvement (ibid.: 11). A worker representative survey, carried out as part of the SALFS, found a much smaller proportion of companies (17%) with mechanisms for management-employee discussions (apart from committees that dealt with negotiations or single topics, such as health and safety) (Macun, Rosenthal and Standing, 1997). *SAJLR 21(1)* Given the likelihood of divergent views on the nature of employee involvement between workers and senior managers, this is hardly surprising. This conflicting finding merely serves to emphasise the ambiguity surrounding expectations and the role of such initiatives.

Second, the most common function of the joint committees identified in the SALFS survey was consultation. Some were also concerned with negotiation, information-sharing and, in some cases, joint decision-making, but these were all a smaller proportion than those concerned with consultation. The survey by Veldsman and Harilall also found that a relatively small proportion of employees were actually involved in these initiatives which were predominantly production-oriented, for example, feedback mechanisms, quality circles and quality of work life committees (ibid.: 69).

Third, despite an increase in these structures, the information flow between management and workers remains limited. Respondents to the SALFS were asked whether they provide information to employees or their representatives concerning work accidents, labour productivity, labour costs, and sales and financial information on a regular basis. Apart from information pertaining to work accidents (which is subject to the Occupational Health and Safety Act), a relatively small proportion of firms provided information on key economic issues (see Table 6.1). This feature was confirmed both by the Veldsman and Harilall survey and the worker representative survey.

Finally, although it is difficult to gauge the extent of union involvement in these initiatives from the survey findings, it is clear that employee involvement is occurring mainly in unionised firms. Roughly 60% of the 33 companies surveyed by Veldsman and Harilall were unionised, a figure very similar to the SALFS (58,7%). It is possible to interpret this finding to suggest that management use employee involvement to bypass and, possibly, to undermine trade unions. Given the extensive support for COSATU unions in particular, and their majority status in most workplaces, the undermining of unions is unlikely. It is more likely that trade unions treat such initiatives with circumspection, avoid them or find it necessary to engage with them in order to improve their participation rights in companies.

TABLE 6.1:   Per cent of management providing information on selected issues to employees on a regular basis, 1996

Category of information	All employees	Representatives	No information
Work accidents	47	28	25
Labour productivity	39	28	33
Labour costs	18	29	53
Sales	26	24	50
Financial information	17	19	66

CASE STUDIES OF WORKER REPRESENTATION

Sample and method

The companies selected for the study were chosen according to two factors: companies with whom the Sociology of Work Unit (SWOP) had past research contact and companies where the existence of institutions for worker participation was known. A more detailed summary of the sample is presented in Appendix 6.1. Our sample consisted of 11 large national companies: six in the manufacturing sector, two in mining, two parastatals (one electricity, one transport) and one in the retail sector. Interviews were conducted with a representative from the industrial relations or human resources department in each of the companies. The first round of interviews was conducted between February and March 1995, with a second round of interviews being carried out between September and October 1996.[3] Where possible, union officials and shop stewards were also interviewed. A semi-structured questionnaire was used and the interviews were transcribed. All the companies in the sample were highly unionised, with union membership exceeding 50% of the workforce and the majority of companies having a unionisation rate of 80% (see Appendix 6.2 for industrial relations features of the sample).

As Appendix 6.1 indicates, nearly all of the companies are in highly competitive markets including, in many cases, competitive international markets. These are also price-sensitive markets. A number of the companies are large enough to derive economies of scale and competitive advantage given their position as national companies. All the companies in the sample have undergone or are undergoing some form of restructuring, ranging from changes in senior management to international expansion, workplace restructuring and changing corporate culture.

Findings

The findings from our case studies can be divided into four different themes. Why are forums introduced? What form do they take? What powers do they have? How do they deal with conflict? After addressing these themes, we discuss some general observations before drawing conclusions.

Why are forums established?

A variety of factors influence the establishment of new forums. The most useful way of understanding these influences is through the concept of 'breakpoints'. 'Breakpoints', according to Paul Strebel (cited in Stace and Dunphy, 1994: 20), are sudden radical changes in business conditions, changing technologies, changing community and customer attitudes and shifting political frontiers. They can be handled, he says, by anticipating the breakpoints, by exploiting the breakpoints or by creating the breakpoints.

All the companies interviewed began to anticipate 'breakpoints' from the mid-1980s onwards when they began introducing new participatory styles of management. However, two of these – Volkswagen (VWSA) and PG Bison – stand out as organisations which created the breakpoints by developing 'new rules of the game'. By responding creatively to 'breakpoints', these companies changed the playing field for others. 'Breakpoints' force management to make strategic choices. They do not retain a hard line towards employees but seek a solution together, encouraged by the threat of chaos in a continued stalemate. Table 6.2 below lists strikes as the most dramatic example of breakpoints.

TABLE 6.2: Strikes as breakpoints

Company	Date	Duration	Demands
Pick 'n Pay	July 1994	27 days	R229 over 12 mths
Eskom	June 1994	1 day	End to unilateral change
Nampak	Aug 1990	9 weeks	Company bargaining
Transnet	Nov 1989	8 weeks	Recognition agreement
VWSA	Aug 1994	6 weeks	Sector bargaining (NBF)
Mercedes Benz	Aug 1994	6 weeks	Sector bargaining (NBF)

Neil Cummings, Nampak Human Resources Director (Cummings, 1995: interview) reflected on a nine-week strike during 1990: 'You reach a stalemate, and then sit down afterwards, both formally and informally, in various mediating sessions and so on. The blunt reality is: no one won that strike. There were no major achievements by either side'.

It is quite often out of prolonged conflict, for example the VWSA strike in 1994, that the parties come to agree on the need to accept joint responsibility for the future of the company. The Nampak Human Resources Director (ibid.) expressed this point in these words: 'The strike cleared the air and made us realise that we cannot carry on like this and destroy each other. I think if we had not had that strike it probably would have been more difficult for us to embark on our current changes'.

The opening up of the South African economy in 1990 was to provide another 'breakpoint'. In the words of Brian Smith, the Human Resources Director of VWSA (Smith, 1995: interview):

> Suddenly when the whole situation changed, everyone started saying we have got this plant down in South Africa, they have been bumbling along on their own, how do we integrate them into the Group? ... We had a new set of top management who became much more productivity oriented, and would clearly say there is no such thing any more as a national car market, there is just one global car market. It happens to have a surplus production capacity of ten million cars. So suddenly we had this massive focus on our productivity, our integration in the world; we had guys

coming and going and saying, look, you guys are over structured, you are not productive. A German plant producing the same number of cars as you has 2 000 people, you have got 7 000. What the hell are you doing?

The result was a new agreement between VWSA and NUMSA 'forged in the context of a recognition by the parties of the need to ensure the long-term viability of VWSA in domestic and foreign markets' (ibid.). The agreement noted the global over-capacity of motor vehicles of ten million units, and the ongoing eight-year tariff reduction programme for the South African motor vehicle industry, as well as the increased competition from both domestic and foreign manufacturers that this will engender, and committed the parties to 'forge new standards which match those of our world-class competitors' (ibid.). As management explained, a forum was also necessary because 'we had a vacuum – we had the National Bargaining Forum, but no regular in-plant negotiations. No place where we could trade off issues and we wanted a formal in-house committee to do this' (Smith, 1996: interview).

The initiation of workplace representation, at least by companies engaging in strategic re-orientation, dovetails with devolution of managerial authority to lower-level management. The industrial relations manager no longer has sole responsibility for stable and peaceful labour relations. Furthermore, industrial relations is no longer confined to collective bargaining but is integrated into human resources management, corporate strategy and even production issues.

As Volkswagen's Smith (1996: interview) observed:

I remember the old days when I first started in the industry – employee relations or industrial relations was the preserve of a couple of personnel types. I started at Ford and Fred Ferreira sort of ran the thing, and no one else saw the union, but increasingly line management, training specialists, compensation specialists, all sorts are having to mesh and get more involved. There was a recognition that it was important that people management was devolving to toe the line because the nature of that relationship was changing with the move towards more participatory forms of engagement. It became important that first line managers had good people management skills and assumed responsibility for managing people in their areas. So, over the last year, it's been a major focus, with the devolution of human resources management to line, training intervention, etc.

Nampak's Cummings (interview) suggested a similar shift to line managers:

> We used to have thousands of lawyers here... and then we decided that legal industrial relations was a historical thing and the lawyers left. Since then we have never found a need for them. We had a retainer for a legal firm for about eight months and we have abandoned that as well. So symbolically that shift is important. When we decided three and a half years ago that Nampak was no longer going to be a company of the past, one of the things was to abandon legal industrial relations people... The industrial relations functions generally moved into the camp of the managers who manage plants, the so-called line managers.

The need to integrate traditional collective bargaining issues into corporate strategy has now become central:

> What we are finding is more and more, the whole issue of production and human resources is more integrated than it used to be. The newly created employee relations department is tasked with picking up issues with the union, but within human resources, training, the benefit side, the compensation side and then a range of issues on the line side are now involved in industrial and employee relations.
>
> (Smith, 1996: interview)

VWSA's Smith (1996: interview) developed this point further:

> Industrial relations in the old days involved interacting with the union about disciplinary issues, conditions of service, pay, overtime – it was limited to that sort of thing. We were also involved in a bit of training of artisans and apprentices.

That was the extent of our work. But today it's a whole host of issues. Everything now – outsourcing, strategic sourcing, where we buy our parts, how we structure production, productivity, a host of training issues – multi-skilling, adult basic education – so it's really impossible for one or two industrial relations people to handle those things. Whereas in the old days, one person could handle a little bit of training – you know, the old traditional personnel manager, that's really gone now.

In the words of Richard de Villiers the Human Resources Director of Randgold (23 January 1995: interview):

Instead of being second level service departments aimed at record and housing maintenance, labour allocation, hostel management and employee welfare, the human resources departments should be catalysts for cultural change; redesign the labour process; develop strategies for productivity improvements; and manage the consequences of the new South Africa.

It was in the context of these fundamental shifts in the industrial relations functions of firms that the 'new forums' were initiated by management in the late 1980s and early 1990s. Management, in all cases, seized the initiative from the unions and the unions have been perceived as becoming largely reactive in orientation. As Jim Smith, the Human Resources Director of PG Bison remarked (1995: interview) 'Unions have tended to be reactive and lacking in initiative. They lack the capacity to frame creative and imaginative proposals.'

VWSA's Smith (1996: interview) expanded on this point:

We are moving into territory that's difficult for management to understand. Restructuring, outsourcing – the shop stewards are unsure of themselves a lot of the time, for example, Board of Tariffs and Trade recommendations on the future of the motor industry. Quite frankly, these guys do not know what the hell we are talking about. And a lot of them feel very inadequate and it was comfortable in the past.

> They were masters in the art of resistance politics, taking management to the cleaners, whipping up emotions. Now that whole ball game has changed, I think they are very unsure. Now they are having to engage management where we'll present a full financial disclosure. Our finance director and our controller, who are very bright CAs, will come down and meet them with figures. And we will talk about duty-free allowances, tariffs, the fiscus – what all this means for the motor industry – and by their own admission they just say, 'Guys, look we don't know'. We've discussed our submissions with the Board of Trade: they don't understand what we are talking about – whether what we say is right or wrong, they're just going to have to trust us.

As the case studies illustrate, forums arise from 'breakpoints' – understood as radical changes in the external environment of firms, such as the dropping of tariff barriers in the motor industry – that radically change business conditions. These changes, in turn, intensify conflicts in the workplace, as illustrated in Table 6.2. Interestingly, in all the case studies, management responded creatively by introducing new forms of management-union interaction. These initiatives changed the rules of the game. In order to do so, it is not surprising that a central feature of the new forums is a strong emphasis on consensual interaction. Although most have arrangements for third-party intervention (mediation or arbitration), by and large they attempt to avoid conflict by being consensus-driven. This emphasis prevails, even if it means side-stepping or shelving some issues and prioritising others. It is well captured by a clause in the constitution of one of these forums – Samancor Participative Structures – which states:

> Consensus will be sought by way of exhaustive discussion with the parties to the Working Groups, the National Forum and the Strategic Forum. This can include third-party facilitation and referral to the next higher level. Should this process fail, the parties will refer the matter to mediation under the auspices of the Independent Mediation Services of South Africa (IMSSA).

Given the role that overt conflict has played in all the companies studied, the emphasis on consensus is understandable. Moreover, given the high rate of unionisation in these companies and the constant presence of the union as an agent of bargaining, the parties have an incentive to resolve issues within the forums in a consensual manner.

What form do they take?

The 'forums' that emerged in the late eighties and early nineties are different from shop steward committees. Shop steward committees perform a dual function: they engage in collective bargaining and participate in joint problem-solving where problems arise in production. The forums institutionally separate these two functions and focus on problem-solving in production and wider policy issues, particularly in the area of labour relations. Importantly, these forums are linked directly to union structures. They extend, rather than transcend, collective bargaining.

The forums are usually comprised of senior shop stewards drawn from the shop steward committees. Only in one of the plants did we find a non-union member in the forum. Where multi-unionism exists, representation is proportional to union membership. The forums are predominantly based on union members who are employees in the enterprise, with the occasional involvement of 'external' union officials. In one case, union organisers ratify all agreements.

Many of the companies have multiple structures operating at different levels. At the central level, there is a forum that focuses on strategic and policy issues, for example, the National Strategic Meeting of Pick 'n Pay; the National Forum at South African Breweries; the National and Strategic Forum at Samancor; the Central Forum at Nampak; and the Joint Union Management Executive Committee (JUMEC) at Volkswagen. Sometimes ad hoc working groups are established to investigate specific issues or a range of issues, for example, housing loans, affirmative action, training, discrimination, employment equity, job security and the RDP. These companies also have forums that focus on the plant or local level. In addition they often have regional or divisional forums, for example, the regional forums in South African Breweries and Pick 'n Pay.

Only two companies in our sample have worker representatives on their boards of management (Samancor and Eskom). Board representation, however, was proposed by a third company but turned down by the majority union. The relationship between board representation and trade unions is ambiguous at present. In the case of Eskom, a union leader sits on the board in his or her official capacity, whereas in Samancor the position of the worker representative is contested. The union representative at Samancor is a member of the board in his or her 'individual capacity'. However, the representative feels that he is there as a representative of labour: 'I will always emphasise that I am from labour and the views I am expressing are from a particular stakeholder' (quoted in Macun and Buhlungu, 1996: 28).

What powers do these forums have?

One way of measuring the degree of power vested in the 'new forums' is whether they have statutory rights or written agreements. None of the companies sampled had triggered a workplace forum in terms of Chapter 5 of the LRA, but some had formal agreements covering the powers and functions of the forums. For example, in the case of VWSA, the forum (called the Negotiating Committee) had a written agreement between VWSA, NUMSA and the SA Iron, Steel and Allied Industries Union. This agreement prescribes the following role for the Negotiating Committee, namely to:

* discuss, negotiate and agree on operational issues and other matters of plant-wide relevance
* resolve disputes referred by Business Unit Committees
* explore means of promoting co-operation and facilitating a two-way communication process, for example, through the sharing of ideas and success stories through presentations.

However, the constitution governing Samancor's Strategic Forum explicitly defines it as a consultative and information-sharing forum. While the documents give a clear role to the forums, they do not clearly define the powers and responsibilities of these bodies. Not all the companies have formal agreements governing the forums, and some use their recognition agreements with the majority union as a reference point. The absence of strong and binding agreements introduces the risk of the forums having a limited lifespan and being sacrificed to what are perceived as more urgent priorities when companies enter difficult economic times.

Most of the forums are empowered to deal with a range of corporate and industrial relations issues, excluding wages. In many of the cases investigated, bargaining is centralised either at the national company level or in sectoral arrangements, such as the National Bargaining Forum (NBF) established for the motor industry. Bargaining over wages and conditions of employment, therefore, is formally removed from plant-level interaction in forums. Examples of the kind of issues dealt with in the forums include productivity and flexibility in working arrangements (such as outsourcing), training programmes, affirmative action, racism, RDP projects, world-class manufacturing, company financial performance, strategic direction and benefits such as long-service awards.

The flow of information within these forums is relatively high and has tended to increase over time as the parties have developed their working relationships. In some companies, there is still hesitation by management when it comes to full disclosure of financial information. This is not entirely surprising since, outside the context of the LRA, there is no legal obligation to do so, nor are there any arrangements or agreements concerning confidentiality of information within these forums. In the absence of clear guidelines concerning confidentiality, the flow of information is likely to remain uneven and, possibly, limited. Unions can ask for information and, in many cases, management make regular presentations to the union or forum on the financial position of the company, excluding sensitive information on business negotiations and plans.

A central question raised by these forums is whether they operate on the basis of joint decision-making. Although some of the companies do have joint-decision making on certain issues, in general this is not the case. The picture that emerges is one of consultative representation, where workers have gained a substantial degree of influence over a broader range of issues. These concern company policy and operations that traditionally have been the domain of both parties, such as job security, affirmative action and job grading. In some cases, joint decision-making has been extended to issues such as outsourcing and productivity.

The underlying purpose of the forums can best be summed up in the words of Richard Davies, the Human Resources Manager, SA Breweries (19 January 1995: interview): ' … to deal with any issues that are obviously not of a collective bargaining nature, in a collaborative manner to maximise the impact on the organisation of what we want to do.'

From this statement, it could be argued that the emerging forums have significant powers, but these are ambiguous because they are not institutionalised in any formal way and there are no binding mechanisms on the parties. What binds them is an interest, on the part of workers, in exercising greater influence and, on the part of management, in creating greater stability, predictability and co-operation. An implicit rationale for the forums is to change the internal politics of the workplace to ensure that management has greater legitimacy. The forums achieve this by extending the influence of workers, but stop short of real co-determination. It is important to bear in mind that, in all the companies, there are powerful unions which can exercise leverage on management through the collective bargaining process. It is this leverage that remains central in the workplace, notwithstanding the formation of new forums.

By and large, the companies studied typify what Pateman (1971) has characterised as partial participation, that is, situations in which two or more parties influence each other in making decisions but, in the final instance, power rests with one party only. Within this scenario, it is not surprising to find a strong emphasis on co-operation and consensus. While forums open up the potential for the extension of union influence, labour's power remains limited within them.

CHARACTERISTICS AND LIMITATIONS

There are a number of general points concerning the functioning of the forums which give them a particular character and serve to distinguish them from the international experience of workplace representation. First, companies are spending considerable amounts of time and money in running and servicing forums. As pointed out above, most of the companies are large and many have a number of establishments. Given the close link between the forums and trade unions, it is often the members of national negotiating committees who also attend forum meetings with senior management. For example, Pick 'n Pay and Nampak have many different workplaces throughout the country and have to fly delegates to these regular meetings. Estimates of financial expenditure on works councils in countries such as Germany suggest that this amounts to approximately 1% of the annual wage bill.[4] It is possible that the costs of the forums in the sample companies exceed this, but these should be viewed as 'start-up' costs which may decrease over time. Costs are also clearly related to the question of who participates. More decentralised forms of representation would clearly incur lower costs.

A second characteristic of the forums that have been established during the 1980s and 1990s is their vulnerability. In some cases, such as PG Bison, there is a dependence on individuals, for example, the charismatic individual manager who initiates a forum and later leaves the company. Stace and Dunphy (1994) call this 'charismatic transformation'. The problem that arose in PG Bison was that of maintaining commitment when the charismatic leader left to take up a position in government. The problem seemed to have been resolved by an undertaking by the new chief executive to commit himself to the same transformation process. But the vulnerability of the process was underlined when he abandoned the structure, prompted by a downturn in the company's economic performance. In the absence of statutory support or formal agreements, these experiments in participation will always be subject to cycles of changing support by management and labour.

A third characteristic of forums arises from their close link to union structures. Because of this close link, and the structure of trade union organisation in South Africa, white-collar workers and middle management are excluded from the forums. The only exception in our sample was Randgold, where the middle strata were unionised through the Mine Surface Officials Association (MSOA), the Underground Officials Association (UOA) and the Surface and Technical Officials Association (STOA).[5] In all the other cases, these middle strata are neither unionised, nor are they included in the forums. This places management in a dilemma: do they establish a separate forum for this excluded stratum; do they encourage this stratum to unionise; or do they wait for the representative union to trigger a workplace forum? Mercedes Benz have resolved this dilemma by establishing a separate forum for the middle strata 'to hear the concerns of staff' (Knoesen, 2 October 1996: interview). The incentive for all parties to establish a genuinely representative forum is that all parties in the workplace now face the common challenge of international competition and the need, therefore, to develop more co-operative relationships.

In our sample it is clear that, in most cases, a dual structure of bargaining emerged: wage bargaining at the sectoral or central level and bargaining over production at the plant level. Such a structure makes it easier to separate wage bargaining from negotiation over in-plant, production-related issues. Employers, however, expressed concern over the rigidity of centralised bargaining. Ironically, the dual structure of bargaining holds out the real prospect of articulation, that is, increased labour-management interaction at several levels.[6] This approach, which the then Labour Minister Tito Mboweni called 'regulated flexibility', allows plants to modify agreements through a decentralised bargaining structure.

Two important limitations emerged from the case studies. The first relates to the limited capacity of forum members to engage in joint problem-solving. This can best be illustrated through Randgold's Harmony Mine Forum in Virginia. A core item on every agenda is the full disclosure of the company's performance. Management feel that 'slowly a lot more understanding is developing between union and managements on the financial constraints that the mine is under' (Personnel Manager, Harmony Mine, 11 May 1995: interview).

Union representatives saw the forum rather differently. While welcoming the creation of a forum, union representatives complained that decisions made at the forum were never implemented. 'It is nothing more than a talk shop,' one representative said. 'It has got no teeth. Management controls the agenda and uses the forum to lecture to us'. Another complained that meetings do not take place regularly. 'They only call meetings when they want to meet with us. When management has a problem, then they call a meeting'. Another remarked that '99% of the time management has already made the decision. They do not ask us, they tell us. We are a rubber stamp'.

One striking feature of this forum is that the union representatives do not feel they have control over its direction. They feel that the agenda is drawn up by management, who call the meetings and, most importantly, the union representatives do not meet separately as a group. In practice, it is being run by management and workers are treating the forum as if it were a 'liaison committee'.

There are, of course, crucial differences between the Harmony Forum and a liaison committee. First, the forum is non-racial. Second, there is a strong trade union for black workers, the National Union of Mineworkers (NUM). In fact, it was interesting to observe that NUM was the only union in the forum which knew anything about the LRA of 1995 and its provision for workplace forums. This was because the NUM Collective Bargaining Unit had held a seminar on workplace forums shortly before the meeting and the NUM representative had attended this seminar.

This underlines the crucial importance of increasing union members' capacity to engage in these forums, a responsibility that rests with national union structures and which will require substantial change in the operation of national unions. This is well illustrated by Sipho Kubheka, veteran unionist and ex- General Secretary of the Paper, Printing, Wood and Allied Workers' Union (PPWAWU), who said:

> Most of the [union] officials came from a political back-ground, not from an industrial background per se. They were politicians. They were political activists who happened to be much more articulate in making this or that statement in whatever meetings. We were not asking people [when interviewing them for organisers' jobs]: 'what is your experience about the factory situation?' 'Can you tell us about the process of production in the printing industry?' … We were focusing on political issues, apartheid in the work situation.
>
> (Kubheka, 1994: interview)

This limitation places workers at a disadvantage. It is exacerbated by the high turnover of union officials and the inadequate training of workplace representatives. By contrast trade unions in many European countries play a pivotal role in supporting and resourcing works councils and, as a result, members of councils are well qualified to engage with management. The length of service of many works councillors also provides necessary experience in the functioning of the councils.

A second and related limitation concerns the reluctance of employees and their representatives to identify with the goals of the enterprise. This is deeply rooted in the low trust dynamic that arises from the apartheid workplace regime (Von Holdt, 2000), and has resulted in suspicion of any involvement in decision-making. For example, shop stewards at Mercedes Benz SA expressed deep distrust of their works councils' counterparts from Mercedes Benz in Stuttgart when they visited the South African plant. They commented that (Mercedes Benz Shop Stewards Committee, 1997: interview):

> The gap between shop stewards and the people they represent is very large. They [works councillors] dress in suits

> and ties. They look like managers. They are actually involved
> in running the company. They help make the rules. Here,
> our part-time shop stewards still work on the lines alongside
> membership.

Clearly, these shop stewards saw the role that works councillors play in Germany as conflicting with their role as worker representatives. The act of joint decision-making for the shop stewards meant that the works councils had been co-opted by management, not that workers had won greater influence over decision-making. The result of this suspicion is that worker representatives find themselves in difficult situations when companies engage in cost-cutting exercises.

This was clearest in VWSA and Mercedes Benz where the shop steward leadership was overturned due to a belief on the part of the rank and file that the shop stewards were being co-opted into management's strategy (Rosenthal, 1996). Furthermore, the practice of tight mandate and accountability leads shop stewards either to evade tough issues or agree to difficult decisions, but then refuse to accept responsibility for them when faced by their members. A manager (Smith, 1995: interview) captured this tension when he described how shop stewards did not want minutes of sensitive discussions made public:

> They prefer to discuss these things in private because they
> know that if it gets out – that we are discussing the
> outsourcing of the seat area – then they say: 'For goodness
> sake, let's not tell the workers that we are discussing this
> highly contentious topic.' And we say, 'Shouldn't we go out
> and tell them upfront?' 'Woh…,' they say.

The final limitation concerns the unresolved nature of worker representation at board level. As highlighted above, two companies in our sample have worker representatives on their boards. Such representation, however, has developed in an ad hoc way and seems to rely on particular individuals rather than clear policy in law and on the part of trade unions and business. COSATU's September Commission on the Future of Trade Unions has begun to address this. The Commission's report (COSATU, 1997: 124) suggests that:

It should be noted that it would be disastrous for a union to participate on the board of a company if it does not have a clear agenda, and a programme of support for its representatives. The union should define its agenda and programme in terms of clearly defined goals. If the unions decide to go this route, they should seek to have at least two places on the board of directors reserved for worker representatives to ensure some mutual support. A single labour director could become isolated. The representatives may be union officials or workers from the company concerned. The important thing is to maintain strong channels of communication between the labour directors and the shop-steward structures in the workplace, to ensure co-ordination between collective bargaining and board discussions and other participative forums. Labour directors should not forget that they represent workers and must defend their interests. They should always caucus with shop-stewards prior to board meetings, and report back after board meetings.

This proposal has met with opposition from some influential affiliates who think it will be in direct conflict with what unions are supposed to represent. NUMSA, for example, argues that co-determination with the private sector will make workers' interests and agendas similar to that of employers. NUMSA says this will make unions co-participants in sensitive decisions such as retrenchments (*Mail & Guardian*, 15-21 August 1997).

CONCLUSION

In the process of negotiating workplace change, a number of companies have begun to experiment with new institutional forms to deal with the challenge of restructuring. Some have done so in more advanced ways than others. A key feature of these forums is their attempt institutionally to separate collective bargaining from joint problem-solving over production. However, forum members find it extremely difficult to take the initiative as they do not have the resources required to intervene in the restructuring process. They find it difficult to deal with new issues that go beyond collective bargaining, such as team work and productivity, all of which could lead to job losses. In fact, both management and shop stewards are well schooled in adversarial bargaining and find it difficult to adjust to co-determination. Furthermore, these forums are not based on legal rights but on the sheer power (or lack of power) of union representatives in the workplace.

In the past, South African labour law did not provide for adequate workplace representation. Instead, a tradition was built up which rested on strong independent shopfloor structures based around the recognition agreement and the shop steward committee. However, in the process of experimenting with these new institutional forms, the embryo of what the law now calls workplace forums emerged. In so doing, these companies have begun to redefine the playing field for others. This emerges most clearly in the influence these experiments have had on the LRA of 1995. However, as our research suggests, both trade unions and management remain cautious about existing forums and the provision in the Act for workplace forums.

At the core of the unions' caution lies the concern that new forms of workplace representation will undermine established union structures. Given the adversarial nature of workplace industrial relations, suspicion of any form of involvement and taking responsibility for decisions persists among employees and unionists. Managements' uncertainty, especially with regard to the statutory forums, arises from their fear that the proposed forums will substantially curtail their prerogative to make unilateral decisions by giving workers statutory rights to consultation and co-decision-making. These reservations have been bolstered by recent employer arguments that the German model of co-determination is exhausted and that its labour market is too rigid and inflexible (*Mail & Guardian*, 18-24 October 1996).

Comparative research, however, has concluded that institutions such as workplace forums offer a secure basis on which to construct an effective partnership with employees at plant level. Moreover, they hold out the prospect for enhancing efficiency by improving the operation of firms. Current research on the effect of co-determination on European managers supports this argument. Rogers and Streeck (op.cit.) argue that representative consultation contributes to economic performance by improving the flow of information; facilitating the implementation of decisions; reducing absenteeism; helping to handle worker grievances; and assisting firms to move towards a more flexible and decentralised organisation of work. Indeed, from our own research, it emerged that from being the Cinderella of German industrial relations in the early post-war period, co-determination has moved to its current status as the cornerstone of the system (Webster and Macun, *Business Day*, 19 February 1997).

Comparative research also suggests that workplace forums could strengthen unions (Streeck, 1984). First, workplace forums exercise their rights as unitary bodies on behalf of the workforce as a whole. Thus, forums can become the 'extended arm' of unions and deepen their organisational penetration of the workforce in occupational groupings that are less susceptible to unionisation. Given the current low level of unionisation of middle-strata employees by the majority of unions in South Africa, forums could arguably offer the same opportunity to unions as they have in other countries. Second, unions can strengthen themselves by gaining access to information from their forum members. The forums also offer unions the opportunity to increase their capacity through training, paid time off, full-time representatives and administrative facilities.

Of course, there is no guarantee that forums will not lead to a decline of unions in plants. A central criticism of works councils in Europe is their tendency to become management-oriented, concerned too much with promoting management's definition of the enterprise. Indeed, those located within the British labour tradition, such as our own labour movement, may argue that it is collective bargaining, and not co-determination, that provides the key to industrial democracy (Clegg, 1951). One way of meeting union concerns that forums could undermine union structures in the workplace would be to link forum members directly to the union. This is provided for in the Act.

Through the introduction of workplace forums in the LRA of 1995, South Africa has made a tentative step towards co-determination. However, the Act falls short in not making adequate provision for training of members of workplace forums.

An important challenge facing trade unions in South African plants is how they interact with workplace forums, once triggered. Ideally, a close and constructive relationship should be crafted between the union and the forum. The Act also makes no mention of board level representation. The significance of this lies not only in increasing the influence of employees but, more importantly, in widening management's notion of their responsibility beyond shareholders to all stakeholders (Albert, 1992).

This chapter has surveyed evolving forms of workplace representation in South Africa. Though these present possibilities for moving beyond traditional adversarial relations, they carry with them new problems for management and workers, but especially for trade unions. Whether the new forms of representation, as well as the workplace forum provisions of the new LRA, have the potential to take South Africa in the direction of co-determination remains to be seen.

APPENDIX 6.1

Sample classification

Company	Sector	Markets	Degree of competition
AECI	Manufacturing	Domestic International	Very high
Eskom	Electricity	Domestic Regional	Low
Mercedes	Manufacturing	Domestic International	High
Nampak	Manufacturing	Domestic International	Growing
PG Bison	Manufacturing	Domestic International	High
Pick 'n Pay	Retail	Domestic	Low
Randgold	Mining	International	High
Transnet	Transport	Domestic	Low (except road transport – High)
SAB	Manufacturing	Domestic International	Low
Samancor	Mining	Domestic International	High
VW	Manufacturing	Domestic International	High

APPENDIX 6.2

Industrial relations characteristics of sample

Company	Trade union Density	No of trade unions	Affiliation of majority union
AECI	94%	SACWU, NETU, MWU, EWU, CWIU Staff Association	NACTU
Eskom	67%	NUM, NUMSA, MWU, SAAWU, Eskom Employees Association	COSATU
Mercedes	80%	NUMSA	COSATU
Nampak	65%	NUMSA, PPWAWU MWU	COSATU
PG Bison	90% of bargaining unit	PPWAWU, NUMSA UWUSA, SAAWU in Piet Retief, other smaller unions	COSATU
Pick 'n Pay	42% of bargaining unit (66% if casuals are excluded)	SACCAWA	COSATU
Randgold	87%	NUM, Amalgamated Technical and Electrical Association of SA	COSATU
Transnet	60%	SARHWU, SALSTAFF BLATU	COSATU
SAB	FAWU 57% total, and 80% weekly paid; Food and Beverage minimal	FAWU, Food and Beverage Workers' Union	COSATU
Samancor	85%	NUM, NUMSA NETU, Yster en Staal	COSATU
VW	80%	NUMSA Yster en Staal	COSATU

7

DEMOCRATISING THE PUBLIC SERVICE

Co-determination, workplace democratisation and transformation

———— ✦ ————

Imraan Patel

Patel's chapter on engagement in the public service is the first systematic assessment of this issue. He argues that co-determination in the public service is both under- and over-developed relative to the rest of the economy. Although the public service is not included in the LRA's provisions for workplace forums, institutions of engagement are potentially extremely widespread. Interesting institutional innovations – in the form of transformation committees – have, in certain instances, given unions wide-ranging effective co-determination powers at the enterprise level. These include, curiously, participation in governing committees and enterprise boards, rights which are available in Germany but which were not included in Chapter 5 of the LRA of 1995. Furthermore, centralised bargaining in the Public Service Co-ordinating Bargaining Council occurs over issues that extend well beyond wage-setting: qualitative 'non-distributive issues' such as work organisation, as well as the restructuring of the public service itself. It is unclear whether such practices will continue, particularly given fiscal austerity and the trend towards commercialising the public service. Nonetheless, the public service has produced a potentially robust version of engagement that could serve as a model for unions to pursue elsewhere in the economy.

In order to forge ahead with the processes of reconciliation, reconstruction and development, the South African public service will have a major role to play as the executive arm of government. To fulfil this role effectively, the service will need to be transformed into a coherent, representative, competent and *democratic* [emphasis added] instrument for implementing government policies and meeting the needs of all South Africans.

(Dept. of Public Service and Administration, 1995: ll)

INTRODUCTION

In the run-up to the 1994 elections in South Africa, the tripartite alliance (the African National Congress (ANC), the Congress of South African Trade Unions (COSATU) and the South African Communist Party (SACP)) stressed the central role that the public service had to play in addressing the ravages of South Africa's past. The alliance's election manifesto, the Reconstruction and Development Programme (RDP), recognised that the public service would be able to play such a role only if it underwent extensive transformation, and that democratisation was a central element of this transformation. The RDP noted that 'democratisation requires modernising the structures and functioning of government in pursuit of the objectives of efficient, effective, responsive, transparent and accountable government' (ANC, 1994: 120).

But what does democratisation mean, and what is the contribution of trade unions to an agenda of democratisation? The RDP and subsequent policy documents offer a wide definition of this concept. Democratisation is multidimensional and impacts on the development of public policy, the allocation of public resources, as well as the delivery of government services. Because of the influence of labour in the drafting of the RDP and earlier policy documents, it was envisaged that, for labour, democratisation would mean an appropriate role and its active participation in all three of the above processes.

To a significant extent, transformation of the public service meant changing its archaic labour relations framework. Such changes began with the finalisation of the Labour Relations Act (LRA) of 1995. For the first time in South African history, the public service was regulated by the same statute that governed labour relations in the rest of the economy. Workplace forums were a key experiment of the LRA. The forums were an attempt to give effect to the RDP's worker empowerment provisions which noted that 'legislation must facilitate worker participation and decision-making in the world of work' (ANC, 1994: 114).

The real challenge to democratise the public service started immediately after the election of the first democratic government in 1994. Democratisation, however, was a contested terrain between politicians, public service managers, communities and workers. Such competition has resulted in the establishment of a variety of institutional forms, which are somewhat unique to the public service. Yet, in the main, the workplace forum model set out in the LRA was not fully informed by these initiatives.

This chapter reviews efforts at democratisation in the public service in the period 1994 to 1999, and locates workplace forums within this context. It considers the possibilities and limitations of workplace forums as significant vehicles of democratisation and highlights anticipated developments over the next decade. Because of the evolving nature of public service democratisation, however, it can only draw tentative conclusions that will require further debate and research.

CONTEXT

One of the critical challenges confronting the newly-elected South African government in 1994 was the need to overhaul fundamentally existing labour policy. The first step in the reform process was the development of a new labour relations framework consistent with the objectives of the RDP. A Ministerial Legal Task Team was appointed in August 1994 to develop a new policy framework.

The Task Team's proposals were contained in an 'Explanatory memorandum accompanying the draft negotiating document in the form of a Labour Relations Bill'. The memorandum, which was released by the Minister of Labour in February 1995, formed the basis for negotiations between the parties within the National Economic Development and Labour Council (NEDLAC), the then-existing Public Service Bargaining Council (PSBC) and the Education Labour Relations Council (ELRC).

As part of the government's commitment to harmonise fragmented labour laws, the public service was included within the scope of the Bill. Initially the draft Bill entrenched the then existing bargaining arrangements for the public service and therefore provided for a national bargaining council for the public service and one for the education sector (Ministry of Labour, 1995: 23). No specific mention was made of the public service in the provisions on workplace forums. To all intents and purposes, however, the Task Team believed that its proposals on workplace forums would be suitable for the public service.

As a result of the fragmentation of bargaining in the public service, the public service unions focused their demands on ensuring greater co-ordination of collective bargaining and the inclusion of the police within the scope of the Act. On both scores, the public service lobby (comprising both unions and representatives of the government as employer) was successful in having these demands met. The final Act made provision for a Public Service Co-ordinating Bargaining Council (PSCBC), as well as for the establishment of sectoral bargaining councils for educators and police. It provided, furthermore, for additional sectoral bargaining councils.

As far as workplace democratisation was concerned, the debates and negotiations that followed the release of the Explanatory Memorandum in February 1995, and the initial rejection (and later modification) of the workplace forum model, were largely led by private sector unions and management. Public service unions united with their private sector counterparts in rejecting workplace forums. Their objections were based on the legitimate fear that the forums had the potential to weaken militant and democratic unions (Von Holdt, 1995: 61). However, the public service unions failed to appreciate the single most significant safeguard available to them: legislated collective bargaining. In hindsight, these unions could have used the space created by the debate on workplace forums to raise the broader issue of public service transformation and the creation of structures and institutions that would ensure greater worker empowerment in public service institutions.

TRANSFORMATION

Prior to, and concurrent with the NEDLAC negotiations during 1995, the Ministry of Public Service and Administration was engaged in a process of finalising a White Paper on the Transformation of the Public Service. The White Paper's policy framework was significantly informed by the 'new public management' ideology that has dominated the process of civil service reform in developed and certain developing countries alike in the nineties.

The White Paper reaffirmed the importance of the public service and set out a vision for a transformed service. It outlined a comprehensive set of short-, medium- and long-term strategies. These included the devolution and decentralisation of managerial responsibility and accountability, and the introduction of new and participative organisational structures and human resource development (DPSA, 1995: 48). Although the White Paper did not provide a detailed model, it made a vague commitment to an effective role for workers and organised labour.

Workplace forums are dealt with separately. The White Paper anticipated 'that such forums will play an important role in improving efficiency and effectiveness, by providing workers with a say in the day-to-day matters which affect them' (DPSA, 1995: 71). However, it reaffirmed the dominant thinking that saw workplace forums purely in terms of labour relations, and failed to link them with the broader agenda of developing new forms of management and governance for public service institutions. There is no doubt that the new LRA in November 1996 heralded a new phase in public service labour relations. It is clear, however, that the public service was marginalised in the drawing up of the new legislation. It was not sufficiently integrated into the new statute, and labour relations reform was not effectively linked to the broader process of administrative reform.

The public service was specifically *excluded* from Section 80 of the LRA which sets out the guidelines for the establishment of workplace forums. Section 80(12) places the onus on the Minister for Public Service and Administration to regulate workplace forums in the public service through the promulgation of a separate schedule to the Act. The development of the schedule must be guided by Section 207(4) which states that the Minister *may* attach a schedule to the Act after consultation with the Public Service Co-ordinating Bargaining Council (PSCBC), the succesor to the PSBC.

Satgar (1997, and Chapter 3 in this collection) quotes Professor Halton Cheadle, the convenor of the Task Team, on the reasons for the absence of detailed provisions for the public service:

> A task team was established to look at industrial relations issues in the public service ... unfortunately, when the drafting was completed, the public service task team had not completed its work.

Ambivalence

At the time of writing (1999), almost three years since the proclamation of the LRA, the Minister has not yet promulgated a schedule to guide the establishment of workplace forums in the public service. The reason lies in the ambivalent attitude on the part of both government and the public service unions to the forums.

The decision not to issue a schedule was not made by the Minister alone, but was based on a recommendation made at a consultative workshop on workplace forums convened by the DPSA in August 1996. The workshop was attended by employer and employee parties of the PSBC, the ELRC and the National Negotiating Forum (NNF). It agreed that regulations for the functioning of workplace forums would only be agreed upon once the PSCBC had been established and was fully functional (Adair, personal communication).[1] Nor does it appear that any actor will place the issue on the agenda in the foreseeable future.

The reasons for this ambivalence can be explained by three inter-related issues: the particular nature of the public service and the differences and similarities in the policy-making process between public service institutions and private sector firms; the nature of collective bargaining in this sector; and administrative reform in the current transformation process.

THE NATURE OF THE PUBLIC SERVICE

The public service differs from private sector firms in a number of important respects. This impacts on the institutions that are created to give effect to workplace democracy and the design and operation of these structures.

Public service institutions are not geared towards the maximisation of profit through the production and distribution of goods and services. Instead, workers and management are required to implement government policy and to deliver social and economic services. In the case of basic services, the motivating force is the need to improve the delivery of these services to the community which includes workers, management and their families. It could be argued that workers have as much interest as management in ensuring that the institution delivers effectively since they also benefit from these services.

The effective implementation of government policy, however, does not rest solely on improvements at the institutional level. It also depends on the resources available to the institution and the regulatory framework governing its operations. Resources are allocated through a complex political process involving competing government interests, meshed with a variety of formal and informal pressures exerted by civil society, including the unions. In theory, Cabinet takes the final decisions on the allocation of resources, with Parliament playing the role of overseer.[2]

Take, for example, the issue of providing improved health services to communities through clinics. Service delivery at institutional level can be improved through a variety of measures which can be jointly determined by workers and management, for example, tailoring clinic times to facilitate access by communities. In many cases, however, improving access depends on a range of sectoral or national decision-making processes: achieving service improvement through the reallocation of resources which would allow the construction of clinics in under-served communities; the development of adequate transport systems; etc.

Workplace democratisation models geared towards improving the effectiveness of public service institutions therefore require co-ordination between workplace-level and co-determination structures or other forums at higher levels. Such structures have in fact been established at sectoral and national level. The National Health Consultative Forum and the Public Finance and Monetary Policy chamber of NEDLAC are examples of such structures at these levels. However, these need to be formalised and made part of a wider programme of creating appropriate structures that operate in concert with each other. Although formalised, it is unclear to what extent these structures are indeed facilitating co-determination.

The most fascinating and challenging issue confronting the public service is the role of communities in the governance and management of institutions. The client base of the public service is communities, not simply customers. In private firms, the demand and supply of goods and services is an indicator of the success and relevance of the enterprise. For public services, especially those where government exercises a monopoly, communities cannot use purchasing power to indicate preferences. Forms of direct or indirect control of the institution by the community are desirable to ensure that the institution provides the service the community requires.

This understanding is guiding current government efforts to improve community control over public services. The most significant advances are to be found in education. The South African Schools Act 84 of 1996 (SASA) gives school governing bodies powers to hire teachers and set user fees to fund improvements in education. The Act not only blurs the definition of the primary employer of public servants, but also vests significant governance functions in parents. Education highlights important contradictions between democratic structures and the need to ensure redress and equity in a period of transformation.

Another difference between the public service and private sector firms is the identification of managers and owners for purposes of co-determination. In the current set-up, even senior institutional managers are considered to be workers. They lack the most basic of powers which renders any form of co-determination futile. Changes in public service regulations in 1999 and the isolation of senior management as a group (with individual performance contracts) in 1998 are beginning to address this weakness.

Notwithstanding the differences, there are also considerable similarities between public service workplaces and private sector institutions. Lessons learnt in the private sector can and should be tested in public services – and vice versa. Experiments in capacity-building and information disclosure, for example, are applicable across workplaces.

COLLECTIVE BARGAINING

Understanding collective bargaining is crucial in evaluating workplace forums and co-determination. Satgar and Summers separately conclude that the existence of legislated collective bargaining facilitates the separation of the relationship between workers and management into a collective bargaining channel and a co-determination channel (Satgar, 1997; Summers, 1995: 809).

One of labour's criticisms of the current LRA is its failure to provide for legislated collective bargaining. Instead, the Act relies on voluntarism to provide a general duty to bargain. This failure partly accounts for the scepticism and resistance of the union movement to workplace forums. Unions fear that this failure may blur the lines between bargaining and co-determination. Public service unions, however, have less to fear. Centralised collective bargaining is entrenched through the establishment of the PSCBC. Furthermore, the establishment of workplace forums in the public service (including their powers and the scope of issues to be addressed) is dependent on agreement being reached in the PSCBC or a sectoral council.

The development of collective bargaining in the public service since 1994 has seen a widening of the bargaining agenda in the PSCBC. This is the result of both the relative strength of public service unions, as well as the government's commitment to progressive labour relations for its own employees (Patel, 1998). However, these favourable conditions for labour are not guaranteed. The collective bargaining process will be put under tremendous strain over the next few years as a result of the on-going program of public service reform and the adoption of a conservative macro-economic framework for South Africa.

In many respects, workplace forums are perceived as redundant in the public service. At the DPSA workshop on workplace forums in 1996, as well as at a series of workshops with hospital and health personnel,[3] participants reviewed Sections 84 and 86 of the LRA of 1995, which list the issues for consultation and joint decision-making workplace forums. Participants concluded that issues such as mergers and transfers of ownership, export promotion and product development plans did not apply to the public service. Furthermore, because of the centralisation of personnel management in the public service at the time, many of the key co-determination issues listed in the LRA are subject to negotiation at the PSCBC. These include job grading, exemptions from collective agreements, merit increases and discretionary bonuses, education and training, partial or total 'plant' closures, disciplinary codes and procedures, affirmative action and employment equity. Finally, in several institutions, issues such as work scheduling and organisation of work are being considered by management committees, which include the union or workers. Participants felt, therefore, that the workplace forum provisions in the LRA would create structures that would consume tremendous resources on the side of both unions and government, with negligible benefits. However, changes in the regulatory framework towards decentralisation and in the collective bargaining systems are changing these parameters. Labour may therefore have to reconsider its position on the creation of workplace forums in the public service.

The LRA makes provision for sectoral bargaining councils. The precise demarcation of powers between sectoral councils and the PSCBC has not been fully resolved. The finalisation of the constitution of the PSCBC provides the foundation upon which sectoral powers can be more clearly defined. An analysis of the National Negotiating Forum (for police) and the ELRC (for educators) reveals significant potential for union input into policy in the sectoral bargaining councils. The PSBC, as the bargaining council for the remainder of the public service, was more limited in straddling the divide between collective bargaining and policy issues. Alternative structures of participation, however, have emerged. The widespread dissatisfaction and strike action by nurses in the wake of the wage settlement in the second half of 1995 led to the establishment of the National Consultative Health Forum (NCHF) to deal specifically with the problems in the health sector. The NCHF was described by the Minister of Health as the first step towards a 'structured co-operative relationship' to deal with the many problems in this sector (Dlamini Zuma, 1995: 4).

On paper, sectoral bargaining allow unions a voice in policy-making. To ensure that this voice is not silenced, the public service unions will need to see that the role of sectoral bargaining councils in policy matters is entrenched as a part of collective agreements at the PSCBC level. This will also encourage the adoption of a common approach across sectors.

Since 1994, the nature of bargaining has shifted towards establishing appropriate frameworks in addition to bargaining about actual levels of wages and conditions of service. This will facilitate greater decision-making at sectoral and workplace levels and assist the introduction of forms of worker participation. For example, the previous grading system was managed through a system of Personnel Administration Standards (PASs). Individual PASs were developed centrally for each of the more than 300 occupations in the public service. The PAS specified in detail the measures that applied to a particular occupational group, including a detailed description of the tasks that could be performed by members of a particular occupational class. The PAS has been identified as a major obstacle to organising work for effective service delivery and human resource development. The introduction of a new 16-band grading system, and the replacement of the prescriptive PASs with an instrument that is more advisory, known as Codes of Remuneration (COREs), are recent attempts to address the problems.

It is anticipated that centrally-determined competency levels will be introduced. A common job evaluation tool has been adopted at central level. Departments, provinces and, in many cases, institutions, will then be required to develop an appropriate work organisation model and to grade individual workers. These developments will hasten the need for the development of a workplace forum – or other appropriate co-determination structures – to enable workers to intervene in, and monitor, the application of these policies.

ADMINISTRATIVE REFORM

The public service inherited by the new government was hierarchical, centralised and, as a consequence, inefficient. It was designed to cater for the needs of a white minority and a small black elite (DPSA, 1996).

The public service is currently managed by the Public Service Act (Act 111 of 1984). This prescribes that the Minister for Public Service and Administration will be responsible for developing policy on employment and conditions of service of public servants. It further demarcates the public service into departments and provinces and provides for executing authorities and heads of departments.

In 1994, the Government of National Unity (GNU) also started a process of reforming the legislative framework governing the public service. The first phase of this process concentrated on the creation of a single, unified public service and the removal of specific discriminatory clauses, for example, the distinction between officers (mainly white, high-ranking civil servants) and employees (mainly black, lower-skilled workers). The second phase was aimed at transferring executive functions from the Public Service Commission (PSC) to the Minister for Public Service and Administration and the establishment of the DPSA. The PSC now performs the role of overseeing and monitoring in the public service as a whole. The Public Service Act of 1984 was amended to give greater responsibility to executing officers (Ministers) and Heads of Departments (Directors-General). There is strong support for completely rewriting the legislation to ensure that it is more coherent and transformative. This is envisaged to be the next phase of reform.

Progressive unions, such as the National Education Health and Allied Workers' Union (NEHAWU), support the general thrust towards decentralisation if it is geared towards greater community participation, service delivery and human resource development (COSATU, 1997).

Decentralisation will not occur overnight because of constraints on capacity and the need to develop appropriate systems. International experience shows that it can take ten to twenty years. These cases point towards a phased process of devolving authority and responsibility. Specific milestones need to be defined for the delegation of further powers. Institutions will have to meet the performance measures detailed in the preceding step, which include the existence of certain competencies as well as systems. The Department of Health has established pilot projects in a handful of major regional hospitals to test and develop the process of decentralisation.

The devolution process offers a unique opportunity to ensure workplace democratisation. Just as the existence of proper financial systems will be a requirement for decentralisation, unions should ensure that the existence of effective worker representation is also a pre-requisite. Such an approach will need to be coupled with training programmes to facilitate the development of the requisite knowledge base amongst workers.

The old PSBC was unable to deal effectively with these policy issues. The creation of appropriate structures through which unions could influence the direction of the transformation process at the macro level has been the subject of debate since early 1994, leading to a proposal by NEHAWU for the establishment of a Public Service Forum (PSF). The PSF was an attempt to create a 'separate forum to negotiate policy and restructuring issues' (Collins, 1994: 25) to curtail the power of conservative unions in the public service. The PSF would embrace unions, government departments, and community and political organisations.

According to NEHAWU, the forum was never established 'because of the resistance of the reactionary forces in the public service and political unwillingness of the Ministry for Public Service and Administration' (NEHAWU, 1996). Progress was made in October 1995 when the White Paper proposed the setting up of a Public Service Transformation Forum (PSTF).

Concrete plans to establish such a forum were only developed by the DPSA a year later, in September 1996. However, the plans did not take into account developments since 1994, specifically the establishment and functioning of NEDLAC. However, changed conditions have rendered the need for such a forum obsolete.

The White Paper also proposed the development of Transformation Units (TUs) in departments and provinces. The TUs would not have decision-making powers but would act as facilitating organs of transformation. The DPSA specifically stated that organised labour would only be represented indirectly through unionised staff members, and not as unions per se (DPSA, 1997). These proposals were guidelines to assist departments and provinces. Initial outside evaluation of TUs shows that, in many cases, they have become parallel management structures with an undefined mandate which do not function in a focused and strategic fashion. In addition, they are also elite-driven with little or no active involvement by lower-level workers and unions (Patel, 1998).

Concurrent with the establishment of TUs, institutional managers and workers at hundreds of institutions have taken the initiative and established structures and processes. There has been no systematic assessment of the extent of such developments, of their detailed method of operation, their successes and failures, or of their impact on unions.

PUSHING THE LIMITS

Democratising a public service that employs almost 1,1 million people spread over many thousands of workplaces is no easy task. The task is further complicated by the diversity of workplaces, external political forces, and an intense transformation project. However, it offers considerable opportunities for democratising society.

Successful democratisation will need to ensure effective co-ordination between the policy process and the processes of management and governance. Furthermore, it requires co-ordination between democratisation initiatives aimed at the workplace and those aimed at sectoral and national levels.

Workers in public service workplaces are confronted by three types of structural change:

- First, the LRA facilitates co-determination through workplace forums. Some time has passed since the new Act came into operation, however, and the movement towards workplace forums has been negligible.
- Second, departments and provinces are moving towards greater decentralisation of management authority. However, some elements of decentralisation have already begun, for example, the development of institutional governing structures (such as hospital boards), as well as forums to facilitate the participation of stakeholders (such as community policing forums).
- Third, TUs and committees have been suggested to address the specific challenge of transformation. While a detailed evaluation has not been

conducted, it can be reasonably concluded that neither management nor the unions has sufficient capacity to play an effective role in these structures. The creation of alternative, and possibly competing structures does not facilitate effective co-ordination.

Since government owns public services, the scope for a management model that facilitates workplace democratisation is greatest in public institutions. Satgar (Chapter 3) suggests that the workplace forum model can be used to develop autonomous self-management in South Africa. He further suggests that the public service be used as a model that can later be extended to workplaces across the economy. At the current juncture, widespread autonomous self-management may not be possible. Unions will need to explore capacity issues and assess the possibilities that will be created by changes in the regulatory framework to identify possibilities for experimenting with autonomous self-management.

Significant opportunities do exist, however, for unions to advance experiments at specific institutions, particularly those being managed by former unionists. For example, at one time the regional chairperson of the South African Democratic Teachers' Union (SADTU) in the Eastern Cape was also the principal of a school, and the general secretary of the Health Workers' Union (HWU) was the superintendent of a major regional hospital in the Western Cape. Whether or not it is 'politically correct', or in line with values nurtured during the struggle for democracy, a significant number of new managers are open to ideas of workplace democratisation and worker participation. Progressive unions should be able to build on relationships with innovative managers and use these institutions as pilots to develop new forms of managing public services.

Pilot projects need to be sufficiently resourced to improve their chances of success, and unions should be central in this process:

> Employees in single workplaces lack the expertise, capacities, and organisational strength to engage in struggles to change the workplace. Only the organisational power and resources of the union will enable workers to make a real difference.
> (Von Holdt, 1995: 59) .

The need for capacity on both sides to service co-determination is essential. Buhlungu (Chapter 8 in this collection, and 1998) notes that union capacity has four related aspects: structural and organisational; strategic; financial and administrative. Weaknesses in any of these aspects can negatively affect the initiative to democratise.

Pilot projects need to be evaluated regularly. The evolution of co-determination and other models of worker participation will require documentation, analysis and research. Public service unions need to put into place effective short-, medium- and long-term research programmes that will focus on appropriate institutional forums, the development of union capacity, the effective participation of communities, and the impact on service delivery (Kester and Pinaud, 1994).

One of the key requirements for effective democratisation of public services is the role of communities. In the former Yugoslavia, self-management had been extended since 1953 to non-economic activities such as public administration, education, health and social security services, and scientific institutions. Unlike other undertakings, users are represented alongside workers (ILO, 1981: 51). Given the existence of diverse interests within communities and the skewed distribution of power, unions need to be at the forefront in demanding the effective inclusion of previously marginalised groups.

A potential obstacle to effective worker involvement in the management of public service institutions is that of multi-unionism. Historical conflicts between unions have rendered co-operation at workplace level extremely difficult. Structures which take current realities into account will need to be crafted. At Hillbrow Hospital in Gauteng, for example, an RDP/Transformation Committee was established in 1996. It included NEHAWU, Hospital Personnel of South Africa (HOSPERSA), the South African Democratic Nurses' Union (SADNU), and several other unions, with each organisation represented by two delegates (Mazibuko, 1996: 24). In many workplaces, however, co-operation between unions may not be possible and may even heighten existing tension between unions.

Workplace democratisation is difficult to attain, and requires more discussion within the union movement. The area of greatest influence in the short-term is democratisation at the sectoral and national level. Sectoral bargaining councils offer significant opportunities for worker involvement in policy-making. Public service unions need to evaluate the successes and limitations of the ELRC and the NNF in terms of influencing the policy process. This should inform the debate on the distribution of powers between the PSCBC and sectoral bargaining councils, as well as the demarcation of further sectors as bargaining councils. Such an assessment will need to review union capacity, employer organisation and participation in sectoral bargaining councils, and the relationship of the sectoral bargaining council to the central bargaining process.

The public finance and monetary policy chamber of NEDLAC has a potentially substantial influence on the public service. This avenue is not being used effectively to advance democratisation and transformation of the public service. Workplace experiences need to be communicated effectively to union representatives at NEDLAC to ensure the necessary co-ordination between macro-level reform and workplace initiatives.

CONCLUSION

The introduction of workplace forums in the LRA places the issue of co-determination and the broader issue of worker participation on the industrial relations agenda. In the public service, co-determination can be expanded beyond the industrial relations arena into the realm of broader political power where it can encourage more inclusive and effective methods of management and governance.

The provisions of the LRA focus on the workplace and a limited co-determination agenda. Public service institutions that offer greater scope for democratisation need to be understood and developed. To succeed, 'unions first need to define what they see as worker participation, in terms of both structures and content, outside of their traditional forms of engagement with management. Then they need to develop a broad strategy that encompasses this definition (and which includes workplace forums).' (See Chapter 9 in this collection, and Godfrey et al, 1998.)

Any initiatives being taken by 'progressive' and labour-friendly institutional managers to introduce alternative management models need to be supported by labour, especially at the regional and national levels of the unions. To ensure continuation beyond the term of office of the 'charismatic' leadership, workplace democratisation efforts must be formalised through agreements, entrenched by the establishment of appropriate structures, and sustained through the development of the capacity of workers and their unions.

There is an urgent need for unions to develop positions on decentralisation and ensure that workplace democratisation becomes a central element in these initiatives. Decentralisation will require a strengthening of the policy process at the sectoral and national level, for example, in the establishment of minimum central norms and standards. A clear union position on decentralisation can also feed into the process of reaching agreement at the PSCBC on workplace forums.

Finally – as researchers often argue – there is an urgent need for further research into this important area. Specific areas for immediate investigation include:

- The role and attitude of managers (senior policy-makers as well as institutional managers) on co-determination, autonomous self-management, etc., with particular emphasis on the views and opinions of managers employed during the apartheid era, as compared to the views and opinions of managers appointed after 1994;
- The role of community organisations in the functioning of public service institutions, including an evaluation of structures such as community policing forums, Parent/Teacher Associations (PTAs), Parent/Teacher/Student Associations (PTSAs) and hospital governing structures;
- The development and extent of alternative management models in the public service, a description of these models and an analysis of their strengths and weaknesses;
- The experience of Transformation Units and their potential to play a role in democratising policy formulation, resource allocation and the delivery of services in departments and provinces.

The public service has great potential to live up to the principles of democratisation expressed in the RDP and subsequent policy documents. It may play a path-breaking role in developing democratic practices more broadly in the economy. Successful democratisation will be important, not only for its own sake, but also for achieving effective transformation of the old apartheid state and for ensuring improved delivery of services to the population as a whole. Realising this potential, however, will be no easy task for unions or for managers in the public service. It will be an area to be closely monitored and further researched in years to come.

8

A QUESTION OF POWER

Co-determination and trade union capacity

———— ✦ ————

Sakhela Buhlungu

According to Buhlungu, the debate about industrial democracy and co-determination has been preoccupied with whether worker participation and co-determination co-opt workers or advance the struggle of the working class for greater control in the workplace. Buhlungu argues that this polarity leads to a zero-sum understanding of the outcomes of participation and co-determination. It also fails to take note of the fact that managerial strategies in general, and co-determination in particular, are contradictory in that they contain both dangers and opportunities for labour. This chapter examines the ability of the labour movement to take advantage of the opportunities and avoid the 'risks' which these initiatives inevitably involve. It then argues that labour's ability to take advantage of the opportunities depends, to a large extent, on it building its power resources or capacities in a number of areas. Indeed, successful engagement in any transformative project or struggle depends a great deal on building these resources to ensure effectiveness. This suggests that worker participation and co-determination involve struggles by workers, and that, whether workers win or lose those struggles, is a matter which is decided by the balance of power between labour and capital. Engagement challenges South African trade unions to develop new strategies of organisational rejuvenation. A failure to do this would make the dangers of co-option very real indeed for these unions.

INTRODUCTION

It is now over a decade since some South African companies started experimenting with organisational restructuring to reposition themselves in an attempt to become more competitive nationally and globally. Some of these restructuring processes included the introduction of a different style of management which promised greater participation by workers in decision-making. But it is still very difficult to discern a clear co-determinist model emerging from this complex picture. This is partly due to the fact that many of these experiments are often tentative and half-hearted efforts on the part of management to address organisational efficiency constraints. These strategies have not been accompanied by a clear commitment to co-determination per se. This has often led to failure to win the co-operation of workers to make these efforts sustainable. However, trade unions have not managed to go beyond making calls for 'workplace democratisation' and thus there is no clarity on the actual content of labour's own vision of co-determination (Buhlungu, 1996).

The post-apartheid government has taken the initiative by legislating measures which are intended to entrench co-determinist practices in the workplace through workplace forums. The revamped Labour Relations Act (LRA) of 1995, which many have lauded as a victory for workers and unions (Baskin and Satgar, 1995; Lagrange, 1995), came into effect on 11 November 1996. The Act includes provisions which allow labour to exercise rights which it would have had to fight for in the past, including rights to consultation, joint decision-making and the disclosure of information. But one of the most significant innovations of the Act is the introduction of rights and structures for co-determination. It is this innovation which presents the trade union movement with both opportunities and challenges.

Although there is uncertainty about the sustainability of the above initiatives and experiments, it is possible to categorise them under the rubric of what is termed 'co-determination' or 'workplace participation' because they suggest a shift towards what Pateman (1971: 68) refers to as 'a modification, to a greater or lesser degree, of the orthodox authority structure; namely one where decision-making is the "prerogative" of management, in which workers play no part'. In South Africa, the orthodox authority structure which we have inherited from our past has been called the 'apartheid workplace regime', a social structure which 'allocates rights and resources unequally among differently socialised actors' (Von Holdt, 2000: 201).

The notion of a modification of orthodox authority structures which Pateman uses with reference to decision-making in industry can also be said to be taking place in the sphere of national (governmental) policy formulation, particularly since the inception of the National Economic Development and Labour Council (NEDLAC) in 1995.[1] By agreeing to the establishment of NEDLAC, the post-1994 democratic government gave institutional effect to a demand by civil society organisations to have a voice in national policy formulation.

The debate about industrial democracy has been preoccupied with whether worker participation and co-determination co-opt workers or advance the struggle of the working class for greater control in the workplace (Cressey and MacInnes, 1980). This chapter argues that this polarity is incorrect because it leads to a zero-sum understanding of the outcomes of participation and co-determination. In other words, it fails to take note of the fact that managerial strategies in general, and co-determination in particular, are contradictory in that they contain both dangers and opportunities for labour. This, Cressey and MacInnes (1980: 14) have argued, results from the dual character of the labour process where labour is not fully subordinated to capital. In this context, co-determination and worker participation open up space for struggle, thus presenting labour with opportunities to push back the frontier of managerial control (Buhlungu, 1996).

DANGERS AND OPPORTUNITES

Thus, the emergence of co-determinist practices in South Africa should be understood as a contradictory process which presents both dangers and opportunities for the trade union movement. As one shop steward noted at a workshop convened by COSATU's September Commission in 1997 to discuss workplace restructuring, participation in decision-making through joint structures 'involves taking risks, like swimming'.[2]

This chapter looks at the ability of the labour movement to take advantage of the opportunities and avoid the 'risks' which these initiatives inevitably involve. It then proceeds to argue that labour's ability to take advantage of the opportunities depends, to a large extent, on its realisation that, in order to avoid the dangers of co-determination, it needs to build its power resources or capacities in a number of areas. Indeed, successful engagement in any transformative project or struggle depends a great deal on the building of these resources of power to ensure effectiveness. As one COSATU office-bearer noted in a submission to the September Commission (1997: 167):[3]

> We always talk about transformation of society, transformation of government, transformation of the workplace – we never talk about transforming ourselves. We need to transform ourselves and our organisation before we can transform society. We need to make ourselves effective.

Some have argued that worker involvement in co-determinist processes and structures inevitably leads to the institutionalisation of struggles and the co-option of workers. (See, for example, Lehulere, 1995; and Barchiesi, 1998.) Lehulere (1995: 42) goes so far as to argue that:

> Co-determination disarms workers because workers give up their right to strike on issues covered by co-determination agreements. Co-determination undermines the struggle for socialism because, instead of preparing workers for the struggle against capitalism, it promotes the idea that capitalism and the workers have common interests. It therefore leads to the co-option of the working class.

Within the union movement itself, there is ambivalence towards worker participation and co-determination. Some share the perspective that engagement in joint decision-making structures is tantamount to playing into the hands of capital. This view leads them to conclude that engagement in co-determination inevitably leads to co-option and emasculation of trade unions (Ronnie, 1996). A NUMSA shop steward, Ishmael Makhuphula, also articulated this position at the workshop convened by the September Commission:

> Restructuring is an attempt by capital to survive. But the labour movement has never interrogated capital's agenda. By trying to open up the system they are trying to gain acceptance for it.

But this is by no means the dominant view within the trade union movement. There is also a view held by many workers and shop stewards that participation in decision-making is desirable (Buhlungu, 1996). They argue that the terms of such involvement are decided in day-to-day struggles and in the balance of power between capital and labour.

The discussion in this chapter disagrees with the 'incorporation argument', namely that, under capitalism, industrial democracy in its various forms (co-determination, participative management, etc.) necessarily leads to co-option. It is argued that each situation always presents threats and opportunities, costs and benefits. The question of who emerges as a winner is not determined *a priori* by the structure or process. It is a matter decided in a process of contestation and struggle, in this case between workers and management. Thus, it is argued here that innovative managerial initiatives and the provisions of the LRA of 1995 to set up participatory structures present opportunities as well as threats for the labour movement. Organisational strength and capacity could ensure that labour turns these new structures in its favour. Cressey and MacInnes (1980: 6) have cautioned against a simplistic dichotomy where participation is seen to lead to either 'incorporation' (co-option) or the 'advance of labour'. These authors urge us to understand the real challenge of participation, namely, that it presents the 'material space for struggle at the point of production' which 'cuts both ways' (ibid.: 20). This argument is the basis of their critique of classical Marxist notions of labour subordination in production which allows no space for creativity and control by workers in production:

> If we escape from the notion of a working class which prior to the historical break is merely an 'aspect of capital' but exists politically as a universal force opposed to it, and open up the possibility for a 'practical and prefigurative socialist politics', then it must also be remembered that such a struggle roots itself initially in the workplace rather than in the class struggle as a whole. Just as such struggles are not artificial or 'incorporated', neither are they necessarily 'spontaneously' socialist. They may take either form, and the task before us is surely thus to develop yardsticks for differentiating the two and promoting the latter.
>
> (Cressey and MacInnes, 1980: 20)

CO-DETERMINATION
AND THE WORKERS' STRUGGLE

What the above suggests then is that worker participation and co-determination involve struggles by workers. Whether workers win or lose those struggles is a matter decided by the balance of power between labour and capital. In other words, these strategies, whether they are initiated by management, government or workers and their unions, cannot and should not be separated from the day-to-day struggles that workers wage against capital on the shop floor and in the broader society. Both sides of the debate are guilty of making this artificial separation. This discussion now turns to some of the opportunities available to workers and their unions.

Workers and trade unions have always fought for greater involvement of workers in decisions. This demand featured prominently during the height of worker mobilisation and struggles in the 1980s. At its founding congress in 1985, COSATU passed a resolution on the minimum wage which made reference to the workers' demand for 'workers' control and management of production'. A study of shop stewards by Pityana and Orkin (1992: 68) also found that the majority of COSATU shop stewards preferred worker involvement in decision-making. South African workers and unions have always struggled to destroy authoritarian workplace regimes and to see the introduction of more participatory styles of workplace management. In many respects, co-determination in the form of various managerial initiatives and the provisions of the LRA of 1995, offer them an opportunity to do this, provided that it forms part and parcel of a broader strategy of transforming the relations of production in society, and that workers and their unions continue to struggle to build the necessary capacities to turn the contest in their favour.

Even where participation takes a limited or 'pseudo' form, workers and their unions can exploit contradictions and confusion in management schemes and put forward alternative proposals for workplace democratisation. A study of managerial initiatives at Nampak Polyfoil in Johannesburg showed that shop stewards and workers could redefine the terms of the debate by engaging management on these initiatives (Buhlungu, 1996). Similarly, Maller (1992) has shown that workers and shop stewards at Volkswagen South Africa were able to make use of their involvement in joint committees to influence decision-making in the company.

A further opportunity is offered by the LRA of 1995 in the form of institutional rights for workplace forums. Among these are the management obligations to consult with workers, disclose information and decide certain matters jointly with workers' representatives.

For many years, workers and their unions were excluded from policy formulation. As a result, they have been outsiders, demanding a voice in the formulation of policy, particularly on those issues which directly affect workers. The struggle against the LRA amendments in 1988 and the anti-VAT strike in 1991 included a demand by workers and unions to have a say in economic and labour market policy issues.

Finally, NEDLAC gives labour an institutional voice, not only in labour relations policy issues but by providing trade unions with an opening to influence a whole range of other issues related to the economy of the country.

SERVICING CO-DETERMINATION: A QUESTION OF POWER

Co-determination and managerial schemes of participation have little to do with a 'change of heart' on the part of employers and government. They have more to do with two factors:

* These initiatives are a direct outcome of struggles by organised workers. Where workers are docile and divided, capital tends to prefer more authoritarian means of control. But where workers are strong and combative, they are able to push back the 'frontier of control' and gain greater control of their lives in production.
* The initiatives come from a realisation by capital that despotic control alone is not sustainable. In other words, they represent an admission that capital is not omnipotent.

Thus, if we accept the suggestion made in this chapter that worker participation and co-determination are *not separate* from struggle, then it follows that these strategies are about the demands and aspirations of South African workers and unions, particularly black workers and their unions since the days of the Industrial and Commercial Workers' Union (ICU) in the 1920s. A PG Bison shop steward noted this connection when he observed that the management-initiated change process, Total Productivity and Quality (TPQ), was one of the fruits of their struggles for workplace democracy and a living wage (Joseph Mthembu, 1994: interview). However, the grave mistake made by some in the union, including some workers and shop stewards, was to believe that the change process could be a substitute for struggle.

But, as noted above, co-determination is not just about opportunities. It is about dangers too. Once co-determination and participation are seen as substitutes for building worker power and struggle, then the danger of union substitution and co-option becomes very real.

The PG Bison experience cited above illustrates this danger. Shop stewards became absorbed in participation forums, *bosberade* (strategising workshops at venues away from the workplace) and committees at the expense of union structures. A worker interviewed by the author complained that the change process

> made the shop stewards weak and made them work for management. At some stage the union nearly collapsed here because they were not doing their job.

A similar situation occurred at Nampak Polyfoil, but union strength and the relative sophistication of some shop stewards and workers enabled the union to maintain unity and to frustrate management's attempts to weaken it. One shop steward explained how the shop stewards found themselves mired in countless participation structures:

> So what happened is we had meeting after meeting whenever we had a problem. In the management and shop stewards meeting this guy [from management] will come up and say: 'Why don't we elect a committee that will look directly into that problem?' Comrade, time went on! We ended up having eleven committees. And most of the shop stewards were involved in some of those committees and when we looked at this thing, comrade, we saw it was now creating problems. I mean, we can't be having eleven committees. And then, it seemed as if by that time the union wasn't functioning the way it used to. At the same time there are also [disciplinary] cases and most of the time a shop steward, when he is supposed to go to a case, he is busy in another committee –

planning committee, steering committee, task force, what-what committee, canteen committee. Hey, there were a lot of committees! And then we decided that it [the change process] should be suspended. However, there were hard feelings among the [shop stewards'] committee members.

(Masuku, 1993: interview)

Some have sought to avoid these dangers by proposing what has been termed 'adversarial participation'. For example Ntshangase and Solomons (1993: 35) have argued that:

The union should engage the companies and participate in these processes of change, but on our own terms through collective bargaining, rather than on management's terms. In this way we can achieve the goals of expanding worker power and the role of the union. This is what we mean by adversarial participation. Participation, yes, but in a way which does not ignore the irreconcilable differences between labour and capital.

Proponents of this notion therefore argue for engagement with schemes of co-determination in a way which allows workers to pursue their collective interests through their unions.

However, the notion of adversarial participation neglects to address the organisational capacities which the unions need to develop to ensure that engagement does not lead to co-option and substitution of the union by co-determinist structures. In other words, it does not examine the power resources which unions need to build to service co-determination and to get maximum benefit from the opportunities it offers. This chapter seeks to address this concern by looking at the union movement's capacity to service co-determination.

This chapter is based on research material gathered in the course of several projects on unions and worker participation in the period 1993-1997. These include a Sociology of Work Unit (SWOP) study at PG Bison in 1993, an MA research project on union responses to participation at Nampak and PG Bison (1993-1995), a SWOP / PPWAWU study at Nampak in 1994 and discussions organised by the September Commission in the first half of 1997. It does not concern itself with issues to do with union engagement in national policy-making, but reference will be made to that issue where relevant.

Although the bulk of the information used here applies to one union affiliated to the Congress of South African Trade Unions (COSATU), namely the Paper, Printing, Wood and Allied Workers' Union (PPWAWU), many of the issues raised and conclusions reached in this chapter apply to most of the COSATU unions, albeit with some notable variations which will be noted where relevant.

The discussion that follows draws out the key issues pertaining to whether, and how, unions have been servicing co-determination. In discussing this issue, the chapter identifies *a lack of capacity* by unions to take advantage of the opportunities which co-determination offers. Thus the discussion starts with some remarks on union capacity.

A LACK OF CAPACITY

In the nineties, the term 'capacity' has featured prominently in debates about lack of union strength and the need to rebuild organisational power and vibrancy in the movement. In 1997, COSATU's September Commission investigated a number of strategies to strengthen the trade unions affiliated to COSATU. In its report, the Commission (1997: 168) noted that the advent of democracy in South Africa has 'forced the unions to engage with a tremendous range of issues, many of them more complex than in the past'.

Transitional periods and moments of economic crisis and change often force trade unions to re-examine their current strengths and to explore ways of coping with the challenges thrown up by these crises and changes. Another well-known case in recent years is that of the Australian Council of Trade Unions (ACTU). In 1986, ACTU and the Trade Development Council (TDC) went on a fact-finding mission in Western Europe and Scandinavia to look at different models of unionism and to examine ways in which labour should fashion its relations with government. The result of this mission was a recommendation which urged the Australian trade union movement to adopt what was termed 'strategic unionism' (Ford and Plowman, 1989). Among other things, this strategy involved moving beyond wages and conditions, formulating and implementing centrally co-ordinated goals and integrated strategies, participation in tripartite institutions, and strong union organisation (ibid.: 289).

In the early 1990s, the notion of strategic unionism was used to describe the union movement in South Africa at the height of its power and influence in areas other than traditional collective bargaining (Von Holdt, 1992). However, since then, the deepening of the transition, globalisation and the emergence of forms of co-determination and tripartism have exposed a number of weaknesses which have called into question labour's ability to take advantage of the opportunities which have opened up. This has been termed the capacity problem in the trade union movement (Buhlungu, 2000). The September Commission has recommended a number of goals for the federation. To realise these goals, the report identified the centrality of capacity building within COSATU and its affiliates. It argued that COSATU needs to develop the resources and capacities to engage effectively with the alliance, government, parliament, NEDLAC, provincial and local government, and with employers at sectoral and workplace levels (September Commission, 1997: 23).

Before examining some of the problems facing the trade union movement in servicing co-determination, it is worth recalling a note of caution relevant to our circumstances made by the Australian mission. In its report, the group warned that,

> Effective policy formulation is not a part-time activity. It requires the dedication of relatively large amounts of resources, in both time and money. It also requires input from local union members as well as from properly trained professionals.
>
> (Cited in Ford and Plowman, 1989: 298-99)

This observation also applies to co-determination and workplace democratisation. Drawing from experiences in a number of countries across the world, the International Labour Organisation (ILO) has observed that worker participation in decision-making demands special training to equip workers and their representatives with special skills. The ILO (1989: 39-40) has noted that:

> In order to exert influence, whether through representation on management bodies or in the process of consultation, negotiation or joint decision-making, workers' represen-

tatives must be capable of understanding the questions under discussion and appreciating the effects of the decisions to be taken.

Not only do South African unions fail to channel sufficient resources to service co-determination, they also lack a clear strategy and skilled staff to provide leadership to the rank and file. The September Commission has taken cognisance of this problem, hence the importance it places on capacity-building. In this chapter the term 'capacity' has been used to refer to this situation. Elsewhere, trade union capacity has been referred to as:

> The overall capability or competence to deal with or engage in particular activities and/or issues which are of critical importance to the organisation, running and sustaining of the union movement's strength and influence in relation to employers and the state ... Such a capability depends on structures, processes and human and material resources available to the union to achieve its goals.
>
> (Buhlungu, 2000: 79)

Thus, union capacity can be seen as a set of capabilities necessary to exercise power (power resources). It has four related aspects, namely, structural and organisational, strategic, financial and administrative. A union can lack capacity in one or all these aspects. However, it must be noted that these categories are used here merely as analytical categories; in real life it is difficult to find problems occurring in such a neatly categorised form.

The discussion which follows looks at how the trade union movement has been meeting the challenges presented by the emergence of co-determination since the late 1980s and early 1990s. It looks particularly at the capacity problems unions face as they respond to co-determinist institutions and practices.

Structural and organisational capacity

In 1992 Zwelinzima Vavi, then COSATU's organising secretary (now general secretary), noted that the federation was facing a problem of 'deteriorating organisational capacity'. He argued that there was a problem of organisational decline and weakness at factory, local, branch/ regional and national levels. Workers and shop stewards were battling to understand 'complex issues', and the few unionists who understood these issues were over-stretched and thus unable to find time to share their knowledge with workers and shop stewards (Vavi, 1992: 40-41). Today many of these problems persist and the growth in union membership confronts unions with an even bigger problem.

A second issue related to the above is the fact that many of the existing union structures are inadequate for meeting the current challenges facing the unions. This problem was observed during several research projects in PPWAWU and a number of the workplaces it organises. For example, local and branch structures are often ignorant about what happens in workplaces within their geographical areas and, as a result, are unable to provide guidance and support to shop stewards in those workplaces. Similarly, union training does not cover shop-floor issues sufficiently, resulting in ignorance among organisers and shop stewards. A SWOP/PPWAWU study of Nampak's 'world-class manufacturing and service' strategy (1994: 92) found that many shop stewards do not have the skills to engage in strategic issues. The study then observed that: 'As a result, some shop stewards get tricked into endorsing certain changes without understanding the full implications thereof.'

Over the years, the union movement has built a cadre of leaders who have led the movement during difficult times since the 1970s. However, there is evidence that in the nineties the unions have been losing this leadership (Buhlungu, 1997). This haemorrhage has been occurring at a number of levels, but the most serious losses have been among the ranks of shop stewards and full-time officials. A recent study of full-time union staff has found that there is a 'revolving door syndrome' in the unions with the result that, at the end of 1996, 57% of the current staff in COSATU unions had not completed four years as employees of the union movement (Buhlungu, 1997).

The study also identified what it termed a 'generational transition', a process where the older generation of union officials were being replaced by a new generation who were less experienced in the organisational traditions of the union movement (Buhlungu, 1997). A similar trend can be seen with worker leadership at enterprise level where shop stewards are being promoted to positions above the bargaining unit, thus forcing them to cancel their union membership.

One of the consequences of these developments is that unions have been forced to rely on very few skilled and/or experienced leaders. Vavi (1992) observed that many shop stewards 'cannot grasp the complex issues' which have arisen in recent years. To make matters worse (ibid.: 41), 'Those who understand or have a better education occupy many positions. They are over-stretched and cannot find the time to develop fellow workers and shop stewards'. According to the results of the staff survey, only 35% of current union staff said their unions had strong shop stewards (Buhlungu, 1997).

With regard to national issues and tripartite forums, Keet (1992: 32) also noted a similar problem, namely, that there are very few union leaders at any level who have 'a confident or clear grasp of these and many other strategic options being adopted in the union movement today'. The result is that, once one of these few unionists leaves the unions, the repercussions are felt far and wide in the movement. The independent union movement was built on the principle of leadership accountability. In practice, this meant that every leader had to work on the basis of a mandate by the rank and file and was expected to report back to them on a regular basis. However, there have been signs that this practice is no longer adhered to as stringently as in the past. This is particularly the case with national level negotiations and forums where it was found that the bulk of COSATU's members did not know of their federation's involvement in national forums. More than 80% of the members had never been at a union meeting where there was a report or discussion of the National Economic Forum (NEF)[4] (Ginsburg and Webster, 1995: 67-68).

The move towards co-determination is going to require an aggressive education and training programmes in the unions (Buhlungu, 2000). But many unions do not have adequate numbers of personnel to perform the education and training function. Even those who employ staff to perform these functions, do not have structured programmes to educate shop stewards, office-bearers and full-time officials. Participants at a workshop convened by the September Commission in 1997, all of whom were shop stewards from most COSATU unions, noted that lack of capacity was the biggest problem facing the unions in their struggles to democratise workplace relations. Lesley Nhlapho, a NUMSA shop steward from Highveld Steel in Witbank noted that capacity building through education and training is a pre-condition for involvement in co-determinist processes and structures. 'If we want to participate' he argued, 'then the union must empower factory structures to take decisions on the spot. Otherwise management will take decisions alone.'

Speaking at the same workshop, Joseph Mthembu, a PPWAWU shop steward from PG Bison in Germiston, used his union's experience of board representation to illustrate the same sentiment. In the early 1990s, workers at the company were invited to send two representatives to the board of directors. But these worker directors did not get any training or back-up to assist them in the performance of their duties, with the result that they were completely ineffective. 'We were like lost sheep there. We did not know anything. The only thing we knew was eating time'(1994: interview).

A related weakness is that of research within the unions. The majority of unions do not employ researchers (Buhlungu, 1997). In those few cases where there are staff members employed to do research, they often find themselves drawn into other activities of the union with the result that research suffers.

Another weakness in COSATU regarding capacity is a federation structure which often hampers the co-ordination of certain policy issues. In terms of the COSATU constitution, the federation cannot take binding decisions on issues such as co-determination. This often leads to different unions taking different, and sometimes contradictory approaches, thus leaving rank-and-file members confused.

A number of these structural issues can be observed in the unions today and research done among members and leaders of PPWAWU illustrates the constraints unions face. Existing schemes of co-determination were introduced by management on the shop floor and, in the process, the union's organisational structures were bypassed. But what is of greater concern is that the union has been unable to regain the initiative and put forward its own proposals on co-determination. Part of the problem is that PPWAWU, like other unions, has been slow in taking up production (as opposed to distribution and political) issues. Sipho Kubheka, former general secretary of PPWAWU, noted this in an interview with the author in December 1994:

> Most of the officials came from a political background, not from an industrial background per se. They were politicians. They were political activists who happened to be much more

articulate in making this or that statement in whatever meetings. We were not asking people in the interviews: 'what is your experience about the factory situation?' 'Can you tell us about the process of production in the printing industry?' … We were focusing on political issues, apartheid in the work situation.

But the problem goes beyond one of full-time union officials. It is about the slow pace at which unions have been reorienting themselves such that they pay more attention to issues of transformation of the sphere of production.

Strategic capacity

The absence of a union vision for the workplace is part of a bigger issue, namely, the lack of a political vision for the union movement. The transition to democracy and the crisis of the socialist paradigm has left unions groping for a new vision which informs union work and struggles. This has left a number of unions uncertain about ways of approaching certain issues. Maud Khumalo, a Chemical Workers' Industrial Union shop steward at Adcock Ingram told the September Commission workplace restructuring workshop about her uncertainty regarding her union:

> There is no meaningful opposition from our union. The reason why there is no clear challenge is because the union has no policy positions. Management tries to bribe shop stewards and organisers. Organisers try to avoid these issues.

She did add, however, that her union had realised this problem and was preparing a booklet on workplace restructuring for use by shop stewards.

A related problem is the fact that the union movement has lost the strategic initiative to business and the state. The final report of the September Commission (1997) noted how unions often find themselves having to respond to proposals from employers and the state. With regard to co-determination, unions were caught off-guard by the new managerial initiatives, and found themselves unable to provide answers and guidance to their membership in the workplaces. For example, NUMSA shop stewards at a factory in Durban were approached by management regarding the establishment of team work. The shop stewards were not sure how to respond, so they approached the union official to assist, but found that the union official was also unsure about what to do.

The stock responses have been instant rejection or avoidance. (See for example, Buhlungu, 1996.) Similarly, when the government introduced co-determination through the new LRA, unions were forced to respond. Thus, the lack of a clear programme on co-determination has led unions to tend to respond in ad hoc and short-term ways. In 1993, PPWAWU got PG Bison to agree to a union-led research programme before the company could implement its downsizing plans (Bethlehem et al., 1994). What is interesting was that the union's proposal for research was never a well-considered proposal, but a device to buy more time for the union to consult with its membership. A similar process of research was undertaken at Nampak, but these lessons have never been co-ordinated or used to develop a union-wide strategy on participation. In the September Commission report, this kind of ad hoc and reactive unionism is termed 'zig-zag unionism' (1997: 168-169).

Lack of a clear strategic direction on these issues has forced the union movement to adopt defensive approaches and responses. Even where new approaches have been adopted, such as research, unions have failed to follow these through and to use them to develop a programme of servicing co-determination.

The leadership drain made things worse for the unions as a number of experienced unionists have been moving out of the movement. This has left fewer skilled leaders who could steer the movement towards the development of a clearer strategic direction.

It is the lack of strategic clarity and the absence of a political paradigm noted here, rather than co-determination per se, which makes these new initiatives a dangerous game for the union movement. In this confusion, co-determination and worker participation represent different things to different people. These dangers are accentuated by the fact that the parameters of these initiatives are usually set by management, rather than by the union movement itself. In other words, proposals for co-determination often come from management, the pace of the process is dictated by management, and the way it is conceptualised is such that it dovetails with the objectives of the enterprise in the form of productivity and competitiveness.

But this does not have to be so. A union movement with a clear strategic vision, and which is able to communicate that vision to its rank-and-file membership, can reverse this and turn the situation to its advantage.

Financial capacity

Financial self-sufficiency is the backbone of a union's strength. It ensures that a union can rent offices, set up efficient administrative systems, pay its staff reasonable salaries, employ experts where and when required, and train its membership and leadership. While unions cannot compare themselves with large companies and corporations in terms of resources, they have to strive to match them in terms of expertise, efficiency and power. This often implies that unions have to use their limited financial resources to set up and run unconventional, but effective, systems of education and training, administration, research, and so forth.

Although some unions, particularly the smaller ones, still face serious financial constraints, the majority have succeeded in achieving much higher levels of self-sufficiency. This is due, in part, to the shift towards a percentage subscription rate which has boosted union income and is adjusted annually when workers get a wage increase. As a result, many of the larger unions do not have serious financial constraints. But, in the majority of cases, improvements in the financial situation have not necessarily translated into capacity-building activities and initiatives, such as training and employment of union educators and researchers. The bulk of union income still goes towards running expenses and staff salaries and benefits. Those with limited financial resources often find it extremely difficult to engage with co-determination because they cannot run education, employ professional staff, and so forth. The union staff survey cited above revealed that a number of unions now employ staff in support positions (education, legal services, media, health and safety, etc.), but few of these officials are engaged in education and training functions (Buhlungu, 1997). Financial capacity remains an important area for trade unions, particularly because in most of the existing schemes of participation and in the statutory workplace forums, management is not compelled to provide meaningful resources for participation or co-determination structures. This is in stark contrast to the German system where employers are expected to bear training and other costs for building the capacity of the works councils (Rogers and Streeck, 1994).

But financial stability will not necessarily resolve these issues for unions. As noted above, the unions' lack of capacity is a multi-faceted problem which needs a holistic approach to resolve.

Administrative capacity

The lack of efficient administrative systems and professionalism have been discussed by others (see Baskin, 1991; Vavi, 1992). Baskin (1991) argues that lack of professionalism manifests itself at national, regional and local levels of unions.

Information systems are inadequate or non-existent. Efficiency is rarely practised, nor is it valued. At local level, organisers and officials are generally forced to rely on their own resources and inventiveness. Those unions which have tried to address these problems have often resorted to bureaucratic solutions, further disempowering both local officials and the general membership (ibid.: 458).

Although elements of administrative inefficiency exist in all unions, there are variations according to union size and the amount of resources of each union. For example, the smaller unions tend to have more limited resources and therefore cannot build a stable administrative infrastructure. The magnitude of the problem becomes obvious to a researcher who comes to a union to get information. Information gathering for the staff survey revealed that most union officials do not know the number of paid-up members in their branches and regions or in the individual workplaces they organise. This has wider implications for the union, particularly when it comes to the collection of membership subscriptions. The same confusion exists with regard to the number of shop stewards in factories and branches.

Other problems relate to lack of knowledge and poor communication between the various levels of the union. Workplace change means that many union officials and leaders have limited knowledge of production issues and therefore cannot give appropriate advice to their members. National structures often fail to communicate union decisions to the shop floor. These problems have a bearing on the ability of unions to service co-determination in the workplace. However, their effect is an indirect one.

Attempts to build trade union capacity should therefore include attempts to improve administrative systems and information flow, and to beef up education and training which will engender a more professional approach to union work. Not only are these factors important for the normal day-to-day running of the union, but they are prerequisites for engaging management on complex issues on the shop-floor.

SERVICING CO-DETERMINATION: AN ASSESSMENT

In South Africa, many of those who have engaged in debates about co-determination and worker participation have given these terms perjorative connotations and have tended to use them interchangeably with terms such as co-option, social contract and class collaboration. However, there are those who have been too hasty to embrace notions of co-determination and participation without paying attention to their content and the dangers they pose for unions. Both sides of the debate share two major weaknesses:

- They draw an artificial separation between co-determination and the struggle between capital and labour. The argument in this chapter is that attempts to introduce co-determination and worker participation, whether they emanate from management or from workers and unions, are inextricably bound with the struggle between these two forces.
- They fail to deal with the conceptual aspects of the debate. In other words, they do not explain what they mean by co-determination or worker participation. Where an attempt is made to do so, such attempts at conceptualisation ignore placing the debate within its historical context, namely, militant struggles by workers in different countries for workers' control of production. In these struggles, workers' control was not seen as an end in itself, but a means to an end, namely the total transformation of the relations of production.

Following Pateman (1971), this chapter has argued that co-determination or worker participation is essentially about 'the modification of orthodox authority structures', resulting in further limitation on managerial prerogatives. Although the struggle for workers' control is historically a project of the labour movement, there are numerous examples, including South Africa (see Maller, 1992; Buhlungu, 1996), which show that management can pre-empt that struggle by offering limited or pseudo forms of worker participation and co-determination. Ramsay (1985: 60) coined the term 'cycles of control' to demonstrate that management initiatives are introduced to 'head off or restrain the demand for more substantial changes in authority relations'. He further argued that the co-optive power attributed to participation and, we may add, co-determination, is exaggerated because 'had participation enjoyed the success commonly attributed to it, it is hard to see why once employers had discovered it they should ever lose interest in it thereafter' (ibid: 61).

It has been argued here that the best strategy for labour, even in those situations where co-determination is an initiative of management or the state, is to engage in worker participation and to exploit the opportunities offered by the contradictory nature of such initiatives. But such engagement should be consonant with the goals of, and be on terms set by, the labour movement itself. It is in this regard that the issue of capacity becomes critical for the labour movement. It has been shown that COSATU unions lack capacity in a number of areas which affects the way they engage in, or service, co-determination. This lack of capacity often results in an ambivalent attitude to co-determination. On the one hand, the day-to-day struggles in which the workers and unions are engaged are about limiting the prerogatives of management in the workplace. But, on the other hand, there is a fear that management may co-opt workers.

One of the points made by the Australian mission to Western Europe and Scandinavia in 1986 was strategic unionism and the policies it implied require a number of conditions in order to succeed. These conditions were identified as:

- a high degree of union organisation
- a high degree of membership involvement
- a high degree of knowledge, facilities and sophistication
- a high level of resources made available by relatively high membership fees, supplemented by contributions from the general community through government expenditure
- a high level of expenditure on education and research.

Successful strategic unionism .   (Ford and Plowman, 1989: 292-93)

Although the conditions in Australia in the mid-1980s may have been different to conditions in the 1990s, the above requirements are also applicable to South African unions as they begin to confront new practices and institutions in a rapidly changing political and economic environment.

South African trade unions can no longer take it for granted that they will maintain the degree of influence they enjoyed during the era of resistance. While these unions can still draw from their past and current strengths, they also require a much greater degree of organisational, strategic, financial and administrative capacity to retain their influence

(Buhlungu, 2000). Co-determination and tripartism challenge South African trade unions to develop new strategies of organisational rejuvenation. Failure to do this would make the dangers of co-option very real indeed for these unions.

CONCLUSION

It must be pointed out that the union movement is aware of some of these challenges and has started to address some of the shortcomings raised in this discussion. Most unionists today acknowledge that there is a general lack of capacity which threatens to rob unions of their power in society at the workplace. The September Commission Report (1997) has done the most detailed assessment of these problems and has proposed a number of solutions. With regard to the workplace, the Commission recommends what it terms 'strategic engagement' based on a union agenda and union independence (ibid.: 111). It goes further (ibid.: 112) to assert that:

> A union which pursues strategic engagement sees dangers in company restructuring. But is also sees opportunities. Thus it engages in order to defend workers' interests, but it also engages to increase workers' control of production, to gain access to training and skills, to improve wages and conditions, and to improve the quality of working life and democratise the workplace.

Apart from the September Commission, there are other initiatives by trade unions to address these weaknesses. Two such initiatives are the National Labour and Economic Development Institute (NALEDI), a union research body established by COSATU in 1993 to build research capacity for the labour movement, and the Development Institute for Training, Support and Education for Labour (DITSELA). DITSELA is labour training institute set up in 1996 by COSATU and FEDUSA with some financial backing from the Department of Labour.

Individual unions are also undertaking individual capacity-building initiatives in a variety of areas, including those discussed in this chapter. However, it is still too soon to assess the impact of these efforts. But there is no doubt that unions need to continue building their power resources in order to meet the challenges of the transition.

9

WHERE IS MANAGEMENT GOING?

Employer strategies with regard to worker participation and workplace forums

———— ✦ ————

Shane Godfrey, Philip Hirschsohn and Johann Maree

Godfrey, Hirschsohn and Maree assess the perspectives of management and business-linked industrial relations consultants on the development of institutions of engagement. They argue that the development of workplace forums was not a priority for management, in part because unions were themselves ambivalent about them and unlikely to initiate them. More importantly, many firms prefer participatory structures and processes of their own design which they believe are better suited to enabling management to achieve its own – rather than workers' – goals. The authors find that 'worker participation' has become a managerial orthodoxy to deal with the changing political, legal and economic context facing firms, but that there is no fixed definition to this term and there is considerable diversity in approaches. Firms appear to proceed cautiously and incrementally, and are influenced primarily by the particular set of environmental factors that they each face, including the power of their unions. In most cases, managements are letting go of their prerogatives very slowly. They will continue to pursue initiatives in the direction of what they define as greater worker participation, but the form these take will depend on their goals, the structure of the firm and the way the union responds to management initiatives in this direction.

Pick any management textbook from the 1970s or 1980s and it will tell you that the job of management is Ploc: a manager should plan, lead, organise and control. Later it became fashionable to Plonc: a manager should also nurture his or her people. Many authors suggest that the Plonc model is paternalistic, disempowering and inappropriate for today's business challenges. As Tom Peters says, 'Our so-recently tried-and-true management tools are arguably worthless; many are downright dangerous'.

(Terry White, 'Ditch the old plonc, it's time for managers to change', *Sunday Independent Business*, 13 April 1997)

We are still writing books about participation – call it *empowerment* or *self-management* or *employee involvement* or *participative management* – because we are having a very difficult time choosing to put the idea of participation into practice. The *Age of Participation's* contribution to solving this dilemma is that it makes the practice of participation so reasonable, explicit, and concrete that we no longer have an excuse not to implement it.

(Excerpt from the Foreword, McLagan and Nel, *The Age of Participation*, 1995)

Naked Emperors (i.e. senior managers) do not surrender any turf, possession or privilege. They wrap themselves around their hard-won gains like some kind of exotic monkey, prehensile tail and all, refusing to give an inch unless prised off the branch or murdered. They don't prise off easily. We're going to have to kill them. (Excerpt from Alan Weiss, *Our Emperors Have No Clothes* 1995)[1]

INTRODUCTION

Management, it seems, is under attack from all sides. The traditional challenge to managerial prerogative, posed by union demands for the control of firms by workers, has been paralleled (and almost sidelined) in the last decade by a concerted critique of the prevailing management paradigm by exponents of a new approach to management. In numerous books, journals and magazine articles, and in the business pages of newspapers, managers are being exhorted to develop participative organisations in which employees are free to think for themselves, take the initiative, be creative, and even have fun at work. In the new participative organisations, managers will no longer issue instructions and exercise control from above, but will become 'leaders' or 'mentors' or 'stewards' in co-operative decision-making processes; and hierarchical organisations will be replaced by organisational 'communities'.

In South Africa, the government intervened to open up a third front in the attack on managerial prerogative and the hierarchical organisation of decision-making and control. The Labour Relations Act (LRA) of 1995 introduces workplace forums which, if triggered by a representative trade union, compel senior management to consult or jointly decide with worker representatives over a wide range of issues. The intention is 'to expand worker representation beyond the limits of collective bargaining by providing workers with an institutionalised voice in managerial decision-making'. Workplace forums proceed from the idea that management will not have the 'flexibility to adapt the workplace to its unique circumstances unless employees have a voice in designing these adaptations' (Ministry of Labour, 1995: 292).

While contemporary managerial theorists and the team that drafted the LRA of 1995 have approached the question of participation from different directions, their motivations are much the same. In both cases, the reason behind the push for more participation is the belief that employee management must change fundamentally if organisations hope to survive in today's highly competitive and rapidly changing business environment. Whether these approaches satisfy the aspirations of unions and workers for industrial democracy remains to be seen. What also remains to be seen, as indicated in the excerpts that opened this chapter, is the extent to which managers will act in accordance with the dictates of the 'gurus' of the new approach to management and fundamentally change the way that decisions are made and work is organised. In other words, will managers in fact surrender their traditional decision-making prerogatives or will they resist or only pay lip service to the new approach; and, more specifically, how will they respond to the 'threat' of workplace forums?

The challenges confronting managers throw up three important questions for current research in South Africa. First, what strategies are South African managers pursuing with regard to worker participation? Second, what strategies are managers developing with regard to workplace forums, and are these strategies a continuance of existing strategies on worker participation or are they different? Third, what is motivating these strategies and what are the main influences on management's thinking regarding these strategies? In brief, how is the management of employees actually changing in the current context and what is driving these changes?

In this chapter we address these questions in the light of interviews with managers at leading firms throughout the country. We start by briefly discussing our research method and theoretical approaches to management strategies. This is followed by a section dealing, in broad terms, with how management is thinking about participation and workplace forums, and what they identified as the main influences on their thinking. The next section deals with patterns of managerial practice with regard to participation. We then explain the cause of the trends in managerial practice and give a composite example of each of these trends. Finally, in the conclusion, we discuss the implications of these patterns for labour and make recommendations to the labour movement regarding workplace forums.

RESEARCH METHOD

Our research method was to interview managers at leading firms in the major centres (Johannesburg, Durban, Cape Town and Port Elizabeth) and across key sectors of the economy (automobile, automobile components, confectionery and beverages, chemicals, clothing, electronics, engineering, mining, printing and packaging, and textiles). This spread was intended to cover most of the sectors (outside of the public sector) organised by unions affiliated to the Congress of South African Trade Unions (COSATU). We also interviewed a selection of the management consultants in the country and representatives of the larger employers' organisations. In all, 20 managers were interviewed (generally industrial relations or human resources managers but, in some cases, production managers and managing directors). We also conducted interviews at seven prominent consultancies and at four major employers' organisations.

During the interviews at leading firms, we covered the following topics: their policy on employee participation in general and the types of participatory schemes already in place; their broad responses to the model of worker participation introduced in the LRA of 1995; detailed comment on their strategic thinking on important features of the workplace forum model; and the sources of their thinking on participation and workplace forums. Much of this ground was also covered in the interviews with the consultants and the representatives of the employers' organisations but, in these cases, we also examined what they were doing for clients or members with regard to participation and workplace forums, and in what way they were disseminating their ideas.

Fairly early on in our fieldwork, we found that the delay in the promulgation of the new LRA (the fieldwork was conducted from July to October 1996, at which stage it was unclear when the Act would be promulgated), and the fact that the establishment of workplace forums depended on unions (and most managers perceive that unions were not keen on workplace forums), meant that workplace forums were not a priority for managers. Little or no strategic thinking or planning was taking place. An additional factor at some firms was that they already had participatory structures and processes, in various forms, which they believed more or less matched workplace forums. The managers at these firms argued that these structures could quite easily be converted to, or accommodate, workplace forums and it was unnecessary for them to develop strategies in this regard.

These responses meant that much of our interview schedule was not being answered, or was being answered in very broad and rather vague terms. Our focus then shifted to the existing participatory practices and structures in place at firms; the reasons for introducing these; how they were changing and whether this was part of a strategy; and what the sources of management's thinking had been on the types of practices and structures introduced. From this examination, we sought to discover patterns that could indicate implicit management strategies with regard to workplace forums.

STRATEGIC MANAGEMENT AND MANAGEMENT STRATEGIES

Any discussion of management strategies regarding participation must take account of the adoption of the concept of strategy by the business world, and the rapid spread of this concept in management literature (particularly in a study such as this where the focus is on the intellectual influences on management's approach to participation). Importantly, management theorists have not treated strategy as a discrete programme to achieve a particular objective or overcome a specific competitive threat. Rather, strategy has been conceptualised as an overarching plan and method for the management of all aspects of a business. Management literature, therefore, speaks of strategic management rather than management strategising. This section will mainly focus on this specific concept in order to understand the world of ideas within which management is currently practised, particularly with regard to the management of employees.

The section also deals with criticisms of the way the concept of strategic management obscures the reality of much management practice which appears to be mainly short-term and reactive in its thinking. This criticism has given rise to a new conceptualisation of strategic management which emphasises flexibility in the implementation of strategy by management in a rapidly changing and unstable competitive environment. Finally, the section ends by briefly examining the relationship between strategic human resource management (which forms an important component of strategic management) and industrial relations management strategies (which have not been conceptualised as part of strategic management), since these are the key functional areas of management that deal with the issue of worker participation.

The use and spread of the concept of strategy in the business world

The concept of strategy has a long history of military usage. The word 'strategy' is derived from the Greek *strategos*, which literally means the art of the general, and for centuries it was used solely in the context of the control and direction of armies in the conduct of war (Miller, 1987: 347). More recently, the term 'strategy' has been applied to planning and decision-making in the business world. This began shortly after the Second World War and the term was possibly first used in this context by faculty members of the Harvard Business School (ibid.: 347-348). Since then, the business usage of strategy has spread rapidly from its epicentre in the United States, gaining what Knights and Morgan describe as a 'fashionable bandwagon effect' (1995: 194). The meaning of the word has consequently expanded well beyond its military roots and, by 1986, the *Oxford English Dictionary* had added the following to its existing definition of 'strategy':[2]

In (theoretical) circumstances of competition or conflict, as in the theory of games, decision theory, business administration, etc., a plan for successful action based on the rationality and interdependence of the moves of the opposing participants.

(Quoted in Shaw, 1990: 468)

As the popularity of the term has grown, strategy has come to cover such a variety of meanings (as the above definition indicates) that it has been described as 'accordion-like' (Miller, 1987: 347).

It has been argued that the rapid spread of the concept of strategy in the business world is linked to two developments. First, the emergence of business schools and their propagation of managerialist ideologies that justify management techniques on rational and scientific grounds, has provided the foundation for the notion of strategic management. Second, the separation of the ownership of business from direct managerial control has led to the professionalisation of management and its legitimation as a body of neutral experts (or a professional elite) that has the strategic skills to run firms (Knights and Morgan, 1990: 478).

The spread of the concept is also partly related to and sustains another group of experts, namely, the management consultants whose business it is to provide analysis and advice to organisations which perceive themselves as lacking these skills. These consultants have promoted the concept further, not only to their existing and potential clients, but also to 'the wider business community, in particular those who own or through the management of funds (e.g. the financial institutions) control the ownership of companies' (ibid.).

Strategic management, human resource management and world-class manufacturing

The central strand in the development of the concept of strategy in the business world has been the notion of strategic management. Strategic management is a wider concept than management strategy in that it is presented as a way of managing the entire business. It therefore proposes an overarching strategy for business management, rather than a discrete strategy for a particular management function or objective. It is important to note, however, that much of the literature on strategic management is normative and prescriptive rather than analytical, and therefore presents strategic management as something of an ideal type.

The concept of strategic management can be seen as having three essential features. First, it emphasises rationality in management's decision-making. Second, it is situated at the pinnacle of the business, that is, it is the preserve of senior management. Third, the objective of strategic management is to provide an overall plan that *integrates* the many diverse decisions taking place at various levels and in the different functional areas of the organisation. The aim is to co-ordinate all these layers and functional divisions in the firm's interaction with its present and (predicted) future competitive environment, and thereby optimise its ability to achieve its objectives (Knights and Morgan, 1990: 478; and 1995: 194-195).

As the concept of strategic management has developed over the years, increased attention has been focused on the workers within organisations. Rather than being viewed as a necessary cost, the perception is that the firm's employees are a key resource; in fact, they are the resource with the most potential for giving the firm a competitive edge. Strategic management has therefore sought to develop this resource, to release its potential, and to maximise its performance. The result has been the integration of a new management function, human resource management, as one of the main components of strategic management:[3]

> A comprehensive corporate strategy is essential to continuing business success. However in many cases, human resource planning is not an integral part of strategic planning, but rather flows from it. One consequence is a weakening of strategic planning because, by emphasising quantitative dimensions of marketing, finance and production it fails to take account of more complex issues such as values, power and company culture. Implementation of strategic plans therefore becomes much more difficult than anticipated. Human resources must therefore become an integral component of the strategic planning process. Because they are the most variable, and the least easy to understand and control of all management resources, effective utilisation of human resources is likely to give organisations a significant competitive advantage. The human resource dimension must

therefore be fully integrated into the strategic planning process.

(Guest, 1987)

Much of the literature on human resource management has therefore added the word 'strategic' to the term.

Although the term human resource management is now very widely used, it remains somewhat vaguely defined. Generally it is seen as a managerial function that is qualitatively distinct from its personnel management antecedents (Guest, 1987: 507-508). It is also characterised, as we have noted above, by a strategic approach to the management of employees and integrates this function with the general management of a business (Boxall and Dowling, 1990: 197-200). In addition, human resource management advocates that employees be viewed as investments rather than as costs:

> When an organisation views its present and future employees as resources rather than purchased services, then it has begun a process of human resource development. Employees are thus considered as investments – investments which yield varying results depending on how the investment is treated. Human resources management represents a change in attitude on the part of management towards the workforce, a move away from seeing employees as a necessary expense of doing business to a critical investment in the organisation's current performance and future growth.
>
> (Ross, in Boxall and Dowling, 1990: 197)

Another approach to defining human resource management has been to look at its goals. Guest argues that the major dimensions of human resource management are best illustrated by its four main goals of integration, employee commitment, flexibility/adaptability and quality. The goal of integration has a number of components: first, the integration of human resource management into the overall strategy of a business, that is, the integration of the human resource management function with the financial, marketing and production management functions. Second, the vertical integration of strategic, business unit and operational level decision-making, so that they complement rather than oppose one another.[4]

The third aspect of integration is to get line managers to understand and practise the human resource management policies. The last component proposes that each and every employee should be integrated into the business and have an identity of interest with the goals of the business (Guest, 1987: 512-513).

The goal of employee commitment requires that human resource management must 'develop in individual employees a feeling of commitment to the organisation' (Guest, 1987: 513-514). This will result 'not only in more loyalty and better performance for the organisation, but also in self-worth, dignity, psychological involvement, and identity for the individual' (Beer et al. in Guest, 1987: 514). The goal of flexibility / adaptability has two parts. Adaptability refers to the organisation's ability to respond quickly to competitive pressures, and flexibility refers to a multi-skilled workforce that is willing to move freely between tasks. Finally, the goal of quality refers to the quality of staff and appropriate policies for the recruitment, development and retention of staff, as well as to the quality of performance and the setting and maintaining of high standards.

The influence of the strategic management concept, as well as strategic human resource management, can be clearly seen in a new approach to management known as world-class manufacturing (WCM). Although WCM is primarily a production strategy, it is characterised by the integration of a set of innovative production techniques with a grouping of key human resource management practices that defines a new competitive strategy for the entire firm. The main components of WCM (MacDuffie, 1995a, 1996b) are:

- the use of just-in-time inventory systems and other buffer minimisation techniques that demand smooth production flow and that integrate the activities of firms with suppliers
- quick set-up times to reduce down-time during changeovers, thereby enabling shorter production runs
- the use of work teams and the flexible deployment of multi-skilled workers, coupled with extensive training to make this possible
- off-line problem-solving groups which involve workers in continuous improvement processes.

WCM is therefore a management approach that aims at improving the performance of firms for competition in global markets on the basis of developing a strong commitment to product quality and customer service, flexible production methods, and highly trained, multi-skilled workers (Saban, 1997: 17).

Theoretical approaches to the concept of management strategy

As noted above, much of the literature on strategic management has been normative and prescriptive, emphasising in an ideal way the long-term planning aspect of the concept. This emphasis on an explicit long-term plan was particularly evident in the early approaches to theorising about strategy in the business world. Chandler, for example, stated that 'strategy is the determination of the basic long-term goals of an enterprise, and the adoption of courses of action and the allocation of resources necessary for carrying out these goals' (in Storey and Sisson, 1993: 69). However, the normative nature of much of the early literature on strategy tended to overemphasise the rationality of management decision-making and obscure the fact that managers seldom develop long-term strategic plans and, where they do, they are seldom able to implement them as originally conceived.

Recent theorists of management strategy have argued that the 'rationalistic' models of strategy should be replaced with 'processual' or 'incremental' models that more closely reflect the reality of management decision-making, and which emphasise the implementation rather than the planning of strategies. Quinn, Mintzberg and Pettigrew suggest that strategy as a concept is more complex than a notion of rational planning suggests; a strategy should rather be seen as emerging as a series of steps which 'are influenced by the social and political routines of organisational life' (cited in Storey and Sisson, 1993: 69). Mintzberg has gone further to argue that a strategy is 'a pattern in a stream of decisions' and distinguishes between 'intended' strategies and 'realised' or 'enacted' strategies, which only emerge when a series of decisions are viewed retrospectively (ibid.; Mintzberg, 1989: 27-28 see also Mintzberg, 1978, 1987, 1988; Pettigrew, 1977; and Quinn, 1980).

These latter theorists of management strategy endorse a pluralistic view of organisations, which emphasises the political nature of decision-making within organisations. This approach 'interprets organisations as political entities, with political goals, political decisions and political people' and strategies are seen as 'products of complex political processes'

(Ahlstrand, 1990: 22). Such an approach excludes the notion of strategy as rational planning. Rather, decisions in organisations 'are made through processes of negotiation, compromise, and bargaining and coalition formation', which partially explains their incremental development over time (Zey, 1992: 24). Another important factor that accounts for a more pragmatic approach to explaining strategy is the fluidity of the business environment which requires far more short-term flexibility in management decision-making, although within the framework of an overarching strategic direction.

This more analytical approach to the concept of strategic management is important since it indicates that, despite the intellectual influences on management to manage strategically and integrate functional areas of management and levels of decision-making, it is likely that, in practice, management proceeds in a more piecemeal and incremental fashion. This would be true of general management and a particular functional area of management, such as human resource management. It is probable, therefore, that management would proceed cautiously in looking to increase participation in firms (as much modern management literature exhorts managers to do), testing the process each step of the way. It is also likely that such initiatives would not be integrated into an overall plan, and could be the preserve of one functional area of management acting relatively autonomously from the others.

Human resource management and industrial relations management strategies

While human resource management has been easily integrated into the concept of strategic management, industrial relations management has been largely ignored. Implicit in most of the strategic management and human resource management literature is the assumption of a non-union environment (which largely reflects the situation in the United States where much of the literature has been generated). The consequence has been that industrial relations management is not conceptualised as part of the integrated strategic management approach and, in terms of this approach, 'trade unions are unnecessary or at best marginal' (Guest, 1987: 519). Similarly, in much of the literature on industrial relations management, strategies developed by managers with regard to the collective organisation of workers are seldom seen as part of a broader business strategy. They are usually presented as relatively discrete sets of decisions being taken within a specialised management function, often dealing with the consequences of business decisions where these impact on organised workers, rather than being part of a proactive management plan.

Conceptually, human resource management clashes with industrial relations management in that it has a unitarist, individualistic focus, whereas industrial relations tends to have a pluralist, collective focus. In some cases, particularly in the United States, a strand of human resource management has emerged which seeks 'to prevent unionisation through anticipating and providing for employee needs (such as equity in pay, meaningful work and employment security) more effectively than unions' (Boxall and Dowling, 1990: 205). But, a number of writers have noted that, human resource management and industrial relations management can co-exist both conceptually and in practice. In well-organised firms, the two approaches can be mutually dependent, for example, individualised processes – such as team briefings and quality circles – are unlikely to be implemented without the backing of the trade union (Sisson and Sullivan, 1987: 430; Boxall and Dowling, 1990: 196). Furthermore, one can argue that the two approaches could also be mutually supporting and enhancing, with both individualistic and collective aspects of employee management being optimised in a synergistic way. Of course, this would depend on the union's ability to guard against collectivist structures and engagement being undermined.

The relationship between human resource and industrial relations management is particularly important when considering management approaches to worker participation. This can be seen as lying somewhere between the traditional concerns of human resource management (with its focus on individualised participation in problem-solving) and industrial relations management (with its focus on collective bargaining over distributive issues). Two quite distinct approaches could therefore emerge in practice with regard to participation, according to the nature of the firm's management structure (i.e. whether it has a human resources manager or an industrial relations manager) and the level of worker organisation. On the one hand, human resource management would emphasise individual participation that improved job satisfaction and employee commitment, with the aim of improving the quality of worker performance. On the other hand, industrial relations management would focus on collective engagement, with the main aim of reducing adversarialism in the workplace. Furthermore, depending on how 'strategically' the firm is being managed, these two approaches could be linked to a greater or lesser extent with other functional areas of management, particularly with an integrated production strategy, such as a world-class manufacturing strategy, which could significantly influence the nature of participation.

In South Africa, one would expect industrial relations management to play a more prominent role with regard to the issue of worker participation than much of the strategic management literature (with its exclusive focus on human resource management in non-unionised environments) would suggest. The reason for this is obvious: the rapid growth of unions of black workers and their aggressive pursuit of worker rights and interests has made industrial relations management an essential part of the management teams of most medium to large firms. But the nature of the sorts of strategies being generated by these different management influences, whether they are part of a longer-term plan or develop incrementally, and the extent to which they are integrated with one another, can only be determined through empirical investigation. It is on these questions that the remaining sections of the chapter focus.

MANAGERS' STRATEGIC THINKING ON WORKER PARTICIPATION AND WORKPLACE FORUMS

The interviews with South African managers showed them generally to be in favour of the concept of worker participation. This revealed the influence of the strategic human resource management approach, as well as of the more popular management literature that calls for greater participation by employees in decision-making in firms. Evidence of the pervasiveness of the new managerial approach to the management of employees was the fact that managers were either unable to identify the specific source of their thinking on introducing participation in decision-making, or pointed to a diverse mix of sources.

In one case, a manager stated simply that their sources 'were all around, it's [sic] everywhere you look'. In a number of other cases, managers argued that they were influenced by the fact that this was 'the way things were going'. Other more concrete influences included new ideas brought into the firm by a new managing director or chief executive officer, the influence of a parent company, the examination of overseas models of co-determination, and programmes introduced by different consultants. In many cases, no one source was predominant and sources often appeared to have had a limited individual influence. In other cases, managers acknowledged various influences but stressed that they were following a trial-and-error approach to develop their own firm-specific model of participation. The fact that there was general consensus by managers on the need to move in the direction of increased worker participation, as well as the influence of such a wide set of sources for this approach, suggests that worker participation is becoming something of a broad managerial orthodoxy.

Environmental factors also played an important part in influencing managers to adopt more participatory management styles. These factors were:

• political transition and the realisation by managers that firms must stay abreast of the democratisation processes taking place in the broader society

• the liberalisation of trade taking place throughout the world and the threats that this posed to the survival of companies

• changes in markets and technology that were forcing firms to become more flexible, versatile and dynamic, and the need for workers to be multi-skilled and committed to the goals of the firm in order to do so.

An additional, more recent influence was the Labour Relations Act of 1995, which gave statutory recognition to the preceding two forces and the need to shift industrial relations away from adversarialism to greater co-operation.[5]

As evidence of the support for increased participation, the majority of firms were already implementing some form of worker participation. However, in many cases the introduction of participatory schemes did not appear to be part of an explicit strategy, but were rather ad hoc initiatives. Furthermore, there was considerable diversity in the approaches of firms and in the degree and level of participation that had been initiated. Firms also differed considerably as to when they had started participatory schemes. In some cases they had only just launched schemes, often focusing on fairly limited forms of participation at the operational level, whereas other firms had well-established and extensive participatory structures in place.

The lack of clear strategies and the diversity of participatory approaches point to the fact that, although there is a broad trend towards increased worker participation, no single path or technique or scheme is pre-dominant. In the main, firms appear to proceed cautiously and incrementally, each influenced primarily by the particular set of environmental factors that they face (including the industrial relations situation at the firm). Furthermore, while managers might often be influenced by certain models and what they have seen at other firms, they tend not to adopt these models wholesale, preferring to develop their own in-house schemes that they believe best suit the needs of their firm.

The general support by managers for increased participation extended in most cases to a positive view of workplace forums. Only one firm was opposed to workplace forums. This firm was in favour of employee participation, but saw a workplace forum as representing 'trade union participation'. Two other firms, although not opposed to workplace forums, were somewhat lukewarm about them, envisaging various problems with their establishment.

As mentioned above in the discussion on the research method, little strategic thinking appeared to be taking place on workplace forums. In many cases, managers contended that a workplace forum could only be triggered by the union and that, until they heard from the union, there was little point in spending time developing a detailed position on such a forum, especially since the unions seemed opposed to these structures. Furthermore, if the union wanted to set up a forum, management would seek to establish it through negotiation and, until they heard the union's proposals, it would be a waste of time developing a blueprint of their own.

Only two features of the workplace forum model were of serious concern to some managers (although this was not the case for the majority). The first concern was the role of the Commission for Conciliation, Mediation and Arbitration (CCMA), which was an unknown factor at the time of the interviews, and whether it would have the capacity to fulfil its role effectively.[6]

In some cases, managers stated that they would seek to reach agreement with the union (if a forum was established) to have disputes referred to an outside agency (the Independent Mediation Service of South Africa was often their choice).[7]

The second concern was the provision for disclosure of information. In one case this was seen as problematic because the firm was privately owned. In a few other cases, it was seen as potentially intrusive or as vaguely defined and therefore a probable cause of disputes. No specific strategies to address this concern, however, were mentioned by managers.

The consultants and representatives of employers' organisations that were interviewed were all in favour of workplace forums, but none could be seen as having developed specific strategies for management with regard to them. Rather, their major focus was on offering training or legal advice on the establishment of forums. Andrew Levy & Associates had run widely publicised training seminars on workplace forums that focused on explaining the provisions in Chapter 5 of the LRA. This training neither promoted workplace forums nor suggested ways of avoiding them. The Labour Law Group also ran training seminars, as well as addressing individual companies on forums. This consultancy was more actively promoting the establishment of workplace forums and had developed a quite sophisticated programme for preparing firms for forums and for establishing forums. However, it viewed the union as crucial to this process and saw the establishment of the forum as taking place in partnership with the relevant union. It therefore focused on the process, rather than advocated particular types of forums that would suit firms rather than unions. Both Andrew Levy & Associates and the Labour Law Group had developed training manuals on workplace forums.

The other consultancies were not doing training on workplace forums nor were specifically promoting workplace forums. These consultancies tended to operate in a one-to-one relationship with a client and most were focused on their existing organisational development programmes at their client firms, and were not going out of their way to deal with the question of workplace forums.

The employers' organisations had also not developed explicit strategies with regard to workplace forums. The Steel and Engineering Industries Federation of South Africa (SEIFSA) had run training courses for members (along the lines of the Andrew Levy courses) and had produced a training manual on workplace forums that was generally positive about their establishment. However, this did not advocate any particular workplace forum model or way of establishing a forum. The general approach of employers' organisations was that they would assist a member with advice where a workplace forum was being established. In addition, SEIFSA and the Natal Clothing Manufacturers' Association suggested that they would be open to discussing workplace forums at bargaining council level with a view to establishing a framework agreement for their establishment at firms.

FUNCTIONAL DIVISIONS IN MANAGEMENT AND THEIR PATTERNING OF APPROACHES TO WORKER PARTICIPATION

To summarise, our research has revealed that there was a broad trend in favour of worker participation amongst the managers interviewed, but they did not identify any dominant influences that were promoting particular strategic approaches to participation. Rather, most firms operated in a firm-specific and incremental way on the issue which appeared to be the way they were approaching the prospect of workplace forums. However, an examination of the various schemes that had been introduced showed there were certain patterns in the approaches being adopted by management. The initial pattern that emerged was a tendency for there to be either an emphasis on structures for participation (what we have named the structural approach) or on processes for employee involvement (what we describe as the process approach).

The structural approach tended to emerge in firms where there were powerful unions present with strong shop-floor organisation. In such cases management, in attempting to make changes to respond to environmental pressures, had to engage the union at the collective level to set up structures within which the participation process could take place. The structural approach, therefore, was characterised by largely representative participation, and governed by collective agreements that entrenched structures with clear rights to decision-making over a range of issues. In its most developed form, such structures were situated at a number of levels (for example, the operational, business unit and strategic levels of decision-making).

The process approach saw performance improvement in response to environmental pressures as an ongoing process that utilised a variety of structures at the operational level to increase employee involvement and commitment. Although there were structures for participation, the requirement of performance improvement was dominant and the structures that had been developed were being utilised primarily to advance performance improvement. The process approach, therefore, was characterised by employee participation that was largely individual and direct, through structures that tended to be situated at the operational level. Where there were higher-level structures, these tended to be of the steering committee type which sought to monitor and facilitate the process rather than to firmly entrench worker rights to decision-making.

It is important to note that the process approach did not appear to be directed at marginalising or avoiding unions – the unions were brought on board – but management were the initiators of, and retained more control over, the process of performance improvement and the way in which workers were involved in this process. In cases representative of the process approach, one could therefore interpret participation as being the result of a participative management approach rather than reflecting a more firmly entrenched involvement by workers in decision-making.

We then noted that, to a certain extent, one could link the structuralist approach to those firms which saw participation primarily in industrial relations terms. That is, it was part of an industrial relations strategy in the face of strong and active trade unions and sought to overcome or significantly reduce adversarialism. The process approach however, was more closely related to firms that emphasised the human resource development aspects of participation, that is, participation was seen as a way of improving employee commitment and performance as an important part of the process of improving the firm's competitive performance. It also appeared that both the structural approach, with its industrial relations orientation, and the process approach, with its human resource development orientation, were integrated – to a greater or lesser extent which varied from firm to firm – with the production strategy of the firm.

Our research therefore confirms the points made in the theoretical section above regarding the influence that the human resource and industrial relations management functions can have on the nature of the process initiated at firms. Our interviews with managers showed that the way in which participatory structures and processes had developed at the firms surveyed was largely determined by the functional areas of management that were given primary responsibility for this programme (i.e. human resource management and industrial relations management), and by the degree of integration between these functional areas and the production management function. These functional areas of management, in turn, were emphasising and putting into practice the ideas being generated in that particular field in their approach to participation, namely, industrial relations-oriented ideas of 'co-determinist' structures, and human resource development-oriented ideas of 'individualised' participation processes. Both these sets of ideas were linked to a greater or lesser extent with production-oriented world-class manufacturing (WCM) strategies. So each of the functional areas of management were channelling particular management ideas into the approach being adopted to participation.

In the absence of clear and explicit management strategies for worker participation, the patterns that emerged indicated a linkage between the strategic thinking being disseminated in the latest management literature and the functional areas of management involved in driving the process of organisational change in response to the intensifying pressures of global competition facing South African industry. However, these linkages were seldom overcome by managers adopting an integrated approach to management. Therefore, in most cases, implicit strategies on worker participation were not part of a comprehensive manufacturing strategy, and the patterns that emerged tended to underline a specialisation of management functions rather than an integrated managerial approach.

Before dealing with the particular clusters of firms that showed the influence of the three functional areas of management, we briefly outline the major features of each of these management functions and the way they represent particular streams of management ideas. These will be presented as ideal types.

The *first stream* of management ideas is strongly influenced by the need to come to terms with an assertive union which has the shop-floor power to ensure that management involves worker representatives in co-determination structures on an on going basis. Industrial relations management is strongly developed and adopts a pluralist frame of reference which recognises the inherent differences between management and labour, but seeks to shift their adversarial relationship towards greater co-operation. Fully-developed co-determinist structures involve shop stewards and other worker representatives, rather than individual workers, on an ongoing basis in decision-making from the shop-floor level, through operational management to strategic planning and governance at board level.

The *second stream* of influences on management approaches to participation originates from the ideas professionalised in the human resource development function. Micro-participation initiatives include a broad range of individualistic or team-based techniques, such as green areas, quality circles, total quality management, team-based work organisation and so-called autonomous workgroups which aim, in varying degrees, to ensure that operators are more directly involved in and responsible for the decisions that affect their immediate task environment. These principles may be closely tied to the introduction of a WCM strategy which requires that operators have multiple skills, can be flexibly deployed according to need, and are an integral part of the need to continually improve production efficiencies.

The *third stream* of influences flows from a focus on WCM. It is predominantly a production-driven response to competitive consumer market pressures that demand a move away from mass production methods to a more flexible, specialised production strategy. The shift towards WCM in South Africa is typically driven by the need to move from producing a very wide product range of standard goods for the local market, to producing more specialised and changing product ranges for both domestic and international markets. As noted above, the WCM concept refers in practice to a broad range of production strategies which aim at enhancing the flexibility, quality and efficiency of a firm by introducing production concepts, such as just-in-time materials management and continuous improvement. These techniques are often coupled with strategies to upgrade worker skills and integrate the conception and execution of production tasks.

It should be stressed that elements of all three streams of management thinking and practice are present in all firms, to a greater or lesser degree. The emergence of a number of distinct patterns suggests that, within firms, different aspects are emphasised as managers attempt to move away from their traditional approach to management. From our discussions with managers in South African firms, we identified five distinct clusters of managerial approaches to participation strategies. These reveal differing combinations of the influences of (a) industrial relations management-oriented co-determination structures; (b) human resource development-oriented individualised participation processes; and, where these were integrated with one another, (c) the influence of WCM production strategies. We have named these clusters of firms: Traditional; Participative Structures; Co-determination; Participative Processes; WCM/Partnership. We describe their relationship graphically in Figure 9.1 (each firm is identified by *F* and a number, and each consultancy by *C* and a number).

In the section that follows, we provide composite examples to illustrate the characteristics of each cluster.

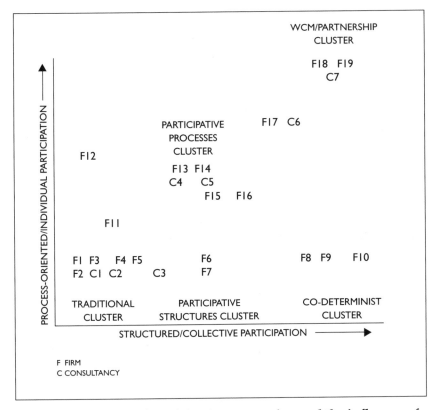

Figure 9.1 Patterns of participative approaches and the influence of different functional areas of management

This seeks to explain graphically the relationship between the sorts of participatory practices that have emerged at firms, and the major influences on these practices emanating from the world of management thinking. The vertical and horizontal axes indicate the structural and process pattern that first emerged, which can be seen as the major trends that participation takes which firms tended to follow. When one includes the three key influences emerging from the functional areas of management (i.e. the human resource development influence, the industrial relations influence, and the WCM influence) – two of which align closely with the structural and process axes, and the last of which introduces a third dimension – the clusters that appeared (which represent different emphases of these influences) can be explained. These clusters are discussed below.

We found that a relatively large number of manufacturing firms have made only moderate moves from the Traditional organisational pattern. In many firms, the Traditional pattern persisted as management reacted hesitantly to environmental change or had yet to be confronted with a fundamental challenge to its way of doing business. In many cases, management perceived that its relationship with the union was not particularly antagonistic and, as a result, did not seem to place a high priority on the need to transform its approach to industrial relations. The production process still largely conformed to Fordist methods, although some pilot initiatives had been undertaken at some of these firms to reorganise workers into teams.

Worker participation was not actively encouraged at the firms in the Traditional cluster and, where green areas had been introduced, they were primarily used for information-sharing, with limited opportunities for communication up the hierarchy. The monthly meetings between shop stewards and management were typically limited to terms and conditions of employment and, on many of these issues, management consulted rather than negotiated. In some cases, senior management was taking hesitant steps towards sharing information on company operational (but not financial) performance with shop stewards on a quarterly basis.

There were two consultancies in the Traditional cluster and one that had moved marginally along the horizontal axis towards the Participative Structures cluster. These consultancies offered standard industrial relations services to firms, with an emphasis on negotiation and dispute resolution, as well as training on various aspects of the LRA. They had little or no involvement with worker participation and, only with the introduction of the new Act, were some of these consultancies starting to address this issue through training and advice on workplace forums.

The evolution away from the Traditional pattern towards more Participative Structures was found in larger plants in the engineering and automotive sectors where the industrial relations function has traditionally played an important role. These industries are facing increasing challenges from international competition as tariffs are lowered, and there is a growing need to shift production to longer runs and to target export niche markets. In most cases, the firms have already embarked on significant restructuring exercises and are showing the benefits of improved performance, but the need to continue to improve remains a priority. However, these firms have not yet adopted a fully-fledged WCM strategy in their pursuit of performance improvement.

In the Participative Structures cluster, firms have developed sound relations with the relevant trade unions and participation follows a more structured and representative route, with management keen to extend the depth and breadth of participation. At one firm, management was taking the initiative to extend the range of issues that are negotiated by the existing participative structure and had tabled proposals in this regard to the union. These proposals were under discussion at the time of the interview. Management's desire to extend the scope of this joint decision-making structure resulted from some of its difficulties with earlier attempts to introduce work organisation changes unilaterally in a top-down approach. This reflects the ability of the union to resist such unilateral initiatives.

This does not mean, however, that firms in this cluster do not have more individualised forms of participation at the operational level. Green areas were present at one firm and work teams were present at another. The work teams had been introduced by management without worker consultation as part of a management initiative to prepare the workforce for an export drive. Depending on line management in a particular area, team leaders, who were hourly paid, had either been appointed or elected by team members. Furthermore, management had not introduced team leaders as part of an initiative to increase worker control and team leaders were not integrated into any worker representative structures.

The Co-determinist cluster consisted of firms facing similar sorts of competitive pressures as those in the Participative Structures cluster. These firms had also engaged in significant restructuring and their production strategies were moving more in the direction of WCM. However, the defining feature of this cluster was the highly structured nature of participation and its foundation in very strong and creative trade union organisation. Participation was rooted in collective agreements and the union was involved in decision-making at all levels of the firm, including the board level. There was also extensive information disclosure. Industrial relations management at these firms was primarily (though not exclusively) responsible for designing and negotiating the participative structures. The attitude of managers in this cluster was one of high commitment to the partnership with unions and to the development of competitive strategies based on the foundation of co-determinist structures.

In moving away from the Traditional pattern, we also observed firms that appeared to be on a fundamentally different path. This is suggested by firms that were pursuing a pattern that emphasised participative processes rather than participative structures. These firms were also facing pressures of international competition, but tended to have somewhat uncertain industrial relations environments. In certain cases the unions, while representative, were not particularly strong (union rivalry was a feature at some of these firms), and management-union relations were poor to average.

Management had introduced a variety of schemes to involve employees more at the operational level, seeking their commitment to the goals of the firm. They also emphasised the need to lay a proper foundation for effective participation, which was preceded by training and capacity building. Participation was seen, therefore, as part of an ongoing process to develop employees and improve their ability to contribute to the performance of the firm. This was part of a move towards more flexible production methods and the pursuit of international best practice in their manufacturing strategy. The human resource development function emerged as particularly strong in this cluster.

The outlier to the left of this cluster (F12) showed the most extreme form of a human resource development-driven approach to participation. In this case, management was seeking to exclude the union from participatory structures and, at that time, was intent on involving only management and supervisors in participatory processes. Workers were organised in teams, but there was no scope for representative participation.

The two consultancies in the Participative Processes cluster emphasised that their approach was to work with unions at firms, but they tended to be management-oriented and followed a top-down format to participation that emphasised information-sharing, but little or no participation by workers beyond individualised involvement at the operational level. These firms retained some traditional industrial relations services, but had widened their scope to include organisational development. It was the latter focus that had led to their involvement in assisting firms with participative schemes and processes.

Only two firms made up the remaining cluster. This cluster revealed the integration of industrial relations and human resource management functions in the management of employees, with a clear direction being given by the WCM production strategy. These firms displayed the best of both the human resource development-oriented approaches (ongoing investment in human resource development and training, and participation at the operational level), and the industrial relations management-oriented approaches (highly structured participation at all levels of the firm and a commitment by management to working in partnership with the union). These approaches were integrated with a production strategy that emphasised a team-based, multi-skilled workforce.

However, the firms in this cluster were different in a number of respects. One was a world player with major penetration into export markets. It was not therefore pursuing international competitiveness in a survivalist fashion, but was rather seeing it as a way of expanding and growing. Its competitive strategy had evolved over time and had various sources. The other firm was much smaller, and was focused on a relatively specialised section of the domestic market. The main source of its approach to participation had been a head office initiative launched a number of years before, primarily (it appeared) driven by an individual manager. This firm had been under new ownership for a few years, but had continued with the same approach, although it seemed that certain problems were emerging under the new owners because of their lack of understanding of, and commitment to, the participative processes and structures that had been developed.

The two consultancies close to or in this cluster were strongly oriented towards organisational development, and worked closely and over a long period of time with client firms. These clients were major firms that tended to be at the forefront of the drive to build more participative, efficient and competitive organisations. At these firms, the consultancies had facilitated the introduction of comprehensive, multi-layered participatory structures and had changed the organisation of work to utilise labour and technology more efficiently. They worked very closely with the union at every step in this process. Furthermore, at one firm, the entire process was underpinned by a collective 'workplace change' agreement with the union that sought to address any fears that the union might have regarding the implications of the process. For example, such agreements provided that no retrenchments could flow from work reorganisation. In addition, these consultancies placed great emphasis on training both management and workers for participation. Thus, they sought to build capacity within the firm to drive its own continued participatory evolution.

The clusters reveal that, although management is under the influence of the ideas and trends that advocate greater participation, they are in most cases letting go of managerial prerogatives very slowly. Where there are no strong unions present, the human resource development influence was predominant and the firms were adopting limited forms of participation at the operational level that emphasised individual involvement in decision-making in the performance of work. In only a few cases had firms, under the threat of international competition and with a history of strong union organisation, surrendered significant managerial prerogatives in favour of extensive forms of consultation and negotiation of business decisions with workers and unions. In even fewer cases had this partnership with workers and unions been integrated into their WCM strategy in a way that sought to draw on the best aspects of these streams of ideas to achieve international competitiveness.

CONCLUSION: OPTIONS FOR LABOUR

Much of the management literature on strategic management appears to have only a limited impact on management's thinking.[8] In most cases, managers appear to be influenced in a general way by this literature but, in practice, they adopt an incremental approach to management that often shows little evidence of an integrated, overarching strategy for the management of the firm. This is particularly evident in the case of human resource management and industrial relations management, which often appear to be seen as discrete management functions that are only loosely co-ordinated with other areas of management.

The lack of integration is particularly evident when one considers management's approach to worker participation which tends to fall somewhere between the specialist areas of human resource management and industrial relations management, and which should also involve production management to an important degree. Our research shows that many managers have been influenced by the new approach to management being propagated in modern management literature, which draws heavily on the concept of strategic human resource management and, consequently, are broadly accepting the need for greater worker participation in firms. But in South Africa, unlike the United States where much of the management literature (and particularly the strategic human resources literature) is being generated, the union movement is strong and militant. This has led to a cautious and circumspect approach by managers and a more important role for industrial relations managers in moves to establish participatory structures or processes.

There are two important conclusions to note:

- Management will continue to pursue initiatives in the direction of greater worker participation, but the form these take will depend, in the main, on the way management is structured at the firm and the way the union responds to management's initiatives in this direction.
- It is also likely that management will continue to follow a pragmatic, step-by-step approach to the introduction of participative structures and processes at firms.

These findings are important for trade unions that are developing their own strategic approach to worker participation and, more specifically, workplace forums.[9]

First, the research shows that management is generally in favour of increased worker involvement or participation in decision-making and is likely to continue with initiatives in this direction. However, as discussed above, different managements view participation in different ways and are adopting a wide variety of approaches to participation, both in terms of the structures for participation and the content of participation. It is therefore essential that trade unions should develop a comprehensive and all-encompassing strategy on worker participation (including workplace forums). A strategy that focuses narrowly on workplace forums (for example, that workplace forums will not be 'triggered') will not address the many other processes through which workers, to a greater or lesser extent, are being drawn into forms of co-operative decision-making (particularly those deriving from the human resource development influence). This means that unions first need to define what they see as worker participation, in terms of both structures and content, outside of their traditional forms of engagement with management. Then they need to develop a broad strategy that encompasses this definition (and which includes workplace forums).

Once worker participation is defined by the union, a number of strategic options present themselves. First, unions can reject all forms of worker participation and call for members to withdraw from any existing processes or structures that fit the definition. This eliminates the dangers to unions posed by participation, but also blocks any gains that could be made and runs the risk of alienating members who see participation as advantageous for workers. It might also be difficult for unions to enforce such a ban on participation in workplaces where workers believe they have made gains by engaging in a participatory structure.

Second, unions can ignore the issue of participation and focus their attention exclusively on the traditional forms of engagement with management, that is, through shop steward committees and collective bargaining structures. Such an approach means that unions ignore the potential gains that they could make through participation, while not countering any of the dangers that participation poses for collective organisation. It effectively means that unions leave the way entirely open to management and passively allow the current human resource management discourse on participation to dominate in the workplace. We submit that such a strategy (or absence of strategy) carries the greatest risks for the union movement.

Third, unions can decide to accept worker participation in principle and engage in a defined range of structures or participatory processes. However, this raises the problems of which structures or processes they participate in, and how the union manages this engagement if it is taking place at many firms with different firm-specific emphases. One option in such a case would be for unions to choose a single vehicle for participation that can be relatively standardised, and through which all participatory processes can be channelled, screened and monitored. This would allow unions to retain some sort of control over the many participatory approaches being presented by management.

It will also allow unions to develop consistent approaches to servicing such a structure and training members to participate in it. A workplace forum is an obvious and appropriate candidate for such a participatory vehicle. It is a statutory-based model of participation with a set of rights and powers encapsulated in a constitution that (although it can be varied extensively by collective agreement) could provide a relatively standardised benchmark for participation.

Furthermore, the range of issues over which the LRA provides that consultation with a workplace forum must take place (particularly changes in the organisation of work and restructuring of the workplace, including the introduction of new technology and work methods) would include most if not all of the types of Participative Processes identified in this study. However, while consultation with a workplace forum would be a collective affair, most of management's participative processes tend to emphasise individualised participation at the operational level. With a workplace forum in place, the introduction of all such processes would first have to be approved by the forum. This would allow the trade union to keep some control over these diverse management initiatives that have the potential to undermine more structured and genuine forms of participation.

The advent of workplace forums gives unions the means to take the initiative away from management and take the strategic high ground on the issue of participation. Although management generally initiates participation, it does not have clear strategies and is proceeding in an incremental way. So it appears that there is considerable 'space' for unions to make moves of their own and secure rights in decision-making. Unions could therefore drive the participatory processes at firms through the vehicle of workplace forums. And the strong rights-based nature of workplace forums should protect unions and members from being undermined by management initiatives.

Where unions are not representative at a firm and therefore cannot trigger a workplace forum, it is suggested that they could aim for a non-statutory structure which closely resembles a forum. As long as a certain minimum set of requirements are met that will secure workers' rights in decision-making over the types of issues that workplace forums deal with, the structure will provide the sort of base that a union can use to push for a statutory forum. Similarly, if there is a structure in place at a firm which exceeds the requirements provided by the workplace forum model, then this can be left as it is or can be converted to a workplace forum of a particular type to secure the protection of the statutory rights. The important point in the above cases is that unions assess the circumstances in each workplace strategically and make a choice as to the most appropriate participatory structure, with the workplace forum model providing a benchmark.

A further point that unions should note is that it appears from the research that the WCM/Partnership cluster provides a combination that could benefit labour in most respects. It has the potential to create the conditions for the development of an internationally competitive enterprise which is founded on a team-based, multi-skilled workforce, with ongoing extensive investment in human resource development and training, governed through a highly structured partnership between management and organised labour. This represents the integration of a world-class production strategy, and progressive human resource development and industrial relations strategies. It is suggested that a workplace forum attempt to structure its engagement with management in such a way that these three main functional areas of management are represented in the senior management delegation that meets the forum. This will allow for a co-ordination of these functional areas in the deliberations with the forum which will drive participation at the firm along the WCM/Partnership route, and will guard against the overemphasis on the side of management of any one functional area to the possible detriment of labour. In effect, the union would be forcing management through its engagement with the workplace forum to develop an integrated competitive strategy founded on co-determination.

Finally, it goes without saying that if unions do decide to engage with management in certain participatory structures, they should do so from a position of strength. Participation is always open to manipulation and needs to be protected by a strong and active trade union.

Furthermore, participation is unlikely to be meaningful where the union is poorly organised and weakly represented on a forum, where there is trade union rivalry in the workplace, and where the union is unable to service and support its members when they engage in those participation structures. Unions should see participation not only as an inroad into certain managerial prerogatives, but as a way of building shop-floor organisation and capacity. To repeat the point made above: trade unions should view their involvement in participatory structures strategically. Unions, therefore, should only participate where management devotes resources, such as training, to the employees who engage in the participation structures so that they are genuinely empowered and a democratic culture can develop for improving the performance of the firm.

NOTES AND REFERENCES

———— ✦ ————

CHAPTER 1

Notes

1   I wish to thank Jeremy Baskin, Darcy du Toit, Shane Godfrey and David Jarvis for comments on an earlier draft of this chapter.

2   This chapter and the collection will focus on labour's role in extra-parliamentary economic institutions and will spend little time on its involvement in the formal institutions of political democracy, such as the legislature. The focus is an analytical one, and should not be taken to prioritise the extra-parliamentary sphere as a superior form of representation. Rather, the argument advanced here takes as an assumption that the deepening of democracy is dependent upon strong elected democratic institutions, and cannot occur outside of this context.

3   The literature on corporatism is vast. For classic interpretations, see Schmitter, 1974; Schmitter and Lembruch, 1979; Panitch, 1986; Cawson, 1986; Pekkarinen et al. 1992.

4   Labour is divided between three major federations, though COSATU is larger than the other two combined. The federations – even where organised into a single labour caucus in NEDLAC – seldom speak with a single voice, and dissent within the labour caucus is common. Business itself is divided on racial lines into two major organisations. Its peak-level organisations draw extremely weak mandates from their constituents, and have difficulty bargaining beyond a narrow range of distributive issues. Both parties have difficulty making agreements unpopular with their members 'stick'. By 'strong corporatist systems' I have in mind countries such as postwar Sweden, Norway and Austria.

5   The same Act redefined the term 'employee' to exclude all Africans, closing the loophole through which those few Africans who were exempt from the pass laws were able to join registered unions, while ruling out any liberalisation of labour law.

6   The range of issues was determined at NEDLAC. For a complete list, see Satgar's contribution to this collection. However, the Act makes provision for a representative trade union and an employer to conclude a collective agreement to add or remove issues for consultation and joint decision-making. In essence, the division between matters to be decided through industry or enterprise-level collective bargaining or via joint decision-making or consultation in a workplace forum cannot be made without the agreement of a representative trade union.

7   For further discussions of co-determination in Europe, see Schregle, 1978; Schauer, 1973; Swenson, 1989; Pontussen, 1988; and Weiss, 1986. For a discussion of workers' control, self-management and co-determination in the third world, see Bayat, 1991. For the results of an international comparative study of worker participation, see Kester and Pinaud, 1994 and 1994a.

8   For an assessment of the Metal and Allied Workers' Union's decision to enter the Industrial Council, see Webster, 1985.

9   For a frank discussion of the difficulties of accomplishing this feat, see COSATU, 1997 and 1997a.

10   Pressures for an accord in mining were revived in early 1998 due to the continuing fall in the gold price and employers' plans for widespread retrenchments in the industry. The establishment of a tripartite Gold Crisis Committee provides an opportunity for the consensual restructuring and downscaling of the industry while ameliorating the extent of job losses. The mining summit also yielded a major advance in the area of health and safety, though this came about less through the tripartite process and more through the Leon Commission into health and safety in the industry, and the work of former unionists in Parliament who pushed through progressive legislation.

11   For a discussion of the effects of intra-union conflicts over enterprise-level engagement and their impact on implementing an industrial accord, see von Holdt, 2000.

12   At the time of publication, no such schedule had been issued.

13   Representation at NEDLAC includes members who represent organised business, organised labour, organised community and development interests, and the state. According to the Act (section 5(1)) NEDLAC shall: '(a) strive to promote the goals of economic growth, participation in economic decision-making and social equity; (b) seek to reach consensus and conclude agreements on matters pertaining to social and economic policy; (c) consider all proposed labour legislation relating to labour market policy before it is introduced in Parliament; (d) consider all significant changes to social and economic policy before it is implemented or introduced in Parliament; (e) encourage and promote the formulation of co-ordinated policy on social and economic matters'.

14   For further discussion of such transitional institutions, see De Villiers, 1994.

15   The ambiguities concern whether engagement in forums such as the National Manpower Commission and the National Economic Forum was purely defensive in orientation – blocking the apartheid state's ability to embark on unilateral restructuring of the economy – or whether it included a proactive element of involvement in policy-making. Friedman and Shaw (2000) tease out the complications of labour's position: in essence it attempted to do both by furthering the ANC's (and its own) short-term

agenda by blocking state economic policy, while seeking to achieve certain long-term gains by participating in agreements. While the latter produced some important results that were advantageous to workers, the largely defensive posture of blocking unilateral restructuring 'interfered with pursuing a longer term transformative agenda'. Either way, engagement was a function of a strategy of extending worker control.

16   This independence is extremely important: neither labour nor business owe their organisational status to the state; nor is either party – most significantly labour – dependent on the state or the ANC for its funding, leadership selection or for decisions to take collective action.

17   Strangely, the NEDLAC Act (Section 5(1)) more successfully achieves the balancing act Du Toit calls for by giving equal weight to 'the goals of economic growth, participation in economic decision-making and social equity.' It is unclear why the LRA – which after all was negotiated at NEDLAC – does not do the same.

18   In this context, both Parliament and the extra-parliamentary institutions of engagement may well be threatened by the growing power of the executive. Given that the apartheid state granted central state authorities massive formal and informal power, any democratic project must address the restructuring of the relationship between the executive and representative institutions.

19   It is not clear to what extent organised South African business was involved in GEAR's formulation, but the direct involvement of World Bank economists is rather easier to discern. For a discussion of insulating economic policy-making, see Gelb and Bethlehem, 1998.

20   In contrast to those state officials looking to end or downgrade engagement, the Director General of the Department of Labour, Sipho Pityana, made a sophisticated assessment of the possibilities and problems of engagement. In distinguishing NEDLAC from collective bargaining between labour, business and the state, he has called instead for 'the three parties together [to] define a vision of what South Africa must be transformed into'. All policies – including those from business and labour – should be up for discussion, but with a clear focus on desired outcomes, tied to extensive and collaborative research (Pityana, 1997, 1997a). These ideas come very close to Friedman's and Shaw's arguments for 'communicative action'.

References

Adler, G. and Webster, E. 1995. 'Challenging transition theory: The labour movement, radical reform and transition to democracy in South Africa'. *Politics and Society*, 23(1).

————1997. 'Bargained liberalisation: The labour movement, policy-making and transition in Zambia and South Africa'. Research report commissioned by the Multinational Working Group on Labour Movements and Policy-

Making in Africa for the Council for the Development of Social Science Research in Africa, Dakar.

Akwetey, E. 1996. 'Hegemonic unilateralism or autonomous multi-actor reciprocity: Dilemmas of labour regime reform in Zambia and Ghana'. Paper presented to the Workshop on Labour Regimes and Liberalisation. Institute for Development Studies, University of Zimbabwe, May.

Barchiesi, F. 1998. 'Trade unions and organisational restructuring in the South African automobile industry: A critique of the co-determination thesis'. *African Sociological Review*, 2 (2).

Baskin, J. 1993. 'Corporatism: Some obstacles facing the South African labour movement'. Research Report no. 30. Johannesburg: Centre for Policy Studies.

——— 1993a. 'The trend towards bargained corporatism'. *South African Labour Bulletin*, 17 (3/4).

——— 1998. 'Labour relations policy and the politics of economic reform'. Paper presented at the conference on the Politics of Economic Reform, University of Cape Town, January.

——— 2000. 'Labour in South Africa's transition to democracy: Concertation in a third world setting'. In Adler, G. and Webster, E. (Eds.), *Trade Unions and Democratisation in South Africa, 1985-1997*. London: Macmillan.

Bauer, G. 1994. 'The labor movement and the prospects for democracy in Namibia'. Ph.D. thesis, University of Wisconsin.

Bayat, A. 1991. *Work, Politics and Power: An International Perspective on Workers' Control and Self-management*. New York: Monthly Review Press.

Bird, A. and Schreiner, G. 1992. 'COSATU at the crossroads: Towards tripartite corporatism or democratic socialism?' *South African Labour Bulletin*, 16(6).

Buhlungu, S. 1996. 'Trade union responses to participatory management: a case study'. MA thesis, University of the Witwatersrand.

——— 1997. 'Working for the union: a profile of union officials in COSATU'. Labour Studies Research Report no. 8. Sociology of Work Unit. Johannesburg: University of the Witwatersrand.

Cawson, A. 1986. *Corporatism and Political Theory*. Oxford: Blackwell.

COSATU. 1997. 'The report of the September Commission on the future of the unions to the Congress of South African Trade Unions'. Johannesburg: COSATU.

——— 1997a. 'Secretariat Report to COSATU 6th National Congress'. Johannesburg: COSATU.

——— 1998. '6th National Congress Resolutions'. Johannesburg: COSATU.

Cronin, J. 1992. 'The boat, the tap and the Leipzig way'. *The African Communist*, 130.

Desai, A. and Habib, A. 1996. 'Labour relations in transition: The rise of corporatism in South Africa's automobile industry'. Working Paper no.13. University of York, Department of Politics.

De Villiers, R. 1994. *Forums and the Future*. Johannesburg: Centre for Policy Studies.

Du Toit, D. 1995. 'Corporatism and collective bargaining in a democratic South Africa'. *Industrial Law Journal*, 16.

Etkind, R. 1995. 'Rights and power: Failings of the new LRA'. *South African Labour Bulletin*, 19(2).

Friedman, S. 1987. *Building Tomorrow Today: African Workers in Trade Unions, 1970-1984*. Johannesburg: Ravan Press.

Friedman, S. and De Villiers, R. (Eds.) 1996. *South Africa and Brazil: Two Transitional States in Comparative Perspective*. Johannesburg: Centre for Policy Studies, Foundation for Global Dialogue, IDESP.

Friedman, S. and Shaw, M. 2000. 'Power in partnership? Trade unions, forums and the transition'. In Adler, G. and Webster, E. (Eds.) *Trade Unions and Democratization in South Africa, 1985-1997*. Macmillan: London.

Gelb, S. and Bethlehem, L. 1998. 'Macro-economics for the masses?' *Siyaya!* 1, Autumn.

Gostner, Karl. 1997. 'Playing politics: Labour's political role in Zambia', *South African Labour Bulletin*, 21(3).

Harris, L. 1993. 'South Africa's economic and social transformation: From "no middle road" to "no alternative"'. *Review of African Political Economy*, 57.

Kester, G. and Pinaud, H. (Eds.) 1994. *Trade Unions and Democratic Participation, Volume 1: Policies and Strategies*. Paris and The Hague: Institute of Social Studies.

———1994a. *Trade Unions and Democratic Participation, Volume 2: Analysis of Experience*. Paris and The Hague: Institute of Social Studies.

Lagrange, R. 1995. 'Workplace forums: Some comments'. In 'Opinions on the new Labour Relations Bill'. NALEDI Information Package. Johannesburg: NALEDI.

Lehulere, O. 1996. 'Social democracy and neo-liberalism: Social democrats in new clothes'. *Debate*, 1.

Lwoga, C. and Mapolu, H. 'Workers' participation and the management of public enterprise in Tanzania'. Unpublished mimeograph. Dar es Salaam.

Maphosa, G. J. 1992. 'Industrial democracy in Zimbabwe?' In Cheater, A. (Ed.) *Industrial Sociology in the First Decade of Zimbabwean Independence*. Harare: University of Zimbabwe Publications.

Maree, J. 1993. 'Trade unions and corporatism in South Africa'. *Transformation*, 21.

Marie, B. 1992. 'COSATU faces crisis: "Quick-fix" methods and organisational contradictions'. *South African Labour Bulletin*, 16(5).

———1995. 'Trade unions in the transition in South Africa'. Sociology of Work Unit. Johannesburg: University of the Witwatersrand.

Panitch, L. 1986. *Working Class Politics in Crisis*. London: Verso.

Pateman, C. 1971. *Participation and Democratic Theory*. Cambridge: Cambridge University Press.

Pekkarinen, J. et al. (Eds.) *Social Corporatism: A Superior Economic System?* Oxford: Clarendon Press.

Pityana, S. 1997. 'NEDLAC: Government by collective bargaining?' *New Nation,* 23 May.

———— 1997a. 'Creative thinking can improve NEDLAC's effectiveness'. *Business Day,* 17 September.

Pontussen, J. 1988. 'Radicalization and retreat in Swedish social democracy'. *New Left Review,* 165.

Psoulis, C., Moleme, K., Spratt, J. and Ryan, E. 1999, 'Workplace forums: What is their future?' Labour Studies Research Report no. 9. Sociology of Work Unit. Johannesburg: University of the Witwatersrand.

Rakner, L. 1992. 'Trade unions in the processes of democratisation: A study of party labour relations in Zambia'. Report no. 6. Bergen, Norway: Chr. Michelsen Institute.

Rogers, J. and Streeck, W. 1994. 'Workplace representation overseas: The works council story'. In Freeman, R. (Ed.) *Working Under Different Rules.* New York: Russell Sage Foundation.

Schauer, H. 1973. 'Critique of co-determination'. In Hunnius, G., Garson, D. and Case, J. (Eds.) *Workers' Control.* New York: Vintage.

Schmitter, P. 1974. 'Still the century of corporatism?' *Review of Politics,* 36(1).

Schmitter, P. and Lehmbruch, G. (Eds.) 1979. *Trends towards Corporatist Intermediation.* London: Sage.

Schregle, J. 1978. 'Co-determination in the Federal Republic of Germany: A comparative view'. *International Labour Review,* 117(1).

Schreiner, G. 1991. 'Fossils from the past: Resurrecting and restructuring the National Manpower Commission'. *South African Labour Bulletin,* 16(1).

Shivji, I. 1976. *Class Struggles in Tanzania.* New York: Monthly Review Press.

———— 1986. *Law, State and the Working Class in Tanzania, c. 1920-1964.* Oxford: James Currey.

Streeck, W. 1992. 'Co-determination: After four decades'. In Streeck, W. *Social Institutions and Economic Performance: Studies of Industrial Relations in Advanced Capitalist Economies.* London: Sage.

———— 1994. Public lecture presented to a workshop on co-determination sponsored by the *South African Labour Bulletin,* the Sociology of Work Unit and NALEDI, Johannesburg.

Swenson, P. 1989. *Fair Shares: Unions, Pay, and Politics in Sweden and West Germany.* Ithaca: Cornell University Press.

Turner, L. 1991. *Democracy at Work: Changing World Markets and the Future of Labour Unions.* Ithaca: Cornell University Press.

Vally, B. 1992. *A Social Contract: The Way Forward?* Johannesburg: Phambili Books.

Von Holdt, K. 1990. 'The Mercedes Benz sleep-in'. *South African Labour Bulletin,* 15(4).

Von Holdt, K. 1991. 'From resistance to reconstruction: The changing role of trade unions'. *South African Labour Bulletin,* 15(6).

———— 1991a. 'Towards transforming SA industry: A "reconstruction accord" between unions and the ANC?' *South African Labour Bulletin,* 15(6).

——— 2000. 'From the politics of resistance to the politics of reconstruction? The union and "ungovernability" in the workplace'. In Adler, G. and Webster, E. (Eds.) *Trade Unions and Democratization in South Africa, 1985-1997.* London: Macmillan.

Webster, E. 1985. *Cast in a Racial Mould: Labour Process and Trade Unionism in the Foundries.* Johannesburg: Ravan Press.

——— 1995. 'NEDLAC – corporatism of a special type?' *South African Labour Bulletin,* 19(2).

Weiss, M. 1986. 'Institutional forms of workers' participation with special reference to the Federal Republic of Germany'. Paper presented to the 7th World Congress of the International Industrial Relations Association, Hamburg, 1-4 September.

CHAPTER 2

Notes

1   This is not to say that the left has uncritically accepted co-determination as the future for the shop-floor, but rather that at this juncture co-determination is seen as an obtainable and immediate goal.

2   For a critical opinion of the Yugoslavian experience, see Eddie Webster's article 'Self-management in Yugoslavia: A failed experiment in democratic socialism?' in *SALB,* Vol 15, No 1, June 1990.

References

Anstey, M. 1990. *Worker participation: South African Options and Experiences.* Cape Town: Juta & Co.

Bahro, R. 1978. *The Alternative in Eastern Europe.* London: New Left Books.

Banks, A. 1994. 'Participating in management: union organising on a new terrain'. *South African Labour Bulletin,* 18(5): 102-106.

Bayat, A. 1991. *Work, Politics and Power: An International Perspective on Workers' Control and Self-management.* London: Zed Books.

Bettleheim, C. 1976. *Economic Calculation and Forms of Property.* London: Routledge and Kegan Paul.

Blauner, R. 1964. *Alienation and Freedom: The Factory Worker and his Industry.* Chicago: University of Chicago Press.

Blumberg, P. 1969. *Industrial Democracy: The Sociology of Participation.* New York: Schocken Books.

Bukharin, N. 1979. *The Politics and Economics of the Transition Period.* London: Routledge and Kegan Paul.

Burawoy, M. 1985. *The Politics of Production-factory under Capitalism and Socialism.* London: Verso.

Ellerman, D. P. 1985. *The Democratic Worker-owned Firm.* London: Allen and Unwin.

Gorz, A. 1973. 'Workers' control is more than just that' In *Workers' Control*. New York: Vantage Books.

Gorz, A. 1989. *Critique of Economic Reason*. London: Verso.

Hobsbawm, E. 1994. *Age of Extremes: The Short Twentieth Century, 1914-1991*. London: Abacus.

Jarvis, D. 1995. Politics and Participation in Two Durban Factories'. Unpublished MSocSci Thesis. Durban: University of Natal Durban.

Joffe, A. 1994. 'Democratising the workplace'. Presentation at COSATU Human Resource Policy Workshop, Durban.

Maller, J. 1992. *Conflict and Co-operation: Case Studies in Worker Participation*. Johannesburg: Raven Press.

Nove, A. 1983. *The Economics of Feasible Socialism*. London: Allen and Unwin.

Ntshangase, W. and Solomons, A. 1993. 'Adversarial participation a union response to participatory management'. *South African Labour Bulletin*, 17(4) :31-35.

Poulantzas, N. 1980. *State, Power and Socialism*. London. Verso.

Sitas, A. 1993. *Etopia: A Week in the Life of a Worker in 2020*. Durban. Madiba Press.

——— 'Managing the democratic revolution' *South African Labour Bulletin*, 17(2): 73-75.

Slovo, J. 1990. 'Has socialism failed?'. *The African Communist*, 128.

Standing, G., Sender, J. and Weeks, J. 1996. *Restructuring the Labour Market: The South African Challenge: An ILO Country Review*. Geneva: International Labour Office.

Streeck, W. 1994. 'Co-determination and trade unions'. *South African Labour Bulletin*, 18(5): 87-101.

Turner, R. 1981. *Eye of the Needle: Towards Participatory Democracy in South Africa*. Johannesburg: Raven Press.

Von Holdt, K. 1991. 'From resistance to reconstruction'. *South African Labour Bulletin*, 15(6): 14-25.

CHAPTER 3

Notes

1   S80(12) Labour Relations Act of 1995

2   *NUM v East Rand Gold and Uranium Co Ltd* 1991, 12 *ILJ* (A) 1239 A –D.

3   *CSFWU v Aircondi Refrigeration 1990*, 11 *ILJ* 532 (IC) at 547 C where retrenchment, even if informed by an anti-union intent, was allowed by the Industrial Court. Second, the LRA of 1956 did not outlaw scab labour and even the countervailing strategem for labour – picketing – was criminalised. Third, employers had recourse to an interdict in terms of S17(11)(Aa) of the LRA of 1956, when a strike did not conform to Section 65 or was prohibited. Finally, the patchwork jurisprudence developed around collective or strike dismissals provided employers with an opportunity to dismiss workers and ultimately weaken the strike weapon.

4   See *SASBO v Standard Bank* 1993, 14 *ILJ* 706 (IC), in which a distinction was made between mandatory and permissive bargaining topics.

5   Statutory agreements concluded at industrial council or conciliation board level had to be promulgated by the Minister of Manpower in terms of S 48 of the previous LRA.

6   Comprising the following members: Professor H. Cheadle (Convenor); Mr R Zondo; Ms A Armstrong; Ms D Pillay; Mr A van Niekerk; Professor W le Roux; Professor A Landman (President of the Industrial Court); Mr D van Zyl (State Law Advisor seconded to the team). Assisting the team were advocates M Wallis, J Gauntlett, Professors SM Brassey and S Ngcobo, Attorney Ms H Seady, and a researcher, Ms C Cooper. The Task Team was also assisted by the ILO which provided resources for a ten-day stay at the ILO in Geneva, as well as gave the Task Team an opportunity to consult internationally renowned experts within the ILO itself. The task team was also assisted by three experts: Professor B Hepple, Master of Clare College, Cambridge; Professor A Adiogun, University of Lagos, Nigeria; and Professor Manfred Weiss, JW Goethe University, Frankfurt, Germany.

7   In the end though, watching for this danger is not new to the labour and shop-floor tradition in South Africa, and was apparent in the opposition displayed by unions to works and liaison committees.

8   According to Cheadle, it was Minister Mboweni who stressed the imperative of crafting a worker participation institution into the LRA. Interview, February 1997.

9   Amanda Armstrong and Helen Seady, interview, September 1996. Also see Andre van Niekerk, interview, October 1996.

10 Interview, September 1996.

11 This is apparent from the policy thrust emanating from the government's macro-economic policy framework, known as GEAR. As a macro-economic policy GEAR, has all the hallmarks of a homegrown stabilisation and structural adjustment programme.

12 This is notwithstanding the provision for a union trigger.

13 The challenges confronting autonomous worker self-management also pertain to the realisation of co-determination in some respects.

14 Relevant in this regard is the policy framework governing worker pension and provident funds. It might be necessary for the Finance Ministry to play a more active role in structuring worker buy-outs with this money.

References

Anstey, M. (Ed). 1990. *Worker Participation.* Cape Town: Juta.

Bayat, A. 1990. *Work Politics and Power: An International Perspective on Workers' Control and Self-management.* New York: Monthly Review Press.

Braverman, H. 1974. *Labour and Monopoly Capital: The Degradation of Work in the Twentieth Century.* London: Monthly Review Press.

Collins, D. 1994. 'Worker control'. *South African Labour Bulletin,* 18(3): 33-42.

Davis, D. 1991. 'The juridification of industrial relations in South Africa, or Mike Tyson v Johannes Voet?'. *Industrial Law Journal,* 12(4-6): 1181-1191.

Du Toit, D. 1994. 'Towards a critical analysis of labour law in South Africa'. Selected papers from the Labour Law Conference, Durban.

———— 1997. 'Industrial democracy in South Africa's transition'. *Law, Democracy and Development,* (1): 39-68.

Du Toit, D. et al. (Ed). 1996. *The Labour Relations Act of 1995.* Durban: Butterworths.

Gamble, A. and Kelly, G. 1996. 'The new politics of ownership'. *New Left Review,* 220: 62-115.

Hunt, A. 1986. 'The theory of critical legal studies'. *Oxford Journal Of Legal Studies,* 6(1).

Hyman, R. 1977. *Industrial Relations: A Marxist Introduction.* London: Macmillan.

ILO. 1989. *Workers' Participation in Decisions within Undertakings.* Johannesburg: Skotaville.

Joffe, A., Kaplan, D., Kaplinsky, R. and Lewis, D. *Improving Manufacturing Performance in South Africa – The Report of the Industrial Strategy Project.* Cape Town: UCT Press.

Jordaan, B. 1994. 'A new organising theme for labour law'. Selected papers from the Labour Law Conference, Durban.

Klare, K. 1981. 'Labour law as ideology: Toward a new historiography of collective bargaining law'. *Industrial Relations Law Journal,* 4: 450.

———— 'Critical theory and labour relations law'. In Kairys, D. (Ed). 1990. *The Politics of Law.*

Labour Relations Act 66 of 1995.

Maller, J. 1992. *Conflict and Co-operation.* Johannesburg: Ravan Press.

Ministry of Labour. 1995. 'Explanatory memorandum on the draft negotiating document'. January 1995.

Ministry of Labour. 1995. 'Draft negotiating document in the form of a Labour Relations Bill'. *Governement Gazette* 16259, 10 February.

Munck, R. 1988. *The New International Labour Studies – An Introduction.* London: Zed Books.

Patnaik, P. 1995. *Whatever Happened to Imperialism and Other Essays.* India: Tulika.

Rycroft, A. and Jordaan, B. 1992. *A Guide to South African Labour Law.* Cape Town: Juta & Co.

Satgar, V. (Ed). 1995. *Opinions on the Labour Relations Bill.* Johannesburg: National Labour and Economic Development Institute.

———— 1996. *Towards a Democratic Agenda for Worker Participation: A Radical Critique of the Wiehahn Paradigm of Collective Bargaining.* Cape Town: UCT Press.

Srinivas, B. 1993. *Worker Takeover in Industry – the Kamani Tubes Experiment.* New Delhi: Sage Publications.

Streek, W. 1992 'Successful adjustment to turbulent markets: The German automobile industry in the 1970s and 1980s'. In Streek, W. (Ed.) 1990. *Social Institutions and Economic Performance – Studies of Industrial Relations in Advanced Capitalist Economies.* London: Sage.

Von Holdt, K. 1992. 'What is the future of labour?'. *South African Labour Bulletin,* 16(8).

—— 1993. 'The challenge of participation'. *South African Labour Bulletin.* 17(3): 45-53

—— 1995. 'Workplace forums: Can they tame management?'. *South African Labour Bulletin,* 19(1): 31-34.

Wainwright, H. 1994 *Arguments for a New Left – Answering the Free Market Right.* Oxford: Blackwell Publishers.

Zita, L. 1995. 'The role of trade unions in the new situation'. Unpublished speech presented to the South African Communist Party, Gauteng Regional Congress.

Interviews

Armstrong, Amanda and Seady, Helen. Ministerial Legal Task Team. Johannesburg, September 1996.

Botha, Bokkie. Business South Africa. Johannesburg, February 1997.

Cheadle, Halton. Convenor Ministerial Legal Task Team. Johannesburg, February 1997.

Dobson, Wendy. Convenor NEDLAC Labour Market Chamber. Johannesburg, November 1996.

Shilowa, Sam. General Secretary, COSATU. Johannesburg, October 1996.

Van Niekerk, Andre. Ministerial Legal Task Team. Johannesburg, October 1996.

Cases

NUM v East Rand Gold and Uranium Co Ltd, 1991, 12 *ILJ* (A) 1239.

CSFWU v Aircondi Refrigeration, 1990, 11 *ILJ* 532 (IC) 547.

SASBO v Standard Bank, 1993, 14 *ILJ* 706 (IC).

CHAPTER 4

Notes

1 FEDSAL has since amalgamated with two other union bodies to form a new federation – FEDUSA (Federation of Unions of South Africa).

2 While known as the Committee of Principals during the LRA negotiations, this body is now simply referred to as the overall convenors.

3 Now Deputy General Secretary of COSATU.

4 We could not confirm this since despite repeated attempts we were unable to obtain an interview with the convenor of the labour caucus.

References

Adler, G. and Webster, E. 1995. 'Challenging transition theory: The labour movement, radical reform and transition in South Africa'. *Politics and Society*, 23(1).

────── 1996. 'Exodus without a map? Participation, autonomy and labour's dilemmas in a liberalising South Africa'. Paper presented at the workshop on Labour Regimes and Liberalization in Africa. Harare: Institute of Development Studies, University of Zimbabwe, 16 May.

Baskin, J. 1996. *Against the Current: Labour and Economic Policy in South Africa*. Johannesburg: Ravan Press.

Business Day. 13 March 1997.

Friedman, S. and Shaw, M. 2000. 'Power in partnership? Trade unions, forums and the transition'. In Adler, G. and Webster, E. (Eds.). *Trade Unions and Democratization in South Africa, 1985-1997*. London: Macmillan.

Gomomo, J. 1997. 'Address to the second NEDLAC summit'. Johannesburg: NEDLAC.

Gostner, K. 1997. 'Organised labour and globalisation: A case of David and Goliath?' Unpublished MA research report. Johannesburg: Department of Sociology, University of the Witwatersrand.

Macun, I. 1997. 'Does size matter? Union size, majoritarianism and the new Labour Relations Act'. *Law, Democracy and Development*, 1(1).

National Economic, Development and Labour Council Act 35 of 1994.

NEDLAC. 1996. *NEDLAC Annual Report*. Johannesburg.

Rosenthal, T. and Gostner, K. 1996. 'Focus on NEDLAC: Progress on all fronts' *South African Labour Bulletin*, 20(4): 49-54.

Interviews

Bethlehem, Lael. Research Co-ordinator, NEDLAC. Johannesburg, 11 February 1997.

Botha, Bokkie, and Du Plessis, Adrian. Business South Africa. Johannesburg, 19 February 1997.

Heintz, James. Senior Researcher, NALEDI. Johannesburg, 12 December 1997.

Kettledas, Les. Deputy Director-General, Department of Labour. Pretoria, 21 February 1997.

Lekwane, Aubrey. Development Chamber, NEDLAC. Johannesburg, 11 February 1997.

Monnokgotla, Lucky. General Secretary of BIFAWU. Johannesburg, 19 February 1997.

Naidoo, Jayendra. Executive Director, NEDLAC. Johannesburg, 17 February 1997.

Ngcukana, Cunningham. General Secretary, NACTU. Johannesburg, 18 February 1997.

Nhlapo, Vusi. President of NEHAWU. Johannesburg, 10 February 1997.

Ramburuth, Shan. Trade and Industry Chamber, NEDLAC. Johannesburg, 10 February 1997.

Sellers, Christian. Research Officer, Chemical Workers Industrial Union. Johannesburg, 17 January 1997.

Van der Merwe, Dannhauser. General Secretary FEDSAL. Johannesburg, 17 February 1997.

Wolmarans, Joshua. Public Finance and Monetary Chamber, NEDLAC. Johannesburg, 7 February 1997.

CHAPTER 5

Notes

1   An earlier version of this chapter appeared as a 1997 NALEDI working paper titled 'Muddling through tripartite industrial policy-making: the auto, textile and clothing sectors'. A subsequent version appeared as Industrial policy-making in the auto, textile and clothing sectors: Labour's strategic ambivalence'. *Transformation* (41) 2000

2   NUM and the Chamber of Mines organised a Mining Industry Summit in 1991 to which all role-players were invited. A number of task groups were established to deal with issues on an ad hoc basis. With the exception of the Health and Safety task group which recommended the establishment of a government Commission of Enquiry, the task groups made little headway in dealing with the challenges despite intense efforts by the union. The Ministry responsible – Mineral and Energy Affairs – took no initiative in the process. The Commission of Enquiry resulted in legislation introducing joint labour-management control over health and safety at industry, mine and shaft level. The initial summit is discussed in 'Summit on the mining crisis', *South African Labour Bulletin*, 15(8), 1991.

3   Because the interviews were conducted in 1996, the chapter does not fully reflect all subsequent developments.

4   We thank the anonymous reviewer for pointing out that, in corporatist literature, the term 'social partners' connotes a commitment to work towards consensus in their engagement. While we agree that it is debatable whether the basis for such a style exists in South Africa, we use the term for the convenience of identifying the key role-players.

5   In the emerging context of hyper-competition, corporatist-style industrial policy-making often conflicts with the competitive instincts of individual firms in many industries. However, because many South African industries have long been protected by tariff barriers, firms have recognised that they must supplement their competitive strategies by pursuing their collective interests through their industry associations.

6   Employer associations primarily deal with labour issues and industry associations primarily deal with tariff and trade issues.

7   The Australian experience was regarded as illustrative for South Africa for a number of reasons. Its industry faced similar problems in the 1980s and had made some progress towards addressing them on an industry-wide basis. Other factors were the lessons of 'strategic unionism', the Accord with the Australian Labour Party, and the influence of Chris Lloyd, an Australian unionist seconded to NUMSA.

8   In the auto industry, industrial relations and human resource management specialists represent firms at the NBF and training specialists represent their firms at AMIETB, while chief executives represent firms at NAAMSA meetings and technical specialists represent the industry on the MIDC.

References

Adler, G. and Webster, E. 1995. 'Challenging transition theory: the labour movement, radical reform and transition to democracy in South Africa'. *Politics and Society*, 23(1).

Allen, C. 1990. 'Trade unions, worker participation and flexibility: Linking the micro to the macro'. *Comparative Politics*, 22(3): 253-72.

Amsden, A. 1992. 'A theory of government intervention in late industrialisation'. In Putterman, L. and Rueschemeyer, D. (Eds.). *State and Market in Development: Synergy or Rivalry?* Boulder, Colorado: Lynne Rienner Publishers.

Atkinson, M. and Coleman, W. 1985. 'Corporatism and industrial policy'. In Cawson, A. (Ed.) *Organised Interests and the State: Studies in Meso-Corporatism*. London: Sage.

Bethlehem, L. and von Holdt, K. 1991. 'A new deal for a new era? The auto industry settlement'. *South African Labour Bulletin*, 16(2): 25-28.

Grant, W. 1985. 'Introduction'. In Grant, W. (Ed.) *The Political Economy of Corporatism*. London: Macmillan.

Kraak, A. 1992. 'Human resource development and organised labour'. In Moss, G. and Obery, I. (Eds.) *South African Review 6*. Johannesburg: Ravan Press.

Maree, J. 1993. 'Trade unions and corporatism in South Africa'. *Transformation*, 21: 24-53.

Maree, J. and Godfrey, S. 1995. 'Toward meso-corporatism: From labour exclusion to union intervention in the South African textile industry'. In Frenkel, S. and Harrod, J. (Eds.) *Industrialization & Labor Relations: Contemporary Research in Seven Countries*. Ithaca, New York: ILR Press.

Meyerson, D. and Scully, M. 1995. 'Tempered radicalism and the politics of ambivalence and change'. *Organization Science*, 6(5): 585-600.

Ministry of Trade and Industry. 1995a. 'Strategic plan for the restructuring of the textile and clothing industries'. *Government Gazette*, 12 June. Pretoria: Government Printer.

Ministry of Trade and Industry. 1995b. 'Government's final decisions on a long-term strategy for the clothing and textile industries'. *Government Gazette*, 10 August. Pretoria: Government Printer.

Mollett, A. 1995. 'Outlook for textiles and clothing in South Africa', *Textile Outlook International*, July.

NAAMSA. 1996. *Annual Report 1995/96*. Pretoria: National Association of Automobile Manufacturers of South Africa.

NUMSA. 1993. 'Restructuring'. Internal union document, June.

Oberhauser, A. 1993. 'Semi-peripheral industrialisation in the global economy: Transition in the South African automobile industry'. *Geoforum*, 24(2): 99-114.

Patel, E. 1993. *Engine of Development? South Africa's National Economic Forum*. Cape Town: Juta.

Schmitter, P. 1981. 'Interest intermediation and regime governability in contemporary Western Europe and North America'. In Berger, S. (Ed.) *Organising Interests in Western Europe*. Cambridge: Cambridge University Press.

Swart Commission (Panel and Task Group for the textile and clothing industries). 1994. *Long-term Strategic Plan for the Textile and Clothing Industries in South Africa*.

Urquhart, R. 1996. 'Lessons from the Mining Summit – achieving successful tripartism'. Unpublished mimeograph, Sociology of Work Unit. Johannesburg: University of the Witwatersrand.

Womack, J. Jones, D. and Roos, D. 1990. *The Machine that Changed the World*. New York: Rawson Associates.

Interviews

Baard, Johan Seardel, and Chairman of National Employers' Caucus (clothing industry). Cape Town, 7 November 1996.

Baxter, Quintin. Human Resources Director, Frametex. Durban, 26 August 1997.

Bennett, Mark. National Official, SACTWU. Durban, 27 August 1996.

Best, Peter. Human Resources Director, Nissan SA, and Chairman of AMIETB. Pretoria, 30 August 1996.

Bird, Adrienne. Director of Training, Department of Labour. Pretoria, 29 August 1996.

Black, Anthony. Chairman, Motor Industry Development Council. Cape Town, 13 August 1996.

Claasens, Helena and Metz, Ingrid. Director and Deputy Director, Auto Sector, Department of Trade and Industry. Pretoria, 29 August 1996.

Clark, Mel. Former SACTWU official. Durban, 28 August 1996.

De Klerk, Leon. Training Manager, Volkswagen SA. Port Elizabeth, 19 August 1996.

Ditsele, Peter. NUMSA shop steward, Nissan SA, and AMIETB member. Pretoria, 30 August 1996.

Ehrenreich, Tony; Lloyd, Chris; and Kgalema, Victor. National Officials, NUMSA. Johannesburg, 4 September 1996.

Erwin, Alec. Minister of Trade and Industry. Cape Town, 18 November 1996.

Gazendam, Harry. Human Resources Director, Toyota SA. Sandton, 2 September 1996.

Goldman, Tanya. National Official and CITB member, SACTWU. Cape Town, 16 August 1996.

Handlinger, Peter. Training Manager, Toyota Manufacturing SA. Durban, 27 August 1996.

Hankinson, Mike. CEO, Romatex, and Chairman of Texfed. Cape Town, 7 October 1996.

Hartford, Gavin. Former National Organiser, Auto Assembly, NUMSA. Vanderbijlpark, 4 September 1996.

Heyns, Ruel. Chairman of Board of Tariffs and Trade. Pretoria, 29 August 1996.

Jordaan, Danie. Chief Director, Industrial Sectors, DTI. Pretoria, 30 August 1996.

Keller, Errol. Economist, Texfed. Johannesburg, 3 September 1996.

Kopke, Christoph. Chairman of Mercedes Benz SA and NAAMSA representative on MITG. Pretoria, 2 September 1996.

Lynch, Albert. CEO, Dorbyl Automotive Products, and NAACAM Executive Member. Port Elizabeth, 20 August 1996.

Magugu, Freddie. Regional Secretary and Swart Commission member, SACTWU. Port Elizabeth, 20 August 1996.

Marais, Eben and Van der Merwe, Susan. Director and Deputy Director of Clothing, Textiles and Footwear Sector, Department of Trade and Industry. Pretoria, 29 August 1996.

Meyer, Johan. Chairman of T&N Holdings and Chairman of NAACAM. Durban, 23 August 1996.

Parfitt, Judy. Former Industrial Relations Manager, Volkswagen SA. Vanderbijlpark, 4 September 1996.

Pearce, Alan. Executive Director, Wool Board, and Swart Commission member. Port Elizabeth, 20 August 1996.

Pitot, Roger. Samcor representative on MIDC. Pretoria, 30 August 1996.

Plummer, Alan. CEO, Metair, and NAAMSA representative on MITG. Johannesburg, 3 September 1996.

Richards, Bernard. Managing Director, Seardel, and Chairman of Clofed. Cape Town, 10 October 1996.

Riches, Peter. Director, Clothing Industry Training Board. Cape Town, 3 October 1996.

Smith, Brian. Human Resources Director, Volkswagen. Uitenhage, January 1995.

Smith, Percy. Industrial Relations Manager, Volkswagen SA. Uitenhage, 21 August 1996.

Soni, Shirish. Consultative Business Organisation (small clothing firms). Durban, 23 August 1996.

Smart, Len. Executive Director, Natal Clothing Manufacturers Association. Durban, 26 August 1996.

Swart, Nic. Chairman of Swart Commission and member of BTT. Pretoria, 2 September 1996.

Van Zyl, Hennie. Executive Director, Clofed. Johannesburg, 3 September 1996.
Vermeulen, Nico. Executive Director of NAAMSA. Pretoria, 28 and 30 August 1996.
Williams, Clive. Executive Director of NAACAM. Johannesburg, 5 September 1996.

CHAPTER 6

Notes

1   The authors would like to acknowledge the assistance of Tanya Rosenthal in researching and writing this chapter. The interpretations remain those of the authors.

2   The term 'forum' emerged in the early 1990s to describe a wide range of representative institutions that were established to give voice to the disenfranchised, such as the National Economic Forum, the Housing Forums and a wide variety of forums in the workplace. The term 'workplace forum' was drawn from these examples and used in Chapter 5 of the LRA. We use the term loosely to capture the variety of workplace initiatives.

3   Initial reflections on the first round of interviews were published in Webster, 1996.

4   Personal communication: Dr Claus Schnabel, Head of Industrial Relations Department, Institut der Deutshen Wirtshaft, Cologne, 13 December 1996. See also: W. Muller-Jensch, 1995.

5   These organisations merged in 1996 to form the Amalgamated Technical and Electronic Association of South Africa.

6   Recent research has challenged the simplistic proposition that enhanced international competition is producing a general decentralisation of industrial relations. The general trend is not toward decentralisation, but rather towards articulation, that is, interaction at many different levels (Crouch and Traxler, 1996).

References

Albert, M. 1993 *Capitalism Against Capitalism*. London: Whurr Publishers.
Bendix, S. 1991. *Industrial Relations in South Africa*. (2 Ed.) Cape Town: Juta.
Clegg, H. 1951. *Industrial Democracy and Nationalisation*. London: Blackwell.
Crouch, C. and Traxler, F. (Eds.) 1996. *Organised Industrial Relations in Europe*. Aldershot: Avebury.
COSATU. 1997. 'The report of the future of the September Commission on the future of the unions'. Johannesburg: COSATU.
Labour Relations Act 66 of 1995.
Macun, I. 1997. 'Evolving practices in industrial relations and collective bargaining: the SALFS results'. Paper prepared for the Conference on Labour Markets and Enterprise Performance in Pretoria, South Africa, January.

Macun, I., Rosenthal, T. and Standing, G. 1997. 'Trade unions in crisis? Findings from the worker representative survey'. *South African Journal of Labour Relations*, 21(1).

Macun, I. and Buhlungu, S. 1996. 'Interview with Gwede Mantashe'. *South African Labour Bulletin*, 20(1).

Mail & Guardian. 1996. 18-24 October.

Mail & Guardian. 1997. 'Unionists want say in boardroom'. 15-21 August.

Maller, J. 1992. *Conflict and Co-operation: Case Studies in Worker Participation*. Johannesburg: Ravan Press.

Ministry of Labour. 1995. 'Explanatory memorandum on the draft negotiating document in the form of a Labour Relations Bill'. *Government Gazette* 16259. Pretoria: Government Printer.

Muller-Jentsch, W. 1995. 'Germany: From collective voice to co-management'. In Rogers, J. and Streeck, W. (Eds.) *Works Councils: Consultation, Representation and Co-operation in Industrial Relations*. Chicago and London: University of Chicago Press.

Pateman, C. 1971. *Participation and Democratic Theory*. Cambridge: Cambridge University Press.

Rogers, J. and Streeck, W. (Eds.) 1995. *Works Councils: Consultation, Representation, and Co-operation in Industrial Relations*. Chicago and London: University of Chicago Press.

Rosenthal, T. 1996. 'Worker control and democracy: Shop-steward elections in the auto sector'. *South African Labour Bulletin*, 20(2).

Stace, D. and Dunphy, D. 1994. *Beyond the Boundaries: Leading and Re-creating the Successful Enterprise*. Sydney: McGraw-Hill.

Streeck, W. 1984. *Industrial Relations in West Germany*. Oxford: Heinemann.

——— 1995. 'German capitalism: does it exist? Can it survive?' Unpublished paper. University of Wisconsin-Madison.

Veldsman, T. and Harilall, R. 1996. *Benchmarking Study of Employee Involvement Efforts by South African Organisations*. Johannesburg: Ernst & Young Management Consulting Services.

Von Holdt, K. 2000. 'From the politics of resistance to the politics of reconstruction? The union and "ungovernability" in the workplace'. In Adler, G. and Webster, E. (Eds.). *Trade Unions and Democratization in South Africa: 1985-1997*. London: Macmillan.

Webster, E. 1996. 'Changing industrial relations in South Africa'. In Lessem, R. and Nussbaum, B. *Sawubona Africa: Embracing Four Worlds in South African Management*. Johannesburg: Zebra Press.

Webster, E. and Macun, I. 1997. 'Lessons learnt from workplace forums'. *Business Day*, 19 February.

Interviews

Botha, Bokkie. AECI. Johannesburg, 31 January 1995.

Cummings, Neil. Nampak. Johannesburg, 26 January 1995.
Davies, Richard. SA Breweries. Johannesburg, 19 January 1995.
De Villiers, Richard. Randgold. Johannesburg, 23 January 1995.
De Wet, Andre. Greater Johannesburg Transitional Council. Johannesburg, 30 January, 1995.
Ewart, Anthony. PX Group. Johannesburg, 26 January 1995.
Knoesen, Brian. Mercedes Benz. East London, 14 February 1995 and 2 October 1996.
Kubheka, Sipho. PPWAWU. Johannesburg, 28 November 1994.
Macilwaine, Bob. Eskom. Johannesburg, 25 January 1995.
Mercedes Benz Shop Stewards Committee. East London, 11 July 1997. (Conducted by B. Kenny).
Mdluli, Joseph. PG Bison shop steward. Johannesburg, 20 June 1994.
Ngoasheng, Moss, Gencor. Johannesburg, 10 February 1995.
Smith, Brian and Parfitt, Judy. Volkswagen. Uitenhage, 15 February 1995 and 3 October 1996.
Smith, Jim. PG Bison. Johannesburg, 12 January 1995.
Volkswagen Shop Stewards Committee, Uitenhage, 15 February 1995.

CHAPTER 7

Notes

1   Barbara Adair is the former Chief Director: Labour Relations, Department of Public Service and Administration.
2   At the time of writing (1999), proposed legislative amendments that would allow Parliament to make adjustments to the budget were being debated but had not yet been passed.
3   Provincial workshops on the LRA of 1995, facilitated by the author, were held during 1996 as part of the National Hospital Strategy Project.

References

African National Congress. 1994. *The Reconstruction and Development Programme: A Policy Framework*. Johannesburg: Umanyano Publications.
Buhlungu, S. 1998. 'Servicing co-determination'. Report commissioned for the NALEDI long-term research project on co-determination and tripartism in South Africa. Johannesburg: NALEDI.
Collins, D. 1994. 'Stuck in the stone age? The public sector in the new South Africa'. *The Shopsteward*, 3(6).
COSATU. 1997. 'Submission to the Presidential Review Commission'. Cape Town: COSATU Parliamentary Office.
Department of Public Service and Administration. 1995. 'White Paper on the Transformation of the Public Service'. *Government Gazette* 16838. Pretoria: Government Printer.

―― 1996. 'Policy framework for transformation units and co-ordinating committees'. Unpublished mimeo.

Dilts, D.A. 1993. 'Labour-management co-operation in the public sector'. *Journal of Collective Negotiations*, 22(4).

Dlamini Zuma, N.C. 1995. 'Speech by the Minister of Health, Dr NC Dlamini Zuma at the opening of the National Consultative Health Forum on 3 November 1995'. Pretoria.

Godfrey, S., Hirschsohn, P. And Maree, J. 1998 'Surrendering prerogatives? Management strategies with regard to worker participation and co-determination'. Report 6 of NALEDI's long-term research project on co-determination and tripartism in South Africa. Johannesburg: NALEDI.

Heinecken, L. 1992. 'Labour rights for the public service: a future challenge'. *Industrial and Social Relations*, 13.

International Labour Office (ILO). 1981. *Workers' participation in decisions within undertakings*. Johannesburg: Skotaville Educational Division.

Kearney, R.C. 1994. 'Labor-management relations and participative decision-making: Toward a new paradigm'. *Public Administration Review*, 54 (1).

Kester, G. and Pinaud, H. (Eds.) 1994. *Trade Unions and Democratic Participation: Policies and Strategies Vol. I.* Paris and The Hague: Institute of Social Studies.

Mazibuko, S. 1996. 'Bringing democracy into the workplace'. *NEHAWU Worker News*, 4(6).

Ministry of Labour. 1995. 'Explanatory memorandum on the draft negotiating document in the form of a Labour Relations Bill'. *Government Gazette* 16259. Pretoria: Government Printer.

NEHAWU. 1996. 'NEHAWU national transformation forum meeting: Main document'. Unpublished mimeo.

Olsen, T. (Ed.) 1996. *Industrial Relations Systems in the Public Sector in Europe.* Norway: European Public Services Committee, FAFO Institute for Applied Social Science.

Patel, I. 1996. 'Changing apartheid's bureaucracy: the transformation of the public service'. In Baskin, J. (Ed.) *Against the Current.* Johannesburg: Ravan Press.

―― 1998. 'Review of public service transformation'. Unpublished commissioned report. Johannesburg: NALEDI.

―― (forthcoming) 'Growing pains: Collective bargaining in the Public Service'. In Adler, G. (Ed.) *Public Service Labour Relations in a Democratic South Africa.* Johannesburg: Witwatersrand University Press.

Satgar, V. 1997. 'The LRA and workplace forums: legislative provisions, origins, and transformative possibilities'. Report 2 of NALEDI's long-term research project co-determination and tripartism in South Africa. Johannesburg: NALEDI.

Summers, C. 1995. 'Workplace forums from a comparative perspective'. *Industrial Law Journal*, 10(6).

Von Holdt, K. 1995. 'Workplace forums: undermining unions?' *South African Labour Bulletin*, 19(6).

Personal communications

Adair, Barbara. Advisor to the Minister for Public Service and Administration. September 1996.

CHAPTER 8

Notes

1 For a detailed discussion of NEDLAC, highlighting the role of labour, see the chapter by Gostner and Joffe in this collection.
2 Willie Mokgeti, PPWAWU shop steward at Nampak Corrugated, Wadeville, speaking at a workshop convened by the September Commission in March 1997.
3 The September Commission was a 12-member body set up by COSATU to investigate and recommend strategies for the future of unions. COSATU's second vice president, Connie September, chaired the Commission, hence the name. The Commission's final report was published in August 1997.
4. The NEF was a national forum set up for government, business and labour to negotiate economic policy. In 1995 the body dissolved into the new National Economic Development and Labour Council (NEDLAC).

References

Barchiesi, F. 1998. 'Trade unions and organisational restructuring in the South African automobile industry: A critique of the co-determination thesis'. *African Sociological Review*, 2(2).

Barret, J. 1993. 'Participation at Premier: Worker empowerment or co-option?' *South African Labour Bulletin*, 17(2).

Baskin, J. 1991. *Striking Back: A History of COSATU*. Johannesburg: Ravan.

Baskin, J. and Satgar, V. 1995. 'South Africa's Labour Relations Act', Unpublished research report. Johannesburg: NALEDI.

Bethlehem, L. Buhlungu, S., Crankshaw, O and White, C. 1993. 'Co-determination vs. co-option: PPWAWU and PG Bison negotiate restructuring'. *South African Labour Bulletin*, 18(1).

Buhlungu, S. 1995. 'Workplace change for whom? Interviews with shop stewards at a Johannesburg company'. *South African Labour Bulletin*, 19(6).

———— 1996. 'Trade union responses to participatory management: A case study'. MA thesis. Johannesburg: University of the Witwatersrand.

———— 1997. 'Working for the union: A profile of full-time officials in COSATU'. Labour Studies Research Report no. 8. Sociology of Work Unit. Johannesburg: University of the Witwatersrand.

———— 2000. 'Trade union organisation and capacity in the 1990s: Continuities, changes and challenges for PPWAWU'. In Adler, G. and Webster, E. *Trade Unions and Democratization in South Africa, 1985-1997*. London: Macmillan.

COSATU. 1985. Resolution on National Minimum Wage. Johannesburg: COSATU.

Cressey, P. and MacInnes, J. 1980. 'Voting for Ford: Industrial democracy and the control of labour'. *Capital and Class*, 11.

Department of Labour, RSA. 1995. Labour Relations Act, no. 66, 1995.

Ford, B. and Plowman, D. 1989. *Australian Unions: An Industrial Relations Perspective.* (2 Ed). Melbourne: Macmillan.

Ginsburg, D. and Webster, E. 1995. *Taking Democracy Seriously: Worker Expectations and Parliamentary Democracy in South Africa.* Durban: Indicator Press.

Keet, D. 1992. 'Shop stewards and worker control'. *South African Labour Bulletin*, 16(5).

Lagrange, R. 1995. 'Workplace forums: some comments'. In 'Opinions on the new Labour Relations Bill'. NALEDI Information Package. Johannesburg: NALEDI.

Lambert, R. and Webster, E. 1988. 'The re-emergence of political unionism in contemporary South Africa'. In Cobbet, W. and Cohen, L. (Eds). *Popular Struggles in South Africa.* Oxford: James Currey.

Lehulere, O. 1995. 'Workplace forums: Co-determination and the workers' struggle'. *South African Labour Bulletin*, 19 (2).

Macun, I., Joffe, A. and Webster, E. 1995. 'Negotiating organisational change in the South African workplace'. Labour Studies Research Report no. 5. Sociology of Work Unit. Johannesburg: University of the Witwatersrand, May.

Maller, J. 1992. *Conflict and Co-operation.* Johannesburg: Ravan.

Nampak/PPWAWU. 1995. 'Agreement between PPWAWU and Nampak Operations where PPWAWU is recognised on the process of world-class manufacturing and service within Nampak'. August.

Nampak/NUMSA/MWU. 1995. 'Agreement between NUMSA/MWU and Nampak Operations where NUMSA/MWU are recognised on the process of world-class manufacturing and service within Nampak'. August.

Ntshangase, W. and Solomons, A. 1993. 'Adversarial participation: A union response to participatory management'. *South African Labour Bulletin*, 17(4).

Pateman, C. 1971. *Participation and Democratic Theory.* Cambridge: Cambridge University Press.

PG Bison. 1994. 'Employee participation in decision-making within PG Bison: A discussion Paper'. June.

Pityana, S.M. and Orkin, M. (Eds). 1992. *Beyond the Factory Floor.* Johannesburg: Ravan.

Ramsay, H. 1985. 'What is participation for? A critical evaluation of "labour process" analyses of job reform'. In Knights, D., Willmot, H. and Collinson, D. (Eds). *Job Redesign: Critical Perspectives on the Labour Process.* Aldershot: Gower.

Rogers, J. and Streeck, W. 1994. 'Workplace representation overseas: The works councils story'. In Freeman, R.B. (Ed.) *Working Under Different Rules.* New York: Russell Sage.

Ronnie, R. 1996. 'For defensive unionism and socialism'. *South African Labour Bulletin*, 20 (2).

September Commission on the Future of Trade Unions. 1997. The report of the September Commission on the future of the unions. Johannesburg: COSATU.

Streeck, W. 1994. 'Works councils in Western Europe: From consultation to participation'. In Rogers, J. and Streeck, W. (Eds) *Works Councils: Consultation, Representation and Co-operation*. Chicago: University of Chicago Press.

SWOP/PPWAWU. 1994. 'Restructuring at Nampak: A strategy for worker involvement'. Research Report. November.

Vavi, Z. 1992. 'The name of the game is membership'. *South African Labour Bulletin*, 16(8).

Von Holdt, K. 2000. 'From the politics of resistance to the politics of reconstruction? The union and "ungovernability" in the workplace'. In Adler, G. And Webster, E. (Eds.) *Trade Unions and Democratization in South Africa, 1985-1997*. London: Macmillan.

———— 1992. 'What is the future of labour?'. *South African Labour Bulletin*, 16(8).

Webster, E. 1995. 'Beyond the boundaries: Experimenting with organisational change in the South African workplace'. Unpublished paper.

Interviews

Kubheka, Sipho. Former general secretary, PPWAWU. December. 1994.

Masuku, Zimi. Shop steward committee chairperson, Nampak Polyfoil. Johannesburg, 24 November 1993.

Mthembu, Joseph. Johannesburg, June 1994.

NUMSA shop stewards. Divpac. Durban, August 1994.

CHAPTER 9

Notes

1   The sub-title of this book gives an indication of its contents: *Incredibly stupid things corporate executives have done while re-engineering, downsizing, TQM'ing, team-building, and empowering in order to cover their ifs, ands or buts.*

2   In 1964, the *Concise Oxford English Dictionary* defined strategy as: 'Generalship, the art of war … management of an army or armies in a campaign, art of so moving or disposing troops or ships or aircraft so as to impose upon the enemy the place and time and conditions for fighting preferred by oneself' (quoted in Shaw, 1990: 468).

3   The starting point for human resource management is conventionally seen as the 1981 launch of compulsory MBA course in human resource management at the Harvard Business School. The importance of this

development is underlined by the fact that this was the only new compulsory course to be introduced into the Harvard MBA for nearly 20 years (Boxall and Dowing, 1990: 196).

4   The strategic level of decision-making is situated at head office and is relatively long-term; the business unit level is situated (as its name suggests) at the level of a particular business unit and is short to medium-term; and the operational level of decision-making related to the day-to-day production decisions.

5   One consultant argued that, even if no workplace forums are established, the Act would have done its job because it is pushing parties into a variety of other forms of participation.

6   The LRA provides that an application for the establishment of a workplace forum must go to the CCMA, which must, if the application meets certain requirements, appoint a commissioner to assist the parties to establish a workplace forum by collective agreement or, failing that, to establish a workplace forum in terms of the Act. The various steps that the commissioner must take to achieve these objectives are set out in some detail in the Act. In addition, disputes in respect of workplace forums must be referred to the CCMA (unless a collective agreement or the Act provides otherwise).

7   It is interesting to note that the training manual on workplace forums compiled by the Steel and Engineering Industries Federation of South Africa contained a model workplace forum constitution which provided that disputes about forums would be referred to the National Industrial Council for the Iron, Steel, Engineering and Metallurgical Industry rather than the CCMA.

8   Terry White notes that only 20% of managers buy business books and, of those, only 2% get beyond the first chapter (*Sunday Independent Business,* 13 April 1997).

9   It must be stressed that the research focused on selected leading firms only and was not representative of the broad cross-section of employers in the country. The points that follow must be seen within this context, and other approaches might need to be pursued by unions for many other firms, particularly medium-sized and smaller firms.

References

Ahlstrand, B. 1990. *The Quest for Productivity: A Case Study of Fawley after Flanders.* Cambridge: Cambridge University Press.

Boxall, P. and Dowling, P. 1990. 'Human resource management and the industrial relations tradition'. *Labour & Industry,* 3(2 and 3).

Guest, D. 1987. 'Human resource management and industrial relations'. *Journal of Management Studies,* 24(5).

Knights, D. and Morgan, G. 1985. 'Strategy under the microscope: strategic management and IT in financial services', *Journal of Management Studies*, 32(2).

——— 1990. 'The concept of strategy in sociology: a note of dissent'. *Sociology*, 24(3).

MacDuffie, J. 1995a. 'Human resource bundles and manufacturing performance: organizational logic and flexible production systems in the world auto industry'. *Industrial and Labour Relations Review*, 48(2).

——— 1995b. 'International trends in work organization in the auto industry'. In Wever, K. and Turner, L. (Eds.) *The Comparative Political Economy of Industrial Relations*. Madison WI: Industrial Relations Research Association.

McLagan, P. and Nel, C. 1995. *The Age of Participation*. Randburg: Knowledge Resources.

Miller, P. 1987. 'Strategic industrial relations and human resource management: distinction, definition and recognition'. *Journal of Management Studies*, 24(4).

Ministry of Labour. 1995. 'Explanatory memorandum on the draft negotiating document in the form of a Labour Relations Bill' *Government Gazette* 16259. Pretoria: Government Printer.

Mintzberg, H. 1978. 'Patterns in Strategy Formation'. *Management Science*, 24(9).

——— 1987. 'The Strategy Concept – Parts I and II'. *California Management Review*, 29(3).

——— 1988. 'Crafting Strategy'. *The McKinsey Quarterly*, Summer: 71-89.

——— 1989. *Mintzberg on Management: Inside Our Strange World of Organi-zations*. New York: The Free Press.

Pettigrew, A. 1977. 'Strategy Formulation as a Political Process'. *International Studies of Management and Organization*, 7(2).

Quinn, J.B. 1980. *Strategies for Change: Logical Incrementalism*. Homewood, IL: Irwin.

Saban, A. 1997. 'What is world-class manufacturing?' *Productivity SA*, January/February.

Shaw, M. 1990. 'Strategy and social process: military context and sociological analysis'. *Sociology*, 24(3).

Sisson, K. and Sullivan, T. 1987. 'Editorial: Management strategy and industrial relations'. *Journal of Management Studies*, 24(5).

Storey, J. and Sisson, K. 1993. *Managing Human Resources and Industrial Relations*. Buckingham: Open University Press.

Thurley, K. and Wood, S. 1983. 'Business strategy and industrial relations strategy'. In Thurley, K. and Wood, S. (Eds.) *Industrial Relations and Management Strategy*. Cambridge: Cambridge University Press.

Weiss, A. 1995. *Our Emperors Have No Clothes*. New Jersey: Career Press.

Zey, M. 1992. 'Criticisms of rational choice models'. In Zey, M. (Ed.) *Decision Making*. Newbury Park: Sage Publications.

CONTRIBUTORS

————— ◆ —————

GLENN ADLER is Associate Professor of Sociology and an associate of the Sociology of Work Unit at the University of the Witwatersrand. From 1996 to 1998 he was a part-time senior researcher at NALEDI, where he coordinated its long-term research project on labour's engagement with the state and business. He recently co-edited *Trade Unions and Democratization in South Africa, 1985-1997* (Macmillan), and his research interests focus on the impact of social movements on economic and political liberalisation in Africa.

SAKHELA BUHLUNGU is Lecturer in Sociology and an associate of the Sociology of Work Unit at the University of the Witwatersrand. He is currently completing a Ph.D. thesis on democracy and organisation in the Congress of South African Trade Unions. For many years he has been a member of NALEDI's board and a member of the editorial board of the *South African Labour Bulletin*. In 1994 he was appointed as a member of the Presdential Review Commission on the South African labour market.

SHANE GODFREY is a senior researcher in the Labour and Enterprise Project, a research project in the Department of Sociology and the Institute of Development and Labour Law at the University of Cape Town. His current research interests concern the relationship between worker participation and economic performance, and that between labour legislation and the labour market.

KARL GOSTNER is Director of Research at the National Economic Development and Labour Council (NEDLAC). Until recently he was a researcher at Labour Market Alternatives, a Johannesburg-based research organisation servicing the labour movement and government. In 1997 he completed an MA thesis in industrial sociology at the University of the Witwatersrand on the social clause negotiations at NEDLAC.

PHILIP HIRSCHSOHN is Associate Professor in the Department of Management at the University of the Western Cape. His current research projects and interests include union democracy on the shop-floor, life histories of union organisers and work organisation in the auto industry. Recent papers include 'From shopfloor democracy to national mobilisation: COSATU as a model of social movement unionism', *Economic and Industrial Democracy*, 19(4), 1998 and 'South Africa: the struggle for human resource development' in *After Lean Production: Evolving Employment Practices in the World Auto Industry*, Thomas Kochan et al. (Eds.). ILR Press, 1997.

DAVID JARVIS is Research Co-ordinator at the Trade Union Research Project (TURP) based at the University of Natal in Durban. TURP is a labour service organisation committed to strengthening labour's bargaining, policy and organisational work through the provision of capacity building research, education and materials development for trade unions. He is the author of *Making Sense of Workplace Restructuring*, recently published by TURP.

AVRIL JOFFE is a social scientist specialising in labour markets, industry strategy and urban development. Through her consultancy, Creativity avriljoffe, she is currently managing a project to regenerate an inner-city area of Johannesburg focusing on creative industries and residential accommodation. With her background in labour-management issues and skills development she has been involved in numerous policy reviews, implementation projects and evaluations of the skills development strategy of the South African government.

IAN MACUN is Director of the Skills Development Planning Unit in the Department of Labour. He was previously Deputy Director and a researcher at the Sociology of Work Unit at the University of the Witwatersrand, and has published in the areas of labour relations, trade union growth and research methodology.

JOHANN MAREE is Professor of Sociology at the University of Cape Town, with a special interest in industrial sociology. He is a member of the Labour and Enterprise Project, a research project in the Department of Sociology and the Institute of Development and Labour Law at UCT. He is a member of the editorial board of the *South African Labour Bulletin*. His publications include *An Industrial Strategy for the Textile Sector* (UCT Press), *The Independent Trade Unions, 1974-1984* (Ravan Press), and numerous chapters in books and journal articles on labour relations and industrial restructuring.

IMRAAN PATEL is Chief Director in the Department of Public Service and Administration responsible for information and knowledge management. He was previously acting Director of NALEDI where he conducted research into public service labour relations and conditions of service. His research interests include co-determination, collective bargaining, wages, employment and public service transformation.

VISHWAS SATGAR is a policy analyst at the Co-operative and Policy Alternative Centre (COPAC) and a political activist in the South African Communist Party. He worked at NALEDI for five years and was involved in labour market reform negotiations at NEDLAC.

ARI SITAS is Chair of Sociology and Industrial, Organisational and Labour Studies at the University of Natal, Durban. He has been writing in the areas of labour, politics and culture, and is active in Durban's Job Creation Forum and other civil society initiatives, like Jubilee 2000 in KwaZulu-Natal.

EDDIE WEBSTER is Professor of Sociology and Director of the Sociology of Work Unit at the University of the Witwatersrand. He is the author of *Cast in a Racial Mould: Labour Process and Trade Unionism in the Foundries* (Ravan Press) and co-editor of *Trade Unions and Democratization in South Africa, 1985-1997* (Macmillan). His current research interests concern the changing forms of workplace representation and the role of labour in the consolidation of new democracies. He is a founder editor and member of the editorial board of the *South African Labour Bulletin,* and in 1996 was appointed an adviser to the Department of Labour on labour market reform in South Africa.